AF323308

DE-POLITICIZATION OF ETHNIC QUESTIONS IN CHINA

Peking University Series on Sociology and Anthropology
(ISSN: 2335-657X)

Series Editor: Xie Lizhong *(Peking University, China)*

Published

Vol. 1   Social Suffering and Political Confession: Suku in Modern China
           by Sun Feiyu

Vol. 2   De-politicization of Ethnic Questions in China
           edited by Xie Lizhong

DE-POLITICIZATION OF ETHNIC QUESTIONS IN CHINA

Edited by

Lizhong Xie

Peking University, China

World Scientific

NEW JERSEY · LONDON · SINGAPORE · BEIJING · SHANGHAI · HONG KONG · TAIPEI · CHENNAI

Published by

World Scientific Publishing Co. Pte. Ltd.

5 Toh Tuck Link, Singapore 596224

USA office: 27 Warren Street, Suite 401-402, Hackensack, NJ 07601

UK office: 57 Shelton Street, Covent Garden, London WC2H 9HE

Library of Congress Cataloging-in-Publication Data
De-politicization of ethnic questions in China / edited by Lizhong Xie, Peking University, China.
   pages cm. -- (Peking university series on sociology and anthropology, ISSN 2335-657X ; vol. 2)
   Includes bibliographical references and index.
   ISBN 978-9814513852 (alk. paper)
   1. China--Ethnic relations. 2. Multiculturalism--China. I. Xie, Lizhong, 1957–
   DS730.D42 2014
   951.004--dc23
                          2013042870

British Library Cataloguing-in-Publication Data
A catalogue record for this book is available from the British Library.

The Yu Tianxiu Fund of Peking University provided funding for the translation of this book series. We are grateful to Mrs. Helen Woo, the founder of the Yu Tianxiu Fund, for her financial support.

In-house Editor: Dong Lixi

Printed in Singapore by World Scientific Printers.

EDITORIAL COMMITTEE

CONTENTS

PREFACE: MY VIEWS ON THE DEBATE OVER "DEPOLITICIZING ETHNICITY IN CHINA"

XIE LIZHONG

Department of Sociology, Peking University

In his essay "A new perspective in guiding ethnic relations in the 21st century: "Depoliticizing" ethnicity in China" (Ma Rong, 2004; Ma Rong, pp. 1–27), Professor Ma Rong of the Department of Sociology, Peking University, questions the ethnic policies adopted by the Chinese government since 1949, going on to propose a new ethnic perspective, shifting from the current policies that "politicize and institutionalize" ethnic minority issues, to ones that gradually "depoliticize" ethnicity. Since its publication, his essay has aroused intense debate among PRC ethnologists, drawing both approval and censure. This book collects some major writings contributing to this debate. To aid readers' understanding, I set out here to straighten out and explore some of the main contents and opinions of the debate purely from the angle of an outsider (new to the debate) and a layman (not a specialized researcher in the field of nationality or ethnic issues).

1. Ma: Why Depoliticize Ethnic Issues?

This essay, Ma's most influential work, is by no means the only one setting out his position: he has expounded it in many others. Taken together, we see that his proposed "depoliticizing"[1] of ethnic issues relies mainly on

---

[1]Translator's note: "depoliticize" and its cognates are placed in quotes the text. A common practice in Chinese, quotation serves little purpose in English and is discarded after the first occurrence.

two aspects of evidence:

1.1. *Difference between the concepts of "nation" and "ethnic group"*

The two Chinese words *minzu* ("nation") and *zuqun* ("ethnic group," "ethnicity") have, argues Ma, totally different meanings. He believes that "nation" and "ethnic group" are distinct concepts in western literature.

> Given their respective time of appearance and inner meaning, they represent human groupings at totally different levels and reflect different forms of identity in human society under different historical conditions. "Nation" is related to "nationalism" and the political movement for "national self-determination" taking place in Western Europe in the 17th century. The term "ethnic group", in contrast, only appeared in the 20th century and is commonly used in the U.S., being gradually adopted by other countries. It refers to groups that exist and identify with a pluralist country with various historical backgrounds, cultures, and traditions (including language, religion, and place of origin), and even distinctive physical features (Ma Rong, p. 3).

These ethnic groups may to some degree be perceived as "sub-cultures" of these societies. In simpler terms, the term "nation" mainly refers to human groupings that emerge from and correlate to "nationalism" and political movements for "national self-determination" originally taking place in the 17th century in Western countries, then gradually spreading to non-western countries, and often identify with a political entity (i.e., the nation-state) with territorial borders. The term "ethnic group", in contrast, refers mainly to human groupings that exist within a nation-state and are tied together by cultural, physical, and other non-political factors.

> Therefore, there are important differences between ethnic groups, which are characterized by distinct cultural traditions and histories, and nations, which are political entities tied to a more or less stable territory (Ma Rong, p. 4).

Given the fundamental distinctions between the concepts of "nation" and "ethnic group", overlooking such differences, or making indiscriminate uses of the two, or otherwise replacing one with the other, may result in undesirable outcomes in social practices. For example, if we make no distinction between the two by using the term "nation" to refer to both human groupings which identify with a political entity with territorial borders, such as a nation-state, and those that exist within a nation-state and are tied together by cultural, physical, and other non-political factors, then it is very likely to instil, among some members of the latter, an awareness of "national self-determination", or even "national independence", that often accompanies with strong political implications and territorial claims. This is exactly what has happened for many years in Mainland China. For years, we in Mainland China have used the term *"minzu"* to refer to both the people ("Chinese nation", or *zhonghua minzu*), which identifies with "China" as a territorial state, and all ethnic groups (i.e., Han, Tibetan, Mongolian, Hui, Yao, Miao and Uygur, etc.) that exist within the territory of "China" and are tied together by cultural, physical, and other factors. And this may have resulted in the "national consciousness" among some members of the "ethnic groups" and created an excuse to be taken advantage of by Xinjiang and Tibetan separatists.

The primary aim of Ma's theory on depoliticizing of ethnicity, therefore, is to try to remind us of the existence of such distinctions and the possibility of us getting into unnecessary trouble and "politicalizing" the "ethnic" issues that would bear no political implications due to conceptual confusion.

1.2. *Two types of policies for managing ethnic relations and the varied outcomes*

Ma points out that based on historical experiences of both China and abroad, government policy has always played an important guiding role during the evolution and development of ethnic relations.

> Government policy plays an important role in guiding group identity and adjusting the boundaries of a political entity. Throughout the history of social development, governments have generally adopted two contrasting policies for regulating ethnic relations: one views ethnic groups mainly as political entities and the other views them primarily as cultural groups. The former policy emphasizes ethnic groups' integrity, political power, and "territorial" conservation. The latter prefers to treat ethnic relations as cultural interactions, and to deal with the problems between people of different ethnic backgrounds as affairs among individuals rather than between groups as a whole, even though the common characteristics of the ethnic group membership are given recognition. By emphasizing the cultural characteristics of ethnic groups, their political interests are diluted. Furthermore, in the processes of migration, the historical

connection between ethnic groups and their traditional residence is gradually loosened (Ma Rong, p. 6.).

These two contrasting policy orientations are, in Ma's words, "politicizing" and "culturalizing" ethnic policies. Examples of the former orientation include modern European nationalist movements aimed at establishing "nation-states", policies of the former USSR for dealing with domestic ethnic relations, ethnic policies carried out by various countries in recent years, and the *minzu zhengce* ("national policies") of the post-1949 Chinese government. Examples of the latter include ethnic policies of ancient China, ethnic policies of contemporary India, and ethnic minority policies of the USA.

These contrasting policies, Ma notes, will have totally different actual effects on the evolution of ethnic relations. The former policy, in effect, causes members of each ethnic group to envision them as a "nation" with political and territorial connotations, which gradually strengthens their "national self-determination" or "national independence" consciousness. The natural results are waves of nationalist movements aimed at establishing "one nation, one state" and eventually, the formation of new nation-states one after another, or even the disintegration of former multi-ethnic political entities (i.e., the Ottoman Empire and the Austro–Hungarian Empire in modern world history, various modern colonial systems in the world, and some contemporary multi-ethnic nations, like the former USSR, Yugoslavia etc.). The latter policy, on the contrary, does not lead to disintegration of multi-ethnic political entities and may under certain conditions help promote integration or assimilation among individual ethnic groups that belong to different political entities. For example, modern nations, such as the U.S., prefers to treat ethnic differences as cultural differences, therefore, allowing the formation and conservation of a multi-ethnic political entity — nation — while the differences among ethnic groups be recognized and conserved. In ancient China, however,

> although there is always politics in issues concerning race, nationality, and ethnic groups, ideas on "majority–minority relations" or "civilized–barbarian relations" were to a great extent "culturalized" in the Chinese cultural tradition, in both theory and practice. This strategy enabled the civilized group in the core region to unify and embody the ethnic minorities in periphery areas. In addition, the Chinese tradition of treating ethnic differences as "cultural differences" made it possible to

implement the policy of "transforming barbarian into civilized", which resulted in attracting ethnic minorities from the periphery areas and the ultimate formation of a unified pluralist Chinese nation with the Han group in the central plain as the core (Ma Rong, p. 9).

Apparently, for any country that has an existing multi-ethnic presence, it is only wise to adopt as far as possible a "culturalizing" policy, not the opposite, for dealing with ethnic relations, so as to avoid national disintegration. This constitutes one of the main grounds for Ma to advocate his theory on depoliticizing ethnicity.

Ma advances his proposed depoliticizing of ethnicity based on this viewpoint, a fundamental ground for his criticism of "national" policies adopted by Chinese governments since 1949. He believed that the international political situation after the founding of New China in 1949 left the Chinese government with no choice but to ally with the then Soviet Union. The government copied almost all the Soviet models in terms of social organizations and economic affairs and also followed the Soviet model by politicizing and institutionalizing the ethnic minorities in China. Specific measures included organizing large-scale "identification of nationalities", practicing a "regional national autonomy" system for all ethnic minorities, and implementing a series of policies in favor of ethnic minorities in the administrative, educational, economic, and cultural areas. These policies have ever since played an important role in strengthening ethnic consciousness, consolidating ethnic identity, and inevitably politicalizing ethnic issues. Ma believed that "the Chinese should learn from their ancestors and their experience for thousands of years in guiding ethnic relations. They also should look to other nations for both positive and negative lessons. China might in the future consider changing the direction of managing its ethnic relations from the "politicizing" to "culturalizing" route. The de-politicizing route might lead China in a new direction, strengthening national identity among ethnic minorities while guaranteeing the prosperity of their cultural traditions," (Ma Rong, p. 24) and ultimately constructing a "politically united" modern civil nation under the condition of "cultural pluralism".

2. Criticisms of Ma: Can or Should Ethnic Issues be Depoliticized?

Ma's viewpoint on depoliticizing ethnic issues has since its publication quickly attracted criticism from a number of his academic colleagues.

Contrary to the afore-mentioned two arguments, the critics are mainly targeting at the following two aspects:

2.1. *Is there a substantial distinction between the concepts of "nation" and "ethnic group"?*

A thorough review of the critics' articles reveals that one of the primary gaps between them and Ma lies in the fact that the former overlooks or even clearly denies in their articles, wittingly or unwittingly, any distinction between the concepts of "nation" and "ethnic group". In the opinion of critics including Hao Shiyuan, Chen Jianyue, and Wang Xien as opposed to that of Ma, "nation" and "ethnic group" are concepts that are basically interchangeable, or "two different concepts referring to the same matter". For example, in an article Chen explicitly criticized Ma for replacing the term "nation" — which is commonly used (especially to refer ethnic minorities such as Tibetan, Mongolian, Uyghur, and Yao nationalities) in the context of the present Chinese literature — with "ethnic group" and treating "ethnic group" and "nation" separately as cultural and political concepts, and for Ma's conclusion that "ethnic relation" is necessarily a cultural relation given the cultural implication of "ethnic group", and that "regional national autonomy will under certain circumstances inevitably lead to "national independence" or "national disintegration"(Chen Jianyue, p. 78) Chen found "critical errors in logic" in Ma's argument:

> (1) after replacing the term "nation" with "ethnic group", he did not emphasize the identity between these two concepts, but on the contrary placed these two concepts that are originally used to describe the same things as "different points on a continuum";
> (2) he went on to make "nation" and "ethnic groups" opposing concepts, arguing that "ethnic groups" as groups with certain cultural heritage and history, are very different from "nations" which are political entities connected to established lands";
> (3) he connected the concept of nation and national self-destruction, national states and nationalism to stigmatize it, asserting that it "is likely to be associated with a certain political entity and separationist movements that have the power to execute "national self destruction" and establish "national states";
> (4) he completely abandoned the stigmatized concept of "nation" in an attempt to establish the value and significance of "ethnic group" which he place on the same continuum: "the reason we distinguish

> between "nation" and "ethnic group" in the Chinese language
> is because the different use of these terms may actually imply
> varied orientations for viewing understanding and managing ethnic
> relations (Chen Jianyue, p. 79).

Wang Xien, on the other hand, points out that there might be some practical difficulties in replacing "nation" with "ethnic group" in the Chinese context. He argues that

> the concept of "ethno" might be distinguished from "nation", but to
> applying this change to China would be difficult and awkward, such as
> trying to replace "national minorities" with "ethnic minority", "national
> policies" with "ethnic policies", or "national theories" with "ethnic
> theories". The difficulty is that in China, terms such as "national
> groups", "national policies", and "national theories" are so ingrained
> in people's minds that they are not just widely used as policy terms and
> social language, but have also been accepted among scholars. Given that
> the objects described can be expressed clearly, they do not need to be
> replaced (Wang Xien, p. 132).

Chen Yuping expresses his viewpoints in related essays that "there are different scholarly conceptions of the term. Therefore, presently, we try not to accurately define the term. Instead, we should focus on the relations between different definitions, which would be more conducive to furthering research on the matter" (Chen Yuping, p. 139). For the sake of simplicity, therefore, it seems best to retain the term "nation" because everyone is used to it.

Ma proposes to use the term "nation" to refer to human groupings that identify with a political entity ("state") with a territorial boundary, and the term "ethnic group" to refer to those that exist within a "state" and are tied together by cultural, physical, and other non-political factors. Based on this proposal, there could be many ethnic groups (i.e., Tibetan ethnicity, Hui ethnicity, etc.) but only one nation, the "Chinese Nation", within the territory of China. Conversely, in the essays of the above-mentioned critics, as both identity groups, e.g., "Tibetan", "Hui", and the "Chinese Nation" (identity group at the "state" level) are all termed "nation", it is unavoidable to use "multi-national states" to refer to countries like "China", the "Soviet Union", and the "United States", which, according to Ma, would have been more appropriately referred to as "multi-ethnic states".

2.2. *Can "ethnic issues" be depoliticized?*

Nevertheless, most of the criticism tends to concentrate on Ma's policy proposition of "depoliticizing ethnicity (ethnic issues)". Roughly speaking, criticism has mainly centered on the following arguments:

(1) Ethnic issues should not, and are not very likely to, be limited to cultural aspects.

Hao Shiyuan insists in this regard that

> National questions or ethnic problems, however labeled, exist in all multi-national countries. They manifest themselves in many aspects, including politics, economy, culture, and social life, making it hard to sort them into the abstract categories of "politicization" and "acculturation" (Hao Shiyuan, p. 40).

Opposing the idea of culturalizing ethnic issues, Hao quotes D. Smith:

> "Believing that it is possible to "return" nationalism to any arena including the cultural arena is both naïve and fundamentally wrong" (Hao Shiyuan, p. 47).

Zhou Daming also believes that, while currently the broad scholarly consensus is that ethnic groups are population groups segregated by culture, and have culture traditions and historical backgrounds, but we cannot deny or overlook the underlying political nature of ethnic groups, given the innumerable, historically-formed links between ethnic groups and their places of residence (Zhou Daming, p. 58, 59).

Chen Jianyue points out from a political science perspective that like any other human community, "Nation"[2] is also a community of interests, but also a unique community of interests:

> "... as a relatively stable collective form in human society, the nationality offers its members the prospect of a set of interests that no other group can provide: the continuity of a specific economic life, common cultural heritage, and share of political power" (Chen Jianyue, p. 73).

Relations among "nationalites" are in fact interest relations, because "all international interactions are interactions between national interests"

---

[2] As mentioned above, the majority of Ma's critics deny or ignore the difference between "nation" and "ethnic group".

(Chen Jianyue, p. 73). Politics, indeed, "refers to interest-based decisions that people make and implement in human communities" (Chen Jianyue, p. 62).

Hence, national (ethnic) issues are in essence political. "As political, national issues must be solved through political systems and public policies. Attempts to "depoliticize" and "culturize" them are fruitless" (Chen Jianyue, 77).

Chen Jianyue believes Ma's arguments on depoliticizing of ethnic issues "all stem from his failure at the starting point of his research to consider interests as a basic driver for national development" (Chen Jianyue, 77).

"Enculturation" and "politicization" are, Wang Xien argues,

> inappropriate descriptors for classifying national policy orientations for several reasons. First of all, as Ma states, "national and ethnic issues are, at any time and in any country, bound to be political in nature" (Ma Rong, 2007b). Next, policies and institutions aimed at resolving such politicized national and ethnic issues are still political actions set up and carried out by the state. Thirdly, even where these policies were aimed at confining national and ethnic issues within the realm of "culture", their ultimate goal was still political stability. Hence, "enculturation" and "politicizing" cannot be used to categorize national policies; nor can they be used to evaluate their faults and merits (Wang Xien, p. 93–94).

Chen Yuping also explicitly disapproves of the proposition of "depoliticizing" national issues, stating that "the idea lacks theoretical support, hence, cannot and should not be implemented,"(Chen Yuping, p. 142) because most national issues are not likely to be solved without resorting to political platforms such as state power and national policies.

(2) The disintegration of the Soviet Union and ethnic separatist activities in China are not the outcomes of "Politicizing ethnic issues".

Hao Shiyuan believes the failure of the Soviet Union to address national issues could be explained in two different ways.

> Firstly, while the former Soviet Union established policies, laws and mechanisms for solving national issues and promoting national equality, it failed to implement them. Its highly centralized government promoted big-Russian nationalist chauvinism, leading to a lack of cohesion with non-Russian nationalities; secondly, the Soviet Union dealt with national issues using a "politicized" system setup and policy orientation, which

not only fortified the power of each nationality, but even wrote freedom of secession into law; non-Russian nationalities were thus led to start separationist movements claiming "national independence" or "nationalism (Hao Shiyuan, pp. 39, 40).

The first explanation, although not explicitly expressed, was apparently favored more by Hao Shiyuan, who criticized the latter as having no sufficient evidence to make it a more convincing explanation. In other words, Hao doubts that the disintegration of the former Soviet Union was due more to politicizing of its national (ethnic) policies than a highly centralized political system that promoted big-Russian nationalist chauvinism, as well as its failure to effectively implement laws, policies, and mechanisms to promote national (ethnic) equality.

Chen Jianyue using relevant studies to supports this, showing that the break-up was not due to politicizing of ethnic policies; on the contrary, "it might have worked out better for the Soviet Union to have adopted regional autonomy or a regional state system..." (Chen Jianyue, p. 76).

As regards the nationalist-separatist activities in China, Hao Shiyuan also denies any connection with politicizing national issues. Hao believes that compared with social issues like population, poverty, and employment, national issues are characterized by being more universal, long-lasting, complex, global and significant. Given these characteristics, it is hard to establish a set of independent indices and predictable timelines for solving national issues in relation to other social issues like population, poverty, and employment. It is the reason national issues are prevalent in all multi-national states, including developed countries (Hao Shiyuan, p. 33).

Yet, China is currently at the early stage of socialist development, the main conflict is between rapid increase in material demand and slow growth of social productivity. Almost all social issues faced by China are produced due to or in relation to this major conflict; national issues are no exception.

China's national issues thus appear complicated and varied, but fundamentally stem from the conflict between demands for economic and cultural development by nationalities and regions, and their inability to develop, which is — the key theme of national issues in China (Hao Shiyuan, p. 34).

In this process, it is likely that national conflicts arise from the imbalance of development among nationalities and regions. Furthermore, "separatists, religious extremists, and international terrorist organizations are not without impact. They utilize the most prevalent and general social issues to create rumours, confuse the public, initiate dissatisfaction and create trouble. In order to protect the nation from these negative outside influences, we need to fundamentally increase development, implement co-development, and realize mutual prosperity (Hao Shiyuan, p. 36).

Wang Xien also argues that the existence of separationist forces does in fact influence China's national relations and cohesion. However, using the existence of these forces as a measure of the quality of methods to resolve national issues may not be reasonable (Wang Xien, p. 125).

> In today's world, separationist trends and movements are explicitly or implicitly present. They are caused by national awareness induced by the theory of "one nation, one state", and the maximized utilization of this awareness by various social forces and interest parties (Wang Xien, p. 126).

> Fairly speaking, from a worldwide perspective, the Tibet and Xinjiang issues in China are no more serious than similar issues in other nations. Then why do they receive so much attention? There is only one answer, and that is the long-term support, connivance, and speculation by international opposition forces (Wang Xien, p. 126).

(3) The results of "acculturalizing ethnic issues" in the USA and India fall short of Ma's ideal.

A major empirical basis for Ma proposed depoliticizing of ethnic issues lies in America's success in solving racial and ethnic issues by "acculturalizing". Hao Shiyuan finds this dubious: even given that US ethnic policies are "acculturalizing" in nature, the outcomes fall short of the success Ma envisions. On the contrary, its implementation actually produced what Huntington and Brzezinski feared, a politicization of ethnic group relations and challenges to national identity (Hao Shiyuan, p. 43).

From a different angle, Wang Xien discusses "why are there no separationist forces that threatened the integrity of the U. S.", arguing that

> the political reasons behind this cannot be ignored; more importantly, the US is an immigrant country with little over two centuries of history. On coming to the US, immigrant ethnic groups or nations were rapidly disintegrated and swallowed by industrialization and urbanisation. The biggest issue they faced in their new social environment immersion and acceptance in the local society as fast as possible; it was that they lacked opportunities to create their own nationalities and conspire to gain independence. In other words, the immigrant identities of the

majority of ethnic groups and racial groups in the U.S. meant that there were no historical and regional bases for them to engage in national separationist activities. Without this identity, it cannot be guaranteed that there would not be separationist issues. In fact, some aboriginal Indians in the U. S. have long engaged in "separationist" activities, claiming to be the "first nation", and have been making continual efforts in "independence" and "nation-building" (Wang Xien, p. 125).

Chen Jianyue is doubtful, too, about the other success story that Ma advanced in support of his proposed acculturalizing-oriented approach to ethnic issues — India. Examples he cites show that "India is less than perfectly harmonious in its ethnic relations" (Chen Jianyue, 80). He quotes A. H. Sornjee, an Indian political researcher, who clearly states,

> "there exist surprising levels of diversity and disintegration in India, far surpassing Holland, Austria, and Canada in extent. When conflicts based on caste, rank, religion, and region are put in the context of ethnicity, they no longer follow the route of power-sharing for the purpose of unification, but waver between conflict and compromise".

It is hard, Chen argues, "in the face of all these bloody facts of inter-ethnic conflicts, to find traces of the 'important success story of India after its establishment" (Chen Jianyue, p. 81).[3]

How then to understand and evaluate these disputes between Ma and his critics?

3. An Initial Assessment: My Views on the Debate

My initial assessment of Ma Rong's debate between his critics is summarized as follows:

3.1. *The distinction between "nation" and "ethnic group" must be recognized*

Ma Rong proposes distinguishing the terms "nation" and "ethnic group" from each other to refer separately to identity groups that are organized in the form of a political entity such as a "state", and those that are tied together by cultural and physical factors within a "state". This proposal is of great value, in my opinion, for the primary reason — advanced also by

---

[3]Ma refutes Chen's criticism in "Evaluation on the 'Nation Building' of India by the United Nations Development Programme," an article included in this volume.

Ma — that in the present literature, they indeed represent human groupings at totally different levels and reflect different forms of identity in human society; one is organized by political entities like states while the other is not. If we do not use different terms having distinct meanings to represent them separately, we are very likely to cause confusion in expression. For example, if we use the term "nation (*minzu*)" to refer to both the "Chinese nation" and ethnic minority groups like "Tibetan Nation", "Hui Nation", and "Korean Nation", it would indeed be very perplexing: Are the "Chinese nation" and "Tibetan" or "Hui" nationalities the same kind of identity groups? Or are they different? If the former is true, then why is not or could not the latter be organized in the form of individual states? If the former is not true, then what is the reason for they are not distinguished in conceptual terms?

In fact, conundrums like this are to be found in the essays of Ma's critics. For example, in his essay "Establishing a socialist harmonious society and ethnic relations," Hao Shiyuan writes:

> The Han nationality and the national minority groups are interdependent, and the same interdependency also exists between the national minorities, which formed the historical cause for China's multi-national structure, and also propelled China on the road of national revitalization (Hao Shiyuan, p. 36).

> Nationalities do not receive differential treatment based on size, length of history or development stage, but are recognized as a member of the Chinese Nation, this is a reflection of real national equality, and also constitutes the basic requirements for the implementation of the regional national autonomy policy (Hao Shiyuan, p. 45).

> The nation that we are building is an organic collective and innovation of 56 nationalities (Hao Shiyuan, p. 50).

As seen from these three sentences, there is an obvious logical issue in applying the term "nation" both to the "Chinese nation" and "56 nationalities", which are in effect human groupings at two different levels.

Similar predicament is also seen in the articles of other critics. The only difference is that they may have noticed and tried hard to avoid it. Chen Jianyue, for example, states in his article "Establishing a multi-national harmonious society and resolving national issues — 'depoliticizing' and 'culturalizing' national issues", that public policies aimed at adjusting international relations in multi-national states can be categorized into two types: one is community policies aimed at building the *guozu* ("state-nation"); the other is national preferential policies aimed at providing national minorities with preferential terms (Chen Jianyue, p. 70).

Here, apparently, the author encounters the awkward situation of having to differentiate two types of "nation" from each other. To solve it, he has no choice but to adopt a new term, *guozu* (which is exactly what Ma regards as a "nation") to refer to the type of identity group different from an ethnic minority. Likewise, in his "On 'Afterthoughts' of China's national issues and 'being practical' — debating Ma", Wang Xien also has to choose "the Chinese nation on a national level" and "basic nations under the rule of the national state" (Wang Xien, p. 99) to solve that predicament. Therefore, it can be seen that from a logical point of view, it is of high necessity that we adopt different terms to reflect identity groups that are organized in the form of a political entity such as a "state", and those that are tied together by cultural and physical factors within a "state".

But this does not necessarily mean, apart from the "nation-ethnic group" pair as proposed by Ma, we cannot use other concept pairs to represent the two different identity groups. The above-mentioned concept pairs (i.e., "state-nation"/"nation", "nation"/"basic nation" etc.), together with those present in the early 20th century Chinese literature (i.e., "big nationalism"/"small nationalism" used by Liang Qichao, etc.) and those mentioned by certain ethnologists (i.e., "broad nation"/"narrow nation", etc.), share some similarities and cannot, from a logical point of view, be deemed true or false in practice. Given that in the context of current Chinese literature people are accustomed to the usage of "nation" as a representation of objects implied in the English language (that is, any human identity group organized in the form of a political entity such as a "state"), using the term "ethnic group" to refer to any identity group that is tied together by cultural and physical factors within a "state" would seem a simpler and more appropriate option.

3.2. *"Ethnic" issues should not, and are difficult to be depoliticized*

Recognizing "nation" and "ethnic group" as two distinct identity groups does not, of course, entail accepting "depoliticizing ethnic issues". As to whether ethnic issues should be depoliticized, I lean toward Ma's critics: "ethnic" issues should not, and cannot without difficulty, be depoliticized.

The chief reason for this is the fact that ethnic groups and relations do in fact involve interests or interest-based relationships. Solving such problems by political means (political communication, political institutions or public policy, etc.) thus seems inevitable. Given Ma's critics have already discussed it extensively, I shall not elaborate on this, beyond adding that economic, social, political, and cultural issues are never indispensable. Any culture, of any type, always infiltrates into or is embodied in a particular type of economic, social, and political life. Their realization, further, has always to resort to a particular economic, social, and political form. For example, polygamy or polyandry may be deemed a certain type of culture. But once practiced, it may give rise to social and economic forms that differ from those under monogamous arrangements. Furthermore, its legitimacy has to be established and guaranteed by "political" activities such as legislation, administration, and jurisdiction; the same also applies to religious belief. Even if we recognize that "ethnic group" is a different types of identity groups from "nation" are mainly formed on a cultural basis, it does not therefore, mean the former could not at once be a group possessing certain political qualities and demonstrating certain political character; as such, it might be a safer way to say that the issues arising from "ethnic groups" or their relationships could not better be solved by such political measures as making them all independent states, than by treating them as individual subgroups (and relationships among subgroups) within a "nation" (such as the "Chinese" or "American" nation).

The question of whether or not "ethnic" issues could be depoliticized forces us to direct our attention to another relevant question: as Ma points out, the entity to which the term "nation" refers actually is composed of two different identity groups, the distinctions between which require conceptual clarification. Even if we recognize or accept what Ma proposes, however, an important question remains in need of clarification: Is the distinction between these two different groups an objective reality determined by inherent properties of the two? Or a subjective construct determined by the acquired will and practice of their members?

Without question, we have two choices to make before an answer to this question emerges: The first choice is related to what is commonly known as traditional "realism" while the second is to "social constructivism".

Based on traditional "realism", we are able to form a theory on the distinction between "nation" and "ethnic group" that may be described as follows:

    (1) Nation and ethnic group, are, regardless how termed, objective realities that exist naturally and independent of human will.

(2) An "ethnic group" is a type of human community that came into being gradually during the pre-modern period. It has the following basic characteristics: formed mainly on the basis of shared identification factors such as blood relationship, physique, and culture; having no fixed territorial consciousness (an "ethnic group" may live in different geographic locations, or is able to migrate among different places even when living together); not linking itself permanently to a political entity such as a "state" (an ethnic group may live either in different states or within the territory of one state with other ethnic groups), amongst others. In contrast, "nation" is a type of modern community gradually developed during the process of modernization. Its basic characteristics are: formed mainly on the identification of modern sovereign states; having comparatively clear territorial boundaries and sovereignty consciousness; linking itself explicitly to a particular state ("one-nation, one-state"), amongst other characteristics.

(3) An "ethnic group" may evolve into a "nation", but certain economic foundation and social, historical conditions are required for the evolution to occur, with one of the most important conditions being the formation and development of capitalist mode of production. Capitalism required for its development that political institutions (e.g., a modern state characterized by monopoly on the legitimate use of physical force) be utilized to establish unified market economy, civil society and order based on rule of law, maintain the security of people's life and wealth, and safeguard external expansion; this facilitated the formation and development of the "nation", a human community that identified with the modern sovereign state (materials for its formation may either come from pre-existing "ethnic groups" in an earlier capitalist society, or not from them; in the case of the former, either an "ethnic group" or multiple "ethnic groups" can evolve into a "nation"). Hence, the evolution of "ethnic group" into "nation" was a natural, historical process that was independent of the subjective wishes of their members (while forming a "national consciousness" among them remains one of the required conditions, the process as a whole was independent of it).

(4) The formation and development of modern "nations" is a constant process, which will not end in the formation of "state-nations" as we see now. Conversely, with constant expansion of the capitalist production mode in spatial terms, there is a need for the current "state-nations" to further integrate with each other as required by the development needs of the capitalist production mode, which

> will give rise to emergence of bigger, and fewer "nations" than the present ones, and eventually — as perceived under the present and foreseeable technical conditions — to the formation of a "human nation" (all human beings belong to a nation-state, or global nation-state).

If we accept the above theory, then it may be safe to say that the distinctions between "ethnic group" and "nation" resemble the "objectivity" of distinctions between water and water vapor (in spite of certain links between the two, they depend on totally different objective conditions). Were it not for the development of capitalism, albeit to varying degrees, "national consciousness" (i.e., the idea of redefining a non-political identity group such as an "ethnic group" as a political group) alone would not, or would with difficulty, necessitate the transformation of "ethnic group(s)" (non-political identity group) into "nation" (political identity group) in practice. In other words, according to this theory, without the required objective historical conditions, "ethnic" issues could not be depoliticized in reality (which also suggests that serious political consequences would be caused if we confuse the terms "ethnic group" and "nation" at the conceptual level).

In comparison, based on "social constructivism", we are able to form the following theory on the distinctions between "nation" and "ethnic group":

(1) "nation" and "ethnic group", irrespective of appellation, are not "objective realities" that are naturally existent and independent of man's will, but "discursive realities" constructed under the guidance of particular human discourse systems (e.g., "nationalism").

(2) Although the above distinctions between "ethnic group" and "nation" still remain valid — that is, the former is a non-politicalized identity group that came into being gradually during the pre-modern period, while the latter is a politicalized and nationalized identity group gradually developed during the process of modernization — such a distinction is not as a completely natural existence as that between water and water vapour; on the contrary, it is caused due to the distinctions of discourse systems to which the constituent group members belong.

(3) Hence, the evolution of ethnic groups and nations is entirely independent of changes in objective, historical conditions; as a matter of fact, it only stems from changes in the discourse systems of group members. If, under the guidance of a certain "nationalistic" discourse, a strong

sense of "national" consciousness starts to ferment among members of a group previously known to possess only "ethnic" characters, it is very likely that in reality they may shift their perceived group identity from a non-politicalized "ethnic group" into a politicalized "nation". Similarly, if members of any group having already been constructed as a "nation" abandons their "nationalistic" discourse and accepts certain new discourses (e.g. culturalized "ethnic group" discourse), it is also likely that they may redefine the group identity by shifting to a non-political "ethnic group".

(4) Therefore, the historical inevitability of all peoples integrating into a single "human nation" does not exist. Whether or not the mankind will eventually evolve into a unified "nation" is entirely dependent on the discourse system — probably a better way to describe it is "Global Nationalism" — that is formed among the majority of people around the world and accepted by these people. And it is irrelevant to the global expansion process of capitalist production mode (or "socialist production mode" as expected by Marxists).

If we accept the above theory, it seems reasonable to suggest that given that the distinctions between "ethnic group" and "nation" stem completely from discourse construction and no physical barrier exists to separate them from each other, there should be no objectively-existing constraint force that can prevent a previously culturalized "ethnic group" from evolving into a politicized "nation". Answering whether "ethnic groups" should be politicalized should be entirely dependent on the discourse system in question; there can be no such thing as the only correct or appropriate answer. People guided by discourse frameworks like "de-politicizing ethnic issues" tend to favor depoliticizing ethnic issues, while those guided by the opposite tend to firmly support for politicizing them. As regards the question of whether or not "ethnic" issues should be "depoliticized", there is no standard answer as the only correct one that everyone must accept. Hence, "depoliticizing" ethnic issues is in essence an extremely difficult mission, one that is impossible to accomplish, or at the best one of the many policy options to choose from, that is supported by no objective basis in terms of reasonableness, and is entirely dependent on a particular discourse system.

As we can in fact see from Ma's essays, some of his opinions on the relationship between "ethnic group" and "nation" are to a certain degree very similar to the above "social constructivist" position. He points out clearly that there is no impassable gulf between "an ethnic group" and "a nation". With changes in the internal and external conditions (socio-economic development, guidance of government policies and propelling of external forces), an "ethnic group" and a "nation" are transferable (Ma Rong, p. 4, 16). If this is the case, then, as we have perceived, depoliticizing "ethnic" issues would be an undertaking so extremely costly and unbearable that it is nearly impossible to accomplish in the real world.

3.3. *The relationship between "ethnic group" and "nation" is one between "pluralism" and "unity"*

Given the above two points, the following conclusion seems to follow: the core of the question concerning the relationship between ethnic group and nation is not between culturalizing or politicizing, but rather between pluralism and unity. The latter relationship is not the "cultural pluralism–political unity" relationship proposed by Ma, but a pluralism–unity relationship involving economic, political, social, cultural, and other aspects (in the case of individuals, one between "national (or citizen) status" and "ethnic group member status"), or, in Hao Shiyuan's words, between "unification" and "diversification", or "similarities" and "differentiation" (Hao Shiyuan, p. 40). In other words, irrespective of what specific field it might be (i.e., economic, political, social and cultural), there are at least two different levels, i.e., nation-state and "ethnic groups" within a nation-state. At the nation-state level, efforts must be taken to establish a unified pattern that covers all economic, political, social, and cultural fields within the entire range of the nation-state, while at the "ethnic group" level, it is also imperative that sufficient room be left for all "ethnic groups" so that they are able to develop differentiated economic, political, social, and cultural forms and styles on the basis of their respective historical and realistic characteristics. The all-around "unification" (at the nation-state level) and "diversification" (at the "ethnic group" level) in economic, political, social, and cultural fields should be the basic direction for properly addressing the relationship between "nation" and "ethnic group".

In view of the debate between Ma and his critics, I am emphasizing here on two main points:

First, as Ma mentioned specifically in his article, the unification at the state level should not only cover economic, social, and political fields but also include the cultural field. Ma states repeatedly in his article that at the nation-state level, a certain "cultural identity" should also be established;

it would otherwise be hard to establish a new "collective identity" at this level. A nation-state must explore a "common culture" shared by all ethnic groups from its historical development and cultural tradition...

> Much as we divide a "political structure" into different levels, we may similarly divide "culture". Habermas emphasizes that national identity requires a national cultural unity to create a group identity at the nation-state level. "Culture" in a state, therefore, should be regarded as a multi-levelled structure, with at least two important levels comprised by "nation" and "ethnic group"...
>
> If a common culture and shared perception is missing at the nation-state level, conflicts among different cultures at the ethnic group level will be inevitable, making them hard to live harmoniously with each other. Therefore, political systems and administrative restrictions alone are not enough. A certain level of unified cultural identity is also needed at the state level (Ma Rong, p. 27, 28).

He also points out that countries with a strong emphasis on "cultural pluralism", like the United States, "also implement powerful measures for a 'unified national culture'" (Ma Rong, p. 17).

I agree completely with Ma about these statements. Hence, as with Ma's proposal, I fully agree that we must make every effort to build a "Chinese culture" shared by all ethnic groups of the "Chinese nation", which should include the perception of identity with the "Chinese nation", one or several languages and world outlook, values and moral principles mutually shared by members of all ethnic groups, as well as beliefs and customs commonly observed by all ethnic groups, amongst others. And like what Ma describes, there will never be solid economic, social, and political unification until cultural unification is achieved at the state level.

Second, as Ma's critics emphasize repetitively, "pluralism" at the ethnic group level should not merely remain at the cultural field but cover economic, social, and political fields as well. We should allow different ethnic groups to build economic, social, and political forms with their own unique characteristics by enabling them to make choices on their own while taking into account their historical tradition, realistic conditions, and perception without prejudice to the unified nation-state mechanism.

Here, I need to elaborate on three points:

(1) At the ethnic group level, pluralism should be allowed, albeit at varying levels and within a certain range, not only in the cultural field (religious belief, values, etc.), but also the economic (industrial structure,

property forms, etc.), social (marriage, family, community, etc.) and political (legislation, consultation, administration and jurisdiction, etc.) fields (discussed earlier these, will not be revisited here).

(2) Carrying out pluralism at the ethnic group level must observe an absolute precondition of avoiding damage to the unified nation-state mechanism, whether it be in the economic, social, political, or cultural field. Specifically, economic pluralism should not interfere with or damage overall "national economic" operations at the nation-state level; social pluralism should not interfere with or damage social solidarity or social integration at that level; political pluralism should not interfere with cause damage the existence and operation of the nation-state as a political entity (Neil MacCormick, 2009, p. 156)[4]; and cultural pluralism should not interfere with or damage identification and knowledge-sharing at the nation-state level.

(3) this all-around yet measured pluralism at the ethnic group level should not be understood as a mere temporary measure that has to be taken under particular historical conditions, but a permanent necessity that must be carried into the future. Not only out of respect for historical traditions of all ethnic groups, or consideration of the internal and external conditions for them to live and develop, this is due as well to doubts about and renunciation of the "monistic" view of truth and its relevant behavioural patterns (e.g., a "non-discretionary" strategy), as well as understanding and appreciation of the pluralistic perception.

In addressing the "nation-ethnic group" relationship based on the above principles, the biggest problem remains that of properly dividing the duties, rights, and interests of nation-state and ethnic groups in economic, political, social, and cultural terms, i.e., establishing the boundaries of duties, rights, and interests between the two in those terms. It is nothing but a component of the problem concerning the nation–society relationship in the modern history. As with the problem of the nation–society relationship, there may be a lot of perceptual discrepancies and endless detailed disputes over it. We cannot however expect all these problems to vanish completely given a "pluralistic unity" consensus among people. Nevertheless, we can still manage to list some duties and rights that can and must be borne by

---

[4]Neil MacCormick finds a basic principle to be followed here: "self-autonomy" at the ethnic group level neither allows nor needs the form of sovereign state. In this sense, I concur that Ma's proposed "depoliticizing ethnicity" is quite accurate and appropriate in the de-nationalizing perspective.

"nation-states" alone; for example, duties and rights of monopoly of armed force (apart from the state, no ethnic group is allowed to possess armed forces); duties and rights of determining territorial borders, defending territorial security, and resolving territorial disputes; duties and rights of conducting reciprocal exchanges with other nation-states; duties and rights of formulating and implementing legal norms to be observed by all citizens within the state; and duties and rights to handle administrative affairs at the state level, and so on and so forth.

From this perspective, current problems arising from China's ethnic policies may be related, not to "De-politicizing" affairs and relationships of "ethnic groups" which were originally "cultural groups", but to examining whether or not the relationship between the "Chinese nation" and the presently-determined 56 ethnic groups is reasonably and appropriately addressed (in economic, social, political, and cultural terms). On this, we may be facing an incessant discussion. There remains, therefore, a long way ahead of us.

References

Chen Jianyue. Establishing a multiethnic harmonious society and resolving ethnic issues — 'Depoliticising' and 'culturising' ethnic issues. In *De-politicization of Ethnic Questions in China.*

Chen Yuping. My views on 'depoliticizing' ethnic issues. In *De-politicization of Ethnic Questions in China.*

Hao Shiyuan. Establishing a socialist harmonious society and ethnic relations. In *De-politicization of Ethnic Questions in China.*

Ma Rong (2004). A new perspective in guiding ethnic relations in the 21st century: 'depoliticizing' ethnicity in China. *Journal of Peking University* (Philosophy and social sciences), Issue 6. Also see this volume.

Ma Rong (2004). *Ethnosociology: A Sociological Study of Ethnic Issues.* Peking University Press.

Ma Rong (2012a). *Ethnic Group, Nation and State Establishment — Contemporary Chinese Ethnic Minority Issues.* Social Sciences Academic Press.

Ma Rong (2012b). *The Ethnic History and Common Culture of China.* Social Sciences Academic Press.

Neil MacCormick (2009). Does a nation need a state? A review on liberal nationalism. In *People, Nation and State: The Meaning of Ethnicity and Nationalism*, Edward Mortimer and Robert Fine (eds.), pp. 156 (translated by Liu Hong and Huang Haihui). Minzu University Press.

Wang Xien. On 'afterthoughts' of China's ethnic issues and 'being practical' — Debating Ma. In *De-politicization of Ethnic Questions in China.*

Zhou Daming. The two required principles for evaluating national policies from an national perspective. In *De-politicization of Ethnic Questions in China.*

Chapter 1

A NEW PERSPECTIVE IN GUIDING ETHNIC RELATIONS IN THE 21ST CENTURY: "DE-POLITICIZATION" OF ETHNICITY IN CHINA*

MA RONG

Institute of Sociology and Anthropology, Peking University
Beijing 100871, P.R. China

All multi-racial and multi-ethnic nations are confronted with the important issue of how to handle ethnic relations and of the role that the government should play in guiding the direction of such relations. In viewing ethnic minorities, "culturalization" has a tradition of thousands of years in China. Until the late Qing dynasty, that tradition resulted in a united-pluralistic polity with a huge population by assimilation and prosperous economy. Under the new historical conditions of the 20th century, however, China has adopted the policies of the former USSR since the 1950s and given ethnic minorities more political emphasis, what is called the "politicization" of ethnic minorities. This paper proposes that, in the 21st century, China should learn from its own historical heritage and the lessons of the U.S., the former USSR and other nations, and redirect its policy from "politicization" to "culturalization" of ethnic issues so as to strengthen national identity among its ethnic minorities. This new perspective might also be insightful to other multi-racial or multi-ethnic nations around the world in the new century.

1.1. Introduction

Most of the world's countries today are multi-ethnic, due to thousands of years of migration. Some countries have been political entities with

---

*This article was published originally in *Asian Ethnicity*, Volume 8, Number 3, October 2007.

many ethnic groups for very long periods of time. Some countries have accepted "new citizens or permanent residents" from other nations, with various backgrounds in race, national origin, language, and religion. In some countries (such as today's western European countries), the immigrants who have settled down for decades or even generations have become a more or less indispensable part of the local community, even though the receiving country may not have granted them citizenship or "permanent residency". From a sociological point of view, all those societies with the aforementioned features are deemed multi-ethnic societies.

In any political entity with a multi-racial or multi-ethnic composition, the political leaders and elites are confronted with such questions as how to cope with the legal status and basic rights of distinct ethnic groups within its political entity (federation or state); how to regard their socioeconomic structural differences (e.g., in education, industry, occupation, and income) and cultural differences (e.g., in language, religion, and customs); how to understand their existence and evolution (ideology and social norms) and the trends of ethnic-based movement in the future; and the strategies and measures the governments should adopt to guide the trends of inter-ethnic relations for group equality, social justice, ethnic harmony, social stability, and political unity.

A nation with good ethnic relations will be able to strengthen the cohesiveness of its citizens continually through positive internal integration, so as to reduce administrative and operational costs, enhance the efficiency of social and economic organizations, and to strengthen its economic power. In a country where politics, economy, and culture are undergoing positive developments, all ethnic groups will enjoy the benefits brought about by a prosperous economy and by a harmonious society. Although a totally egalitarian distribution of benefits among all members is almost impossible, to a great extent, all ethnic groups are "winners" in the process.

However, a nation with poor ethnic relations will suffer growing social disunity and disintegration caused by internal contradictions, followed by an evident increase in social costs in the forms of money, manpower, and material goods for maintaining social order, which in turn will aggregate the government's expenditures and citizens' tax burdens. In the event that ethnic controversies turn into open political confrontations or separatist movements, the entire society will be turned upside down, which may lead to riots or civil war, or even foreign invasion. Consequently, the state will be quickly weakened or torn apart, the economic foundation and establishments will be destroyed, and all ethnic groups will have to suffer the hardships brought about by social riots, economic collapse and political separation. Then, ultimately, all ethnic groups will become "losers". An apparent example is witnessed in the transformation of ethnic relations in the former Yugoslavia. Hence, ethnic relations have become one of the core problems facing all societies in the 21st century.

1.2. "Nation" and "Ethnic Group"

"Nation" and "ethnic group" are distinct concepts in western literature. In discussing definitions of these terms, Immanuel Wallerstein (1987, p. 380) emphasized that:

> "Race" is supposed to be a genetic category, which has a visible physical form ... A "nation" is supposed to be a socio-political category, linked somehow to the actual or potential boundaries of a state. An "ethnic group" is supposed to be a cultural category, of which there are said to be certain continuing behaviors that are passed on from generation to generation and that are not normally linked in theory to state boundaries ... The last of these three is the most recent and has replaced in effect the previously widely-used term of "minority".[1]

Given their respective time of appearance and inner meaning, these terms represent human groupings at totally different levels and reflect different forms of identity in human society under different historical conditions. "Nation" is related to "nationalism" and the political movement for "national self-determination" taking place in the western Europe in the 17th century. The term "ethnic group", in contrast, only appeared in the 20th century and is commonly used in the U.S., being gradually adopted by other countries. It refers to groups that exist and identify with a pluralist country with various historical backgrounds, cultures, and traditions (including language, religion, and place of origin), and even distinctive physical features. "Ethnicity" only appeared in English dictionaries in the early 1970s (Glazer and Moynihan, 1975, p. 1).

---

[1] All concepts or terms have emerged in human societies under certain circumstances. In other words, they were created to describe a special phenomenon that needs to be distinguished from others. Different groups "learned and borrowed" those terms from each other in the process of interaction. Therefore, the same term (e.g., "ethnicity") might have different meanings in different countries and can be variously interpreted (Fenton, 2003, pp. 25–50).

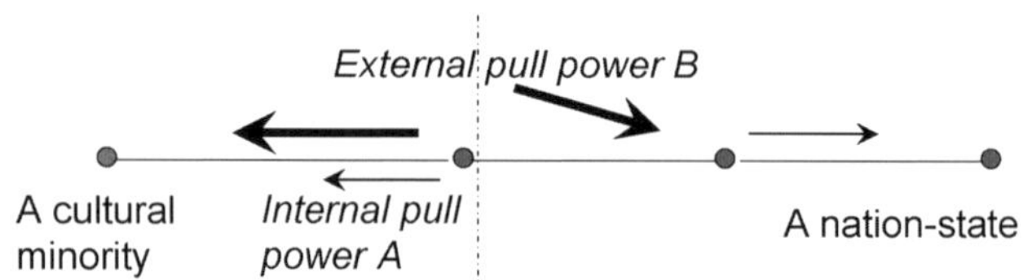

Fig. 1. The "Ethnicity–Nation" Continuum.

There are important differences between ethnic groups, which are characterized by distinct cultural traditions and histories, and nations, which are political entities tied to a more or less stable territory. However, there is no impassable gulf between "an ethnic group" and "a nation". With changes in the internal and external conditions, an "ethnic group" and a "nation" are transferable. Between the "pure" cultural group (a minority group) and the "pure" political entity (state) that can be considered as two "idea types" in ethnic relations, there is a continuum with numerous points or steps of transitions (see Fig. 1). This is a theoretical model in examining the ethnic-nation process. In practice, none has reached either extreme end. In reality, ethnic groups in all countries can be located at various points along this continuum. With economic development, guidance by government policies or endorsement by external forces, an ethnic group would move from its original location toward either end of the continuum; its nature as a "political entity" being either strengthened or weakened.

Therefore, ethnic relations within various nations are multifaceted and dynamic, rather than fixed in a single form. Under the combined pressures of internal and external factors, the quantitative change of a group along this continuum may turn into qualitative change at a certain point. For some ethnic groups, it is possible to split from their home countries and transform into independent nations.[2]

1.2.1. *The terms used in contemporary China concerning "nation" and "ethnic group"*

In China, *minzu* 民族 has been one of the most frequently used terms. Another word *zuqun* 族群 has appeared in the scholarly literatures in recent years. The term corresponding to *minzu* in English is "nation",

---

[2]For example, in referenda in Quebec in 1980 and 1995, if a majority had supported the independence of Quebec, it would have separated from Canada and become a new country.

while the latter corresponds to the English "ethnic group" (or ethnicity). When we speak of the *Zhonghua minzu* 中华民族, the Chinese nation, and the 56 *minzu* or "nationalities" in Chinese official translation, we actually confuse their conceptual difference by using the same word for two different concepts.

Accordingly, some years ago I made the suggestion to keep the term "Chinese nation", and change any reference to the 56 "nationalities" to "ethnic groups" or "ethnic minorities" when these groups are referred to as a whole (Ma Rong, 2001, p. 156). My proposal was based on three considerations. First, the social and cultural connotations of the minority groups such as Mongolians, Manchus, Tibetans, Uygurs, and Hui in China approximate to "racial and ethnic minorities" in other countries, such as the American Indians, African Americans and Hispanics in the U.S.[3] Thus, the term "ethnic groups" reflects the structure of ethnicity in China more accurately. Second, by differentiating among these terms, conceptual confusion resulting from two different meanings (the "Chinese nation" and "ethnic groups" making up the "Chinese nation") for the same term in Chinese will be avoided.[4] Finally, if we translate China's 56 ethnic groups (*minzu*) as 56 "nationalities", and name their requests on behalf of economic and cultural interests as "nationalism",[5] we seriously mislead English-speaking readers who might associate these groups with independent political entities who have the right to carry out "national self-determination" and establish their own independent "nation-states."

The reason we distinguish between "nation" and "ethnic group" in the Chinese language is because the different use of these terms may actually imply varied orientations for viewing, understanding, and managing ethnic relations.

---

[3]There are great variations among the Chinese minorities regarding their population size, residential patterns and historical relationship with the Han majority. These groups may be viewed as spreading along the "ethnic group-nation" continuum in Fig. 1. Tibet was close to the right end (*de facto* independent) before 1951. The Manchus were close to the left end and had largely lost their identity by 1949. Nine minority groups had a population of less than 9,000 in 2000 (Ma Rong, 2004, p. 662).

[4]Some Western scholars used "ethnic relations" to describe majority–minority relations, while using the term "nationalities" in referring to Chinese official statements (e.g., Dreyer, 1976).

[5]"Regional nationalism" of minorities often appeared in Chinese documents. This term in Chinese interpretation only refers to the requests of economic benefits, cultural autonomy, and limited political autonomy within the present system.

1.3. Two Types of Policies for Managing Ethnic Relations: Politicization and Culturalization

Government policy plays an important role in guiding group identity and adjusting the boundaries of a political entity. Throughout the history of social development, governments have generally adopted two contrasting policies for regulating ethnic relations: one views ethnic groups mainly as political entities and the other views them primarily as cultural groups. The former policy emphasizes integrity, political power, and "territorial" conservation of ethnic groups. The later prefers to treat ethnic relations as cultural interactions, and to deal with the problems between people of different ethnic backgrounds as affairs among individuals rather than between groups as a whole, even though the common characteristics of the ethnic group membership are given recognition. By emphasizing the cultural characteristics of ethnic groups, their political interests are diluted. Furthermore, in processes of migration, the historical connection between ethnic groups and their traditional residence is gradually loosened.

1.3.1. *The traditional culture-centered view of ethnic relations in Chinese history*

Historically, the eastern Asian continent has been a motherland to many ethnic groups. Among these groups were more "advanced" Han Chinese and relatively less advanced minority "barbarians", including nomads in grasslands and people living in mountainous areas in the south.[6] In the traditional Chinese cultural norms, ethnic identity rested on the distinction between barbarian minorities and civilized Han. This distinction, according to Confucianism, does not refer to apparent differences in physical features or language. Rather, it is mainly shown in cultural differences with values and norms of behavior as the distinguishing characteristics.

Two contemporary scholars have written (Zhang Lei and Kong Qingrong, 1999, p. 285):

> According to Confucianism, the distinction between "*hua (xia)*" (civilized Han) and *yi* (minority barbarians) was a cultural boundary rather than a racial and national boundary... The barbarian–civilized distinction did not indicate racial or national exclusiveness. Instead, it was a distinction involving differentiated levels of cultural achievement.

---

[6]The terms "advanced" and "less advanced" refer only to the development stage of science and technology, not the nature of "culture".

In other words, the "barbarian–civilized" distinction did not indicate division and exclusivity between different "civilizations" such as that between medieval Christianity and Islam. Instead, it referred to the distinction between highly developed and less developed "civilizations" with similar roots but at different stages of advancement. The less developed minorities ("barbarians") accepted such a distinction, and actively sought knowledge from Chinese civilization. Therefore, although there were conflicts and wars between the dynasties in the "core area" and minorities in the peripheries, what characterized the interaction between the "more civilized" and "less civilized" groups was not mainly hostility and mutual destruction but cultural diffusion and learning.

The ancient Chinese viewed Chinese culture as "the most advanced civilization" of the world, which would sooner or later influence surrounding "barbarians". In this point of view, those who were acculturated by Chinese civilization became "members" of this "civilized" world with "Han" as its "core". Those who were un-acculturated remained "barbarians" who needed to be "educated". Ambrose King (1997, p. 177) argues that, as a political entity, traditional China was unlike any other nation-states, since "it was a political-cultural entity, or what is called the civilized state, which was marked by cultural rather than ethnic differentiations, and consequently followed a unique civilized order".

In discussing "the nature of Chinese nationalism", the great American Sinologist John King Fairbank (1979, p. 98) emphasized that:

> Undoubtedly this universalism has meant that culture (the way of life) has been more fundamental in China than nationalism. Early Chinese emperors asserted that they ruled over all civilized mankind without distinction of race or language. Barbarian invaders who succeeded them found it expedient to continue and reinforce this tradition. To any Confucian ruler, Chinese or alien, the important thing was the loyalty of his administrators and their right conduct according to the Confucian code. Color and speech were of little account as long as a man understood the classics and could act accordingly.[7]

Since culture can be learned and taught, Chinese traditional ideology therefore held that the two sides of the "civilized–barbarian distinction" were transferable. That is to say: "evil Chinese retreat to being barbarians, and fine barbarians advance to becoming Chinese" (Zhang Lei and Kong

---

[7]The fact that most groups in China belong to the Mongoloid also made the physical differences less significant in China.

Qingrong, 1999, p. 285). "Fine" refers to "civilized" whereas "evil" means "uncivilized". This ideology articulates dialectic reasoning and echoes a tolerant attitude on the part of Chinese culture towards other cultures.

Chinese emperors, elites, and people considered ethnic minorities that had accepted Chinese culture as "civilized" citizens and treated them fairly equally. Yet, they adopted a discriminating attitude toward the "barbarian" groups. The foundation of such discrimination, however, was "cultural superiority" rather than "racial superiority". Behind this superiority was a flexible and dialectic view that accepted "barbarian" groups to be "civilized" through acculturation. Following the principle of "teaching without discrimination", it was the Chinese cultural tradition to transform the "uncivilized" minorities into "civilized" members of society through acculturation rather than military conquest.

In the Chinese cultural tradition, the "civilized–barbarian distinction" was advocated along with a unified view of "the world" (*tianxia* or "all under heaven"), which emphasized that "all lands belong to the emperor and all people are his subjects". Both "barbarians" and "civilized" were under the same "heaven", and thus "barbarians" could be "educated". Based on these thoughts, in the Chinese cultural tradition, all ethnic groups were considered equal to each other. This idea was most explicitly expressed in the Confucian saying that "all people around the four seas are brothers", which emphasized that all ethnic groups should be treated equally; that their differences in biological characteristics,[8] language, religion, and customs should not override their common traits in basic ethics and norms or peaceful coexistence among them; and that the main difference between ethnic groups is cultural, with the "superior (more advanced) culture" being capable of integrating all other cultural groups.[9] It is a "diffusion model" (Hechter, 1975, p. 6), but one that only emphasizes the aspect of culture. In Chinese history, it is quite clear that, when acculturation occurred among the "barbarians", a diffusion process followed in other respects.

---

[8] In the Chinese tradition, there was no clear correspondence to the Western term "race" (Stafford, 1993, p. 609). I do not agree with Frank Dikötter's argument about racism in modern Chinese thought. The statements he cites from Kang Youwei (1858–1927), Sun Yatsen (1866–1925), or Su Xiaokang (b. 1949) only expressed the influence of Western categories in modern China (see, Dikötter, 1997, pp. 1–4).

[9] In his study, Frank Dikötter noticed the distinction between "outside barbarians" and "inside barbarians" and he also said that "despite many disparaging comments on the supposedly bestial origins of the minorities, the Han perception of minority Chinese remained embedded in an ethnocentric framework that stressed sociocultural differences" (Dikötter, 1992). Therefore, sociocultural differences, not biological differences, were major indicators of ethnic characteristics and boundaries in ancient China.

American sociologist Milton Gordon classifies ideologies concerning ethnic issues into two categories. One view maintains ethnic inequalitarianism or racism, while the other view supports ethnic equalitarianism or nonracism. Gordon further divides the second view into three sub-categories, namely (1) assimilationist structure, (2) liberal pluralism, and (3) corporate pluralism (Gordon, 1975, pp. 105–106). The Chinese traditional view of ethnicity ("teaching without discrimination") and practice ("transforming barbarian into civilized") belongs to the ideological type of assimilationist structure.

Although there is always politics in issues concerning race, nationality and ethnic groups, ideas on "majority–minority relations" or "civilized–barbarian relations" were to a great extent "culturalized" in the Chinese cultural tradition, in both theory and practice. This strategy enabled the civilized group in the core region to unify and embody the ethnic minorities in periphery areas. In addition, the Chinese tradition of treating ethnic differences as "cultural differences" made it possible to implement the policy of "transforming barbarian into civilized", which resulted in attracting ethnic minorities from the periphery areas and the ultimate formation of a unified pluralist Chinese nation with the Han group in the central plain as the core (Fei Xiaotong, 1989, p. 19). But it should be noticed that the idea of "cultural racism" also emerged among the ethnic groups and their elites throughout the historical interactions among the groups. Sometimes, when the central government was weak, while ethnic minorities became a fatal threat to the Han group, then "barbarians" were viewed as the enemy who could not be "civilized" and become a part of China. For instance, during the late Qing dynasty when the western and Japanese invasions became a fatal threat to China's independence and culture, racism among the Han elites became very strong.

1.3.2. *The European nationalism movement:* *"politicizing" ethnicity*

With industrialization and emergence of capitalism, a trend began in some European countries to "politicize" majority–minority relations. By advocating the regrouping of political entities around the world based on "national identity", the essence of the contemporary "nationalism" became the establishment of "nation-states" through "national self-determination". Thus the "nationalist" movement was an important historical landmark in the "politicizing" of ethnic issues.

Ernest Gellner (1983, p. 1) has remarked: "nationalism is primarily a political principle, which holds that the political and national unit should be congruent.... Nationalism is a theory of political legitimacy, which requires that ethnic boundaries should not cut across political ones". Nationalism did not exist in the past, emerging only in the process of industrialization. Gellner (1983, p. 40) also states,

> The age of transition to industrialism was bound ... also to be an age of nationalism, a period of turbulent readjustment, in which either political boundaries, or cultural ones, or both, were being modified, so as to satisfy the new nationalist imperative which now, for the first time, was making itself felt.

With the emergence of "nationalist" ideologies and political movements in western Europe, "nation-states" were established. European capitalism was first developed in the Netherlands in the early 17th century. Holland was considered the "first capitalist nation-state". Dutch jurist Hugo Grotius treated the independent "nation-state" as the principal unit of international law or the sole authority of the state. In France, the French Revolution overthrew the Bourbon Dynasty's Louis 16th in 1789. In resistance against the armed forces of other monarchical states, the French "citizens" were enthused with nationalism in defending their motherland. During the American War of Independence in the 18th century, the idea that "all men are created equal" inspired the people to establish their own independent state. Consequently, the American War of Independence and the French Revolution were regarded as important landmarks or pioneers for the construction of contemporary nationalism.

The 20th century witnessed three waves of nationalist movements. The first wave took place at the end of World War I. With the collapse of the Ottoman and Austro-Hungarian Empires, a number of "nation-states" were established in eastern and southern Europe.

The second wave arose in the mid-20th century following World War II. With the weakening of the global colonial system, "nationalist" movements were launched in colonies in the African, Asian, Latin American, and Pacific regions. Those educated in European countries or influenced by western ideologies became indigenous elites who promoted the local "nationalist" movement.[10] Under these new historical conditions, the colonial countries

---

[10]There were political maps in the mind of these indigenous elites, which referred to the administrative boundaries of colonies, not to cultural, linguistic or tribal boundaries. The new "nation-states" were "imagined communities" rooted in colonialist education and administration (Hobsbawm, 1990, p. 138; Anderson, 1991).

had no choice but to consent to the independence of the former colonies. As a result, a large number of newly independent states were established in the colonies, some of them copying the political and administrative structures of western "nation-states". Theses newly independent states are the "liberated type" of "nation-states", regardless of whether they are ethnically more homogeneous (such as Iraq, Egypt, and Algeria) or heterogeneous (such as India, Indonesia, and Malaysia).

The collapse of the USSR started the third nationalist wave of the 20th century. National separatist movements took place in the former USSR and some eastern European countries, such as former Yugoslavia and Czechoslovakia. During this movement, 23 newly independent states were established on the territory of the former three states. Separatist movements have continued to cause instability in some of these states.

1.3.3. *Continuation of the European tradition of "politicizing" ethnicity by the former USSR*

Communism is deeply tinted with ideology and thus has a tendency to "ideologize" cultural or social differences among ethnic groups, using political measures to deal with these differences or issues. After the October Revolution of 1917, imperial interventionists employed "national self-determination" as a political slogan to instigate the ethnic groups' rivalry in Russia against the new proletarian regime. To counteract this trend, Vladimir Ilyich Lenin decided to support "national self-determination" selectively on the basis of whether it would be beneficial to the proletarian revolution or not. In the political climate of the time, the Soviet leadership used the idea of the Federation or the Union to unite those ethnic groups under the rule of the former Tsarist Russia (Wang Liping, 2000, p. 151). However, as one specialist has written (Rakowska-Harmstone, 1986, p. 239):

> The convergence of ethnic and administrative boundaries results in politicization of ethnicity and emergence of nationalism. The identification of ethnic with political and socioeconomic structures sharpens the perception of each group's relative position in the competition for the allocation of social values.

Various groups were linked together under the Federation or the Union, while maintaining their own republics or autonomous regions and a full range of political rights. It was exactly this type of institution that later provided legal grounds for these groups to separate themselves from the

USSR and to establish their own independent states. Vladimir Ilyich Lenin pointed out clearly that the Union is, under unique historical conditions, a "transitional" form toward complete unification (a unitary state) (Vladimir Ilyich Lenin, 1920, p. 126). After Vladimir Ilyich Lenin's death, the Soviet regime was consolidated, with the Communist Party enjoying high prestige among the people, especially after World War II. Joseph Stalin had many opportunities to lead all groups from this "transitional" stage into a unified nation, but he and his successors failed to do so.[11] Instead, the transitional stage became permanent and persisted for several decades until the Soviet Union's last days.

In handling ethnic relations, the Soviet government emphasized the political power of minority groups, either consciously or unconsciously, and institutionalized such power. Minority groups were treated as political units and thus "politicized". At the macro level, political entities such as "Soviet republics", "autonomous republics" or "autonomous states" led to the establishment of autonomous administrations and the identification of nationalities or ethnic groups connected with their own territory. These groups thus became "territorialized", which implied "a nation".

At the micro level, in the 1930s, a "nationality recognition" campaign was implemented, and every resident's "nationality status" was identified and formally registered in his/her internal passport. The internal passport system that lists the owner's nationality "has had a negative impact on integration", because it has created a "legal–psychological deterrent" (Rakowska-Harmstone, 1986, p. 252).

Thus, the individual's nationality status became evident and permanent, and membership boundaries between ethnic groups became unambiguously marked and fixed. Government policies favoring minorities in terms of language, education, the promotion of cadres and financial aid further strengthened clear group identification and boundaries. The USSR Government also tried to establish a new identity for the "Soviet People (Soviet man)" among all ethnic groups, but this identity was mainly based on political–ideological ties (Sovietism or communism). When people

---

[11]There might be several reasons why Joseph Stalin did not change the system. First, the USSR took control of several East European countries, so to maintain individual republics in the USSR lessened these countries' concerns about formal Soviet expansion. Second, the three Baltic nations (Estonia, Latvia, and Lithuania) had just recently become union republics of the USSR, and a change in the system could bring about desires for independence. Third, since the Cold War had begun just after World War II, the votes of Ukraine and Byelorussia might be helpful in the United Nations in negotiations with the U.S.

lost belief in Sovietism and communism during the reforms promoted by Gorbachev and the rise of Russian nationalism promoted by Boris Yeltsin, the base of the new identity also collapsed.

The Soviet practice of "politicizing" minority groups and the corresponding institutionalization of minority groups greatly influenced Chinese policy after 1949.

1.3.4. *The "Politicization" of ethnic groups re-emerges in the process of globalization*

With the end of the construction of nation-states, globalization has become a universally popular topic. Some scholars have noticed that, in the processes of globalization, a new tendency towards "politicizing" ethnicity has reappeared both within multi-ethnic nations and between states. "National self-determination" has once again become a political weapon for domestic groups or external hostile powers to split or weaken some multi-ethnic nations. Joseph Rothschild (1981, p. 2) has stated:

> In modern and transitional societies — unlike traditional ones — politicizing ethnicity has become the critical principle of political legitimation and delegitimation of systems, states, regimes, and governments and at the same time has also become an effective instrument for pressing mundane interests in society's competition for power, status, and wealth.

In the process of modernization, societal–institutional change and readjustment of power and interest give rise to opportunities for various ethnic groups to acquire and defend power and resources. The ethnic group thus becomes an ideal cohesive group unit and an effective tool for social mobilization. Ethnic groups advantaged and disadvantaged in social competition will all strive to "politicize" ethnicity in order to mobilize their followers and establish ethnically based political and economic interest groups. Under such circumstances, ethnic conflict becomes one of the major sources of social instability, violent conflicts, and state break-up.

Rothschild (1981, pp. 6–7) states further,

> Many observers, indeed, have been so fascinated and/or alarmed by this initially destabilizing impact of freshly politicized ethnicity that they have interpreted it as launching an absolutist, zero-sum type of politics over uncompromisable values and rights (for example, to self-determination, group status, territorial control) and, hence, as more dangerous to civic order than class and functional interest-group politics are...More seriously, it is also true that the energies of ethnic politics have sometimes produced catastrophic violence.

The above analysis provides us with some insights for understanding the effects and ideological basis of the "politicization" of domestic ethnicity, as well as its potential to damage national stability. Such trends are visible in many countries.

1.3.5. *The policy of "acculturation" in the U.S.*

In industrialized countries, the U.S. in particular, the idea of "nation" has increasingly become a symbol of a stable political entity. The concept of "racial and ethnic groups", in contrast, has gradually been faded out in its political meaning. With more frequent interactions and intermarriages, boundaries separating ethnic groups have become blurred, with members of all ethnic groups being acculturated by one another. Members from all racial and ethnic groups have been led to look upon themselves as equal citizens. The Constitution and government protect the rights of minority group citizens.[12] In daily life or social events, members of minority groups are officially treated as individual cases rather than collectives of an independent political group. Problems (such as inadequacy of the English language or lower levels of education) faced by disadvantaged groups are not perceived as "political interests" and regulated through government policies. Rather, these problems are resolved through assistance from public or semi-public social welfare programs. As a result, ethnicity-related issues are shown as individual or social problems, not political issues facing the entire ethnic group.

For a long time, the U.S. government and the mainstream society have operated on the policy of assimilation without enforcing an identical majority–minority culture through administrative measures. Enforced assimilation is in essence an indication of "politicizing" ethnicity. In promoting a unified political entity, the U.S. government and the mainstream society direct the public to look upon differences in ethnicity and religion mainly as "cultural diversity" within a "pluralist society".

Considering the long-term existence of racial and ethnic diversity and conflicts, American academic circles proposed in the mid-20th century the goal of achieving "cultural pluralism" (Gordon, 1964, pp. 157–159), and of perceiving ethnic groups as "sub-cultures". There are three measures for achieving the goal. The first is to enforce a unified federal law and the mainstream culture (English as the *de facto* official language

---

[12]Of course there are still racial/ethnic prejudice and discrimination in the U.S., but the situation has improved greatly since the Civil Rights Movement of the 1960s.

and the Christian culture). Secondly, preservation of certain traditions by ethnic minorities is permitted. Finally, to avoid race/ethnicity-based discrimination in employment and in other aspects of social life, Americans are not required to identify their racial-ethnicity status for job applications and, for school admission application, this item is optional. In the census questionnaire, the item on "race/ethnicity" is optional and filled out by the informant himself/herself.[13] The government also purposefully de-stresses or blurs ethnic boundaries through reducing residential and school segregation and adopts a neutral attitude towards intermarriages and other practices (e.g. interracial adaptation).

In the past half-century, the U.S. has emphasized "pluralism" in dealing with racial and ethnic relations. "Pluralism", of course, does not indicate any form of division by ethnic groups, either politically or geographically. Instead, American "pluralism" is overseen by a strong unified political entity at both the federal and state levels. Although the government sanctions the establishment of ethnically based, inclusive informal cultural organizations, the setting up of racial/ethnic-exclusive organizations with tendencies towards political and economic "self-determination" is prohibited. Obviously, the U.S. government stresses a "unified politics" by all racial and ethnic groups, although such a view is not openly communicated in the discussion of ethnic issues. Yet, with its advanced economy and a strong armed force, the tendency of "self determination" and of establishing an independent state still exists among certain minority groups and their organizations living at the bottom of the society, such as the African-Americans and American-Indians, even if in a very weak form.[14] The U.S. government keeps a close eye on any organizations with this tendency.

In addition to political and economic unification, the U.S. also imple-ments powerful measures for a "unified national culture". For example, the most popular language in public is English. Fundamental values and norms of behavior — the core of culture — are also shaped by mainstream society. In fact, members of minority groups will hardly advance in society unless they learn English. Also, they will face tremendous difficulties in interaction with mainstream of the community and government agencies unless they

[13]That was why 2.4% of the respondents of the 2000 U.S. Census reported their racial status with two or more races, 823 respondents even reported six races in their census reports of racial/ethnic status (Farley and Haaga, 2005, p. 335).
[14]"In the United States, only among the most disadvantaged minorities do we find such separatist tendencies" (Yinger, 1986, p. 25).

accept and learn Christian values and norms. Therefore, "pluralism" does not help to preserve independent "cultural groups"; it only permits the existence of "sub-cultural groups" and preservation of certain aspects of their tradition. The U.S. government and politicians will not accept any "cultural groups" with tendency of self-determination, as they will endanger the political unity of the U.S.

In sum, since the Civil Rights Movement of the 1960s, a fundamental policy and the guiding ideology of the U.S. Government in handling racial and ethnic issues has been to develop minority groups into "sub-cultural groups" within a pluralist society, or to "acculturate" and to "de-politicize" ethnicity in the U.S.

1.4. The Political and Cultural Levels of "Ethnicity"

1.4.1. *"An ethnic group" might become a "nation" and re-write its history*

Indigenous ethnic groups have their traditional area of residence. Immigrant groups have their place of origin. Wallerstein (1987, p. 385) states:

> The concept "ethnic group" is therefore as linked in practice to state boundaries as is the concept "nation", despite the fact that this is never included in the definition. The difference is only that a state tends to have one nation and many ethnic groups.

This means that "ethnicity" is not only meaningful at a cultural level but at a political level as well. It indicates that, under favorable conditions, "an ethnic group" has the potential to become a "nation". Therefore there is no impassable gulf between the "ethnic group" and a "nation". The leaders and elite of ethnic minorities will fight for their power and space in a national political structure, and they are also given some political space by the government in some nations.

Wallerstein (1987, p. 384) provides a vivid case of the Sahrawi people in northern Africa.

> Is there a Sahrawi nation? If you ask Polisario, the national liberation movement, they will say yes, and to add that there has been one for a thousand years. If you ask the Moroccans, there never has been a Sahrawi nation, and the people who live in what was once the colony of the Spanish Sahara were always part of the Moroccan nation. How can we resolve this difference intellectually? The answer is that we cannot. If by the year 2000 or perhaps 2020, Polisario wins, there will have

been a Sahrawi nation. And if Morocco wins, there will not have been. Any historian writing in 2100 will take it as a settled question, or more probably still as a non-question.

In order to make their independent movement legitimate, some ethnic groups will work very hard to "prove" that their group established a legitimate and independent "nation" a long time ago. Meantime, governments and other groups rarely accept the "evidence" they provide. But if one such group successfully becomes an independent nation, the materials that prove "the history of this ancient nation" would become the new official historical record.

1.4.2. *Practical measures of "politicizing" ethnicity: Institutionalization of ethnic status and ethnic relations*

One important measure was that governments can identify and recognize an "ethnic status" for each of its citizens as part of a political system. Any citizen who wants to change his/her ethnic status applies for permission from government offices with certain criteria. In China, for instance, some applicants switch from the ethnic status of one of his/her parents to that of the other, after the applicant reaches the age of 18 in the case of intermarriage. Also, in cases where the government was mistaken in a previous status allocation in the 1950s, then the relevant person might like to apply for "correction" of his/her status, in order to obtain some benefits assigned to minorities. This situation happened after the "Cultural Revolution" when CCP called to "correct" the political mistakes during the "Revolution".[15]

The institutionalization of ethnic groups systematically creates institutional barriers for the interaction and integration between the members of different ethnic groups. This official system always reminds them that they belong to "a specific group". Clarifying the boundaries between ethnic groups and fixing the "membership" of each ethnic group makes the ethnic boundaries become a social issue, and when the ethnic status is related to some favorable or discriminatory policies, ethnic boundaries will become a political issue.

The measure of institutionalizing ethnic relations might have both a positive and negative impact. Favorable policies toward disadvantaged

---

[15]That policy resulted in millions of people changing their status from Han to a minority in the early 1980s.

groups might improve the situation in ethnic stratification and reduce the structural differences in education, industry, occupation, and income among groups. Discriminatory policies towards disadvantaged groups might worsen the situation in ethnic stratification and provoke ethnic tension. In both cases, these policies designed for ethnic groups as a whole will certainly strengthen ethnic identity and consciousness. Under certain historical and social circumstances, policies favorable toward minorities might effectively improve ethnic relations and reduce tensions and promote cooperation, but these policies will certainly not weaken ethnic consciousness or promote integration.

The former Soviet Union politicized and institutionalized its minority groups and made great progress in helping minorities to improve their education and socio-economic development in minority regions. The relationship between Russians and other groups was generally improved. But based on the institutionalized ethnic relations (union republic — autonomous republic — autonomous region) and fixed ethnic status, the consciousness and political interests of ethnic groups were obviously strengthened. When international and domestic political attitudes and conditions change, as happened in the USSR in the late 1980s, the political consciousness of ethnic groups will be provoked and turned into "nationalist" movements aiming at independence based on their autonomous "territory".

There are many interpretations among scholars and politicians as to why the USSR and Yugoslavia disintegrated. Ways of treating minorities should be considered one of the most important factors. There is a great contrast between the Soviet Union and the U.S. in the way they handle ethnic relations. The former "politicized" and institutionalized ethnicity/nationality, while the other "culturalized" or "de-politicized" ethnic minorities.

1.4.3. *"Culturalism" and "nationalism" in modern China*

The Indian/American historian Prasenjit Duara has proposed looking at Chinese history from what he terms a "bifurcating linear way", which he believes was how the ideas and narratives of Chinese history were formulated in the past. He recognizes "culturalism" as the core of Chinese traditional views of different groups, and that this was a "mode of consciousness distinct from nationalism". He states (Duara, 1995, p. 56):

> Viewing "culturalism" (or universalism) as a "Chinese culturalism" is to see it not as a form of cultural consciousness per se, but rather to see culture — a specific culture of the imperial state and Confucian orthodoxy — as a criterion defining a community. Membership in this

community was defined by participation in a ritual order that embodied allegiance to Chinese ideas and ethics.

But Duara also claims that there was another "nationalist" route in Chinese history in viewing minorities. When "barbarians" could no longer be educated in the Confucian manner but became so strong militarily as to threaten the existence of Chinese empire and culture, the Chinese elite would be forced to turn to the "nationalist route". For example, "during the Jin invasion of the 12th century, segments of the literati completely abandoned the concentric, radiant concept of universal empire for a circumscribed notion of the Han community and fatherland (*guo*) in which the barbarians had no place" (Duara, 1995, p. 58). Then a defensive "nationalism" emerged among the elite and people.

Towards the end of the Qing dynasty (late nineteenth to early twentieth centuries), "nationalism" emerged among the Han Chinese elite who had supported the Qing for over two centuries mainly because of the failures of the Qing in the wars against imperialist invasions. Sun Yat-sen and his colleagues, who were influenced by this nationalist movement, issued a call to "expel the barbarian Manchus and restore China". By contrast, Kang Youwei, the leader of the ideologically "royalist" defenders of the Qing dynasty,

> cited Confucius to argue that although Confucius has spoken of barbarians, barbarism was expressed as a lack of ritual and civilization. If indeed they possessed culture, then they must be regarded as Chinese... he was convinced that community was composed of people with shared culture and not restricted to a race or ethnic group. (Duara, 1995, p. 74)

When the Qing dynasty was overthrown in 1911, China faced a very different situation, and among its many problems were independence movements by the ethnic minorities. As Duara (1995, p. 76) writes,

> Sun Yat-sen and the leaders of the new Republic sought to supplement their racialist narrative with the culturalist narrative of the nation espoused by their enemies — the reformers and the Qing court itself. The Chinese nation was now to be made up of the "five races" (Manchu, Mongol, Tibetan, Muslim, and Han).

Prasenjit Duara applied his "bifurcating linear way" mainly in examining Chinese history in the late Qing dynasty. But this approach can be applied to the period after the 1911 revolution and even to that after the 1950s.

During the Republican period, Chiang Kaishek followed the "culturalist" framework and denied Mongol, Tibetan, Hui, etc. status as "nationalities/nations", considering these groups as tribes of the Chinese nation. He emphasized that China should be "one nation and one leadership". Meanwhile, the Chinese Communist Party followed the Soviet model and "nationalist" narrative, claiming that these groups were "nationalities". They should have the right to "self-determination" and to establish their own nations.[16]

Sun Yat-sen learned "culturalism" from the royalists, and passed it on to Chiang Kai-shek; the Chinese Communist Party learned "nationalism" first from revolutionists of the late Qing and then from the Russians. This is the unimaginable historical dialect in a nation's development process. It switches its positions continually along a bifurcating linear route (see Fig. 2).

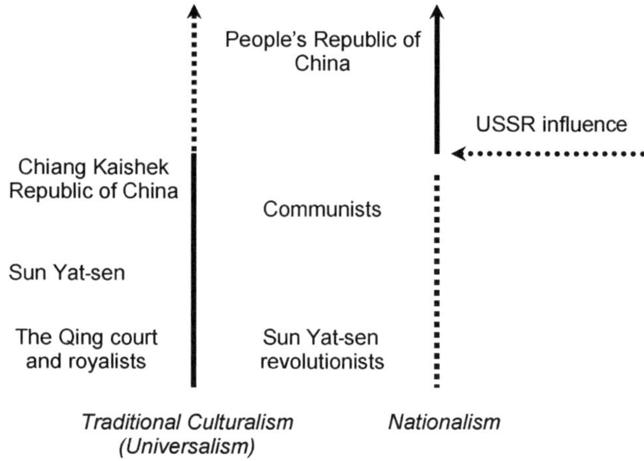

Fig. 2.   The Bifurcating Linear Route in China.

1.4.4. *The policies of the Chinese government since 1949*

Although there were some tortuous periods in ethnic relations in the thousands of years of Chinese history, the mainstream in ethnic relations and integration among the groups has always been "culturalism". This

---

[16]This attitude of the CCP changed after they assumed power in 1949 (Connor, 1984, p. 87).

process lasted until the 1950s. Under the international circumstances at that time, especially the Korean War of 1950–1953, the Chinese leaders, who were extremely inexperienced in administrative matters, had to seek support from the Soviet Union. They copied almost all the Soviet models in terms of administration, education, the economy and military affairs. The government also followed the Soviet model by politicizing and institutionalizing the ethnic minorities in China.

First, the government organized the "identification of nationalities" in the 1950s. Eventually 56 "nationalities" were identified, their population ranging from 718 (Hezhe)[17] to 547,283,057 (Han in the 1953 census). All Chinese citizens were registered by "nationality status" in household registration and personal identification. This system is still in practice today.

Second, the system of autonomy was established for all ethnic minorities. There are five autonomous regions at the provincial level, 30 autonomous prefectures and 120 autonomous counties in today's China. The total areas of these autonomous places together make up 64% of China's territory. The system assumes that the minority groups play a leading role and manage their own affairs in autonomous areas. The National People's Congress adopted the Autonomy Law of Minority Nationalities of the People's Republic of China in 1984. It contains detailed items regarding the administration, jurisdiction, education, religious and cultural affairs, and local regulations in the autonomous places and has become one of China's most important laws.

Third, the government has designed and practiced a series of policies in favor of ethnic minorities in the administrative, educational, economic and cultural areas, and even in family planning programs.[18] The central government provides large amounts of financial aid to these autonomous places each year. Aid accounted for 38–94% of the total budget of the five autonomous regions in 2002 (Ma Rong, 2004, p. 525). These policies helped

---

[17]The Hezhe, a fishing group living along the Amur River, was officially recognized as a "nationality" in the late 1950s and the registration records showed the group with only 718 persons in the 1964 census.

[18]The members of the minority groups were usually allowed to have more children while the Han have been restricted to the policy of "one couple, one child". This was one of the most important reasons why many farmers tried to change their "nationality status" from Han to a minority group. From 1982 to 1990, several minority groups doubled their population size mainly by re-registration (e.g., the Manchu population increased from 4.3 million to 9.8 million, and Tujia increased from 2.8 million to 5.7 million during these 8 years) (Ma Rong, 2004, p. 662).

the minorities to speed up socio-economic development and reduced the disparities between ethnic groups. But since these policies were targeted clearly at specific groups, they also strengthened ethnic consciousness, while the boundaries between ethnic groups became clearer and more stable than they had earlier been.

These policies link each ethnic minority to a certain geographic area, provide these groups with a political status, administrative power in their "autonomous territory", and guarantee ethnic minorities the potential to develop at a higher speed. The process of establishing and implementing these policies and the institutions, with their emphasis on "equality between ethnic groups" rather than "equality among citizens", will inevitably politicize and institutionalize these groups and strengthen their group consciousness. This will have the effect of pushing them away from being "cultural groups" and towards the direction of becoming "political groups" in the "ethnicity–nation" continuum.

One of the reasons why the governments of some nations, including China, pay attention to the political aspects of minorities has been the pressure from western countries to promote human rights and democracy. In response to critical comments from western countries, these governments have tried to enhance the political status and power of ethnic minorities in their countries. They have hoped that these measures would alleviate the criticism, but in fact this has not happened. The result is that minority groups ask for more powers, and their requests are always supported by the western nations. The political concessions of these governments towards minority affairs has done nothing to resolve the tension among their ethnic groups, but instead created a more solid base for future separatist movements.

1.5. The Ideal Nation–ethnicity Framework: Political Unity and Cultural Pluralism

1.5.1. *Political unity and equality among all ethnic groups*

Fei Xiaotong (1989) proposed a framework of "a pluralist-unity structure" to describe the basic pattern of ethnic relations in Chinese history. This theory can be further developed into a framework of "political unity-cultural pluralism", which means strengthening the "national identity" of all citizens at the nation level while promoting cultural characteristics at the ethnic group level. Of course, political and legal equality among all groups should be the precondition and political base for this framework. At the nation-state level, the equality of all citizens (including all ethnic groups) and the political and legal rights asserted by the Constitution should be guaranteed, as well as the rights of all groups to maintain and develop their own cultural traditions (including language, religion, customs, etc.). This framework combines political unity, ethnic equality, and cultural diversity.

1.5.2. *"Ethnic cultural pluralism" and "national cultural identity"*

There are two levels in cultural identities: one is the traditional culture of each ethnic group at the group level; another is the national culture at the national level. Habermas (1998) emphasizes that national identity requires a national cultural unity to create a group identity at the nation-state level. At the national level, the members of all ethnic groups should respect the common social norms; at the ethnicity level, each group should respect, even appreciate, the cultures of other groups.

An Indian scholar, who has spent a long time in the former Soviet Union, has made a comparison between the frameworks in the nation-building process in India and the Soviet Union. He comments (Behera, 1995, p. 31) that

> the Soviet Union came into existence as a multinational nation-state without creating an inter-ethnic, composite culture which would have promoted a common identity of the Soviet people in the form of "Soviet nationalism". In the absence of such a common unifying identity, constituent nationalities were bound to develop separate, distinct identities of their own which led to the growth of separate nationalism.

The former Soviet Union took a great risk by handling its nationality/ethnicity issues the way it did. The assumption that by emphasizing a common ideology (communism) would create a major linkage connecting its ethnic groups was fraught with peril and turned out to be false. The nation was at risk of disintegrating if the ideological linkage among the ethnic groups collapsed, because separate national identity remained strong among these groups.

By contrast, the Indian government tried very hard to create an Indian national identity in the process of its nation-building after independence. There were so many groups in India with different religious, linguistic, ethnic, caste, and even political backgrounds, and India was never unified before British domination. Since independence, "India, though a multinational state, has developed "Indian nationalism" as a common bond, and the "Indian" as the common nationality' (Behera, 1995, p. 6). Another study reported that about 90% of the survey respondents in India said that they were proud of being "Indians"; the percentage of positive response to this question to test "national identification" in India was even higher than that in Spain, Argentina, Brazil, Belgium, Switzerland or Germany (United Nations Development Programme, 2004, p. 49). Nation-building is still in progress in India and there have been ethnic nationalist movements in India among the minority tribes and even guerrilla wars. But these issues have not been internationalized or become a serious threat to Indian unity. However, the caste system is mainly a social structure (hierarchical social status system) with a limited political meaning in any modern sense.

The U.S. is a young nation and its citizens came from all parts of the world with various racial/ethnic, linguistic, religious and cultural backgrounds. Under the framework of "cultural pluralism"–political unity, these immigrants have gradually established their new identity and developed loyalty to the nation. It seems that both India and the U.S. have tried hard to de-politicize and "culturalize" their domestic ethnic minorities and have successfully created a "national identity" among the majority of their citizens. Of course, there have been racial, ethnic and religious conflicts in India and the U.S., as in other nations, but there has been no real threat to national unity from minorities. There must be some lessons the Chinese may learn from these three countries: The Soviet Union, India, and the U.S. in guiding the directions of ethnic relations.

1.6. Discussion

The successful strategy of "culturalizing" ethnic minorities in the Chinese tradition has not been carried on in today's China, but plays a positive role in the U.S. In my opinion, the Chinese should carefully review this historical position. Although in general ethnic relations in today's China are smooth and cooperative, the differences among ethnic minorities in national identification still remain. The Chinese should learn from their ancestors and their experience for thousands of years in guiding ethnic relations. They also should look to other nations for both positive and negative lessons. China might in the future consider changing the direction of managing its ethnic relations from the "politicizing" to "culturalizing" route. The route of "de-politicizing" ethnicity might lead China to a new direction, strengthening national identity among ethnic minorities while guaranteeing the prosperity of their cultural traditions. Of course, how to protect the rights and benefits of ethnic minorities in that process will still be a big task. But to guide ethnic relations according to a modern civic model (citizenship and diversity), instead of the traditional tribal model (group or regional autonomy — separatism) (Gross, 1998) might be an alternative for China in the new century.

There are over 195 members of today's United Nations. They became independent political entities at different times. Many of them are multiracial/ethnic nations. There are tensions among ethnic groups in these nations caused by many factors, but these groups came together to make up a political entity, which has gained recognition from the international community. When a man and a woman come together to create a family, a Chinese phrase has it that the two have fulfilled their "destiny" and that this "destiny" should be prized.

In domestic majority–minorities relations, de-politicizing ethnicity while strengthening national identity might be a strategy for preserving national unity and winning success in the process of nation-building. Meanwhile, no country should intervene in the domestic affairs of other nations, including ethnic relations. The national boundaries recognized by the international community should be fully respected, even if there might be some debates about them. If nations handle both their domestic ethnic relations and their relations with other nations in such a mature manner, then a peaceful international order might be achieved.

When social development, economic prosperity, democracy, and cultural diversity reach a high level in most nations, and equality among different groups has been reached, then the tension among ethnic groups will fade and finally vanish, because there will be no need to encourage minorities to fight for their rights and benefits. When that stage has been reached, the concept of ethnic identity will lose its political meaning, retaining its linkages only with cultural heritage.

References

Anderson, Benedict (1991). *Imagined Communities: Reflections on the Origin and Spread of Nationalism*. London: Verso.

Behera, Subhakanta (1995). *Nation-state: Problems and Perspectives*. New Delhi: Sanchar.

Connor, Walker (1984). *The National Question in Marxist-Leninist Theory and Strategy*. Princeton, NJ: Princeton University Press.

Dikötter, Frank (1992). *The Discourse of Race in Modern China*. Stanford, CA: Stanford University Press.

Dikötter, Frank (ed.) (1997). *The Construction of Racial Identities in China and Japan.* Honolulu, HI: University of Hawai'i Press.

Dreyer, June Teufel (1976). *China's Forty Millions.* Cambridge, MA: Harvard University Press.

Duara, Prasenjit (1995). *Rescuing History from the Nation.* Chicago, IL: Chicago University Press.

Fairbank, John K. (1979). *The United States and China,* 4th Edition. Cambridge, MA: Harvard University Press.

Farley, Reynolds and Haaga, John (2005). *The American People: Census 2000.* New York: Russell Sage Foundation.

Fei Xiaotong (1989). *Zhonghua minzu de duoyuan yiti geju* [Pluralism — unity structure of the Chinese nation], *Beijing Daxue Xuebao* [*Journal of Peking University*], 4, pp. 1–19.

Fenton, Steve (2003). *Ethnicity.* Cambridge: Polity.

Gellner, Ernest (1983). *Nations and Nationalism.* Ithaca, NY: Cornell University Press.

Glazer, Nathan and Moynihan, Daniel P. (1975). Introduction. In *Ethnicity: Theory and Practice,* N Glazer and DP Moynihan (eds.), pp. 1–26. Cambridge, MA: Harvard University Press.

Gordon, Milton (1964). *Assimilation in American Life.* Oxford: Oxford University Press.

Gordon, Milton (1975). Toward a general theory of racial and ethnic group relations. In *Ethnicity: Theory and Practice,* N Glazer and DP Moynihan (eds.), pp. 84–110. Cambridge: Harvard University Press.

Gross, Feliks (1998). *The Civic and Tribal State.* Westport, CT: Greenwood Press.

Habermas, Jürgen (1998). *Die Postnationale Konstellation: Politische Essays.* Frankfurt am Main: Suhrkamp.

Hechter, Michael (1975). *Internal Colonialism.* Berkeley, CA: University of California Press.

Hobsbawm, Eric John Earnest (1990). *Nations and Nationalism Since 1780.* Cambridge: Cambridge University Press.

King, Ambrose (1997). *Zhongguo Zhengzhi yu Wenhua* [*Politics and culture in China*]. Hong Kong: Oxford University Press.

Lenin, Vladimir Ilyich (1920). Minzu he zhimindi wenti tigang chugao [Draft of the outline on national and colonial issues]. In *Liening quanji* [*The Complete Works of Lenin*] (Vol. 24), pp. 124–130. Beijing: People's Press.

Ma, Rong (2001). *Minzu yu Shehui Fazhan* [*Ethnicity and Social Development*]. Beijing: Minzu Press (in Chinese).

Ma, Rong (2004). *Minzu Shehuixue: Shehuixue de Zuqun Guanxi Yanjiu* [*Sociology of Ethnicity: Sociological Study of Ethnic Relations*]. Beijing: Peking University Press (in Chinese).

Rakowska-Harmstone, Teresa (1986). Minority nationalism today: An overview. In *The Last Empire: Nationality and the Soviet Future,* R Conquest (ed.), pp. 235–264. Stanford, CA: Stanford University Press.

Rothschild, Joseph (1981). *Ethnopolitics.* New York: Columbia University Press.

Stafford, Charles (1993). The discourse of race in modern China. *Man: The Journal of the Royal Anthropological Institute*, 28(3), p. 609.

United Nations Development Programme (2004). *Human Development Report 2004, Cultural Liberty in Today's Diverse World.* New York: United Nations Development Programme.

Wallerstein, Immanuel (1987). The construction of peoplehood: Racism, nationalism, ethnicity. *Sociological Forum*, 2(2), pp. 373–388.

Wang, Liping (2000). *Lianbangzhi yu Shijie Zhixu [Federation and International Order]*. Beijing: Peking University Press.

Yinger, J. Milton (1986). Intersecting strands in the theorization of race and ethnic relations. In *Theories of Race and Ethnic Relations*, J Rex and D Mason (eds), pp. 20–41. New York: Cambridge University Press.

Zhang, Lei and Kong, Qingrong (1999). *Zhonghua Minzu Ningjulixue [Coherence of the Chinese Nation]*. Beijing: Chinese Social Sciences Press.

Chapter 2

ESTABLISHING A SOCIALIST HARMONIOUS SOCIETY AND NATIONAL RELATIONS*

HAO SHIYUAN

*Institute of Ethnology and Anthropology at China
Academy of Social Sciences*

Strengthening and developing socialist national relations is one of the most important tasks in China's effort to establish a harmonious society. In this article, the author analyzes three aspects of this task by adhering to the basic requirements for establishing a socialist harmonious society and the basic theme of collaboration and co-development between nationalities. The three aspects discussed are: Strengthening and developing socialist national relations, carrying forward and improving the policy of regional autonomy for minority nationalities, and promoting the development of those nationalities and the protection of the "two resources". Incorporating Chinese and other countries' theory and practice in national issues, the article analyzes and discusses issues and controversies in China's national issues raised by the academic community and related global comparative research.

The Report of the 16th National Congress of the CPC established the strategic goals for economic, political, cultural and social development for the first 20 years of the century: benefit over one billion people in building a higher level of prosperous society. The basic requirements are: further develop the economy, strengthen diplomacy, carry forward scientific education, promote cultural prosperity, increase harmony within the society,

---

*This chapter is based on an article originally published in *Ethnic Research*, 2005, No. 3.

and make people's lives even more fulfilling. In making the decision to increase the execution power of the party, The Fourth Plenum of the 16th CPC Central Committee stressed the importance of establishing a socialist harmonious society as an aspect of increasing the party's governing power. The Party, this showed, had developed a new understanding of developing a socialist society with Chinese characteristics, which is a reflection of the new practice of people-oriented and all-around coordinated sustainable scientific development adopted by the Party. The socialist harmonious society theme helped us to seize important strategic opportunities; the grand goal of building an all-around prosperous society pointed out the direction for social development, which is to approach the idea of a prosperous society from multiple angles including economic development, political development, culture development and social development. China is a unified multinational state; this is a fundamental and important reality. Establishing a prosperous society is beneficial to and desired by all nationalities. Not only is co-development of all nationalities a central idea for the theme of establishing a harmonious society, but strengthening and developing an equal, unified and collaborative national relations will also have an important impact on how that theme will be carried out.

2.1. Establishing a Socialist Harmonious Society and Nationalities Co-Development

Establishing a socialist harmonious society is an important task proposed by the CPC in accordance with the needs of establishing a prosperous society and creating a new socialist society with Chinese characteristics, and is also a strategic decision conforming to the fact that China's revolution is progressing into a key stage. The CPC pointed out that forming a society in which everybody is contributing what they can, getting what they need and all the while co-existing harmoniously is the social foundation for strengthening the CPC's position and the prerequisite for the CPC to perform its role in history. Therefore, adjusting to the profound changes in the Chinese society, emphasizing the establishment of a harmonious society, promoting social vitality, promoting social fairness and righteousness, increasing legal awareness and credit awareness, and protecting social stability are the manifestations of the determination of the CPC to implement the central ideas of the "Three Representatives".

China's revolution and opening up has entered an important strategic opportunity phase. This is a period full of opportunities for development, challenges and social risks. This is especially true for China, a country with large population, great developmental disparity between urban and suburban areas, and low per-capita resources, after the per capita GDP rises above 1000 dollars, various economic and social conflicts will become more prominent and the task of minimizing regional differences and promoting coordinated economic growth will become more difficult. In this aspect, the economic and social development gap between eastern and western China, especially that between the coastal region and the national minority regions is the most prominent. According to relevant studies and analysis, a series of growth indices for economic and social growth showed that the 5 autonomous regions and a few other provinces resided predominantly by national minorities are behind other regions.

The regional rankings are as follows (China Sustainable Development Strategy Research Report, 2004, 410–425):

Economic development:

Tibet	31
Guizhou	30
Inner Mongolia	29
Xinjiang	28
Yunnan	27
Guangxi	26
Hainan	25
Gansu	23
Qinghai	21
Sichuan	20
Ningxia	18

Social development:

Tibet	31
Qinghai	30
Guizhou	29
Yunnan	28
Hainan	27

(Continued)

	(*Continued*)
Gansu	26
Ningxia	24
Guangxi	21
Sichuan	18
Inner Mongolia	10

Education:

Tibet	31
Qinghai	30
Guizhou	29
Hainan	28
Sichuan	27
Guangxi	24
Yunnan	22
Gansu	21
Ningxia	20
Inner Mongolia	14
Xinjiang	8

Technology:

Tibet	31
Guizhou	30
Qinghai	29
Inner Mongolia	27
Xinjiang	26
Hainan	25
Guangxi	24
Ningxia	23
Yunnan	21
Sichuan	17
Gansu	15

Regional management capability:

Qinghai	31
Guizhou	30
Hainan	28
Inner Mongolia	27
Xinjiang	26
Sichuan	25
Gansu	24
Yunnan	22
Tibet	18
Ningxia	17
Guangxi	16

These rankings reflected the unequal economic and social development between regions, and also reflected the difficulties in solving national issues.

In China, nationalities constitutes a conspicuous social problem of a unique type. In a multi-national state, national issues are part of social issues, but are different from general, periodical or social issues relating to other social groups. Their uniqueness is due of their complexity, which in turn is due to the fact that nationalities retain their unique social structures and functionalities within the larger society. This is to say, nationalities in multi-national states are both components of the larger social mechanism, and also are connected to and interact with the larger society in many aspects. The relations between nationalities thus infiltrate into all aspects of society, influenced by its issues, and are intertwined with its problems. This means that national issues cannot be isolated from the larger society, from all other social issues and global circumstances and solved in a vacuum; nor can we solve them quickly without considering the stage of social development. This is also why it is hard to establish a set of independent indices and predictable timelines for solving national issues in relation to other social issues like population, poverty and employment. It is the reason national issues are prevalent in all multi-national states, including developed countries. For these reasons, China has always viewed solving national issues as critical to the operations of the CPC and the state. The prevalence, persistence, complexity, global reach, and importance (Hao Shiyuan, 2000) of national issues are therefore the main characteristics we need to consider when we are dealing with domestic national issues and studying international trends.

National issues have the features just described, but exhibit different themes in different countries and at different social developmental stages. China is currently at the early stage of socialist development the main conflict is between rapid increase in material demand and slow growth of social productivity. Almost all social issues faced by China are produced due to or in relation to this major conflict; national issues are no exception. China's national issues thus appear complicated and varied, but fundamentally stem from the conflict between demands for economic and cultural development by nationalities and regions, and their inability to develop, which is — the key theme of national issues in China. The focus of China's national work namely, the co-development of all nationalities to achieve mutual prosperity, is set by this theme. Sticking to this focus and speeding up economic and social development of nationalities and regions is not only the basic requirement of the goal of establishing an all-around prosperous society, but for establishing a socialist harmonious society as well.

Hu Jintao[1] stated that a socialist harmonious society should be democratic, fair and justified, trustworthy and friendly, full of life, secure and orderly, and where people and nature co-exist peacefully (Hu Jintao, 2005). In order to achieve this goal, we need to fully implement social democracy and execute the basic strategy of ruling in accordance with law; we need to coordinate social benefits and relations, protect social fairness and promote social justice; to establish a trustworthy social environment where people help each other; to respect labor, knowledge, talent and creation in order to increase the creative vitality of the entire society; to establish and improve social structures and management mechanisms, guarantee people's safety and protect social stability and national cohesiveness; and to introduce the coordinated and sustainable development between man and environment. These essential requirements for establishing a socialist harmonious society not only set the rules for solidifying the equal, unified and collaborative socialist national relations, but also constitute the terms that must be executed in order to develop them.

Equality is the foundation for harmonious national relations. Nationalities are created equal regardless of their size, history and development; this is China's basic stand in solving national issues. Equality is not

---

[1]General Secretary of the Communist Party of China, 2002–2012.

limited to politics: economic, cultural and social equality are also important; co-development to achieve mutual prosperity is the basic route to realizing all-around equality, with the key word being "co-development". For a multi-national country made up of varying geographic distribution, natural environment, history and development levels, co-development anchored on the prerequisite of equality is not, and cannot possibly be, leveled development of all nationalities, nor can it follow a single model. Based on China's national characteristics, the feasible model is to promote regions with developmental advantages to speed up development. The outcomes (like revenue, technology, market, experience etc.) of this rapid development will be re-distributed by the central government to support other less developed regions to speed up development. On this issue, Deng Xiaoping emphasized repeatedly the idea of the "Two big pictures", which offered the most in-depth and realistic understanding of co-development. Therefore, co-development means focusing on the big picture. Co-development is not developing at the same time and at the same pace, but is to reach the goal of equal development through strategically planning which regions should develop first and which regions should be developed later. This is in conformity with the Marxism realistic attitude, and is the most effective way to coordinate the development and interests of all nationalities and regions. After eastern China had been developed sufficiently, we will follow up with the plan to develop the western regions, speeding up the economic and social development of national minority groups and regions, eliminating historic developmental disparities and decrease further disparities brought about by reality. This is the only way to coordinate the developmental needs of all nationalities and regions, and is also the only way to bring about all-around equality and social justice.

Unification is the safety net for maintaining harmonious national relations. Unification among nationalities is the foundation for national cohesiveness, the basic component for comprehensive national power and the most important index for measuring social harmony. Unification is founded on equality, and its the prerequisite is the alignment of basic rights, which translates into making co-development for mutual prosperity a reality. This alignment needs in turn to take into consideration the unique requirements of each nationality for their development, including region-specific economic development models, diverse cultures, languages, religions and social norms. These differences require mutual respect and understanding between nationalities, and protection by the law and policies as well. As China's material goods and cultural life diversify, and as interest relations in society increase in complexity, its nationalities, as minority interest parties in the social structure, have many restrictions in claiming their interests. This is due to a number of factors, including internal factors, regional economic development level and regional cultural development level. Aggravated conflicts between nationalities thus commonly appear. As well, separatists, religious extremists and international terrorist organizations are not without impact. They utilize the most prevalent and general social issues to create rumors, confuse the public, initiate dissatisfaction and create trouble. In order to protect the nation from these negative outside influences, we need to fundamentally increase development, implement co-development and realize mutual prosperity.

Collaboration is the driver of harmonious national relations. The co-development of nationalities to achieve mutual prosperity is achieved through collaboration. Without it, there can be no co-development. Collaboration is a reflection of vibrant national relations, which can be characterized as the increasing interactive and intimate relations between nationalities. The Han nationality and the national minority groups are interdependent, and the same interdependency also exists between the national minorities, which formed the historical cause for China's multinational structure, and also propelled China on the road of national revitalization. National relations refer to the interactive relations between nationalities. Antagonistic national relations are characterized as full of conflict, separation, isolation; while harmonious national relations are characterized as equal, unified and collaborative. China's nationalities have formed the "Three Unifications" relationship, which is different from both the historic hierarchical relations and the dependent relationship in the reality; rather it is a collaborative relationship. The foundation for a collaborative relationship is equality, the guarantee is unification, and the goal is co-development for mutual prosperity. Collaboration is a two-way street, with each party offering the other help and assistance, Chairman Mao had written a famous essay on this. Collaboration among nationalities cannot be measured solely by economic growth statistics, but must be viewed through the big picture of overall interest of national unity and the essential aspects of building a socialist harmonious society, which includes cultural diversity, species diversity and resource diversity. Diversity in communication is the source of creativity; China's national diversity is an important resource in promoting national and social development, as well as the establishment of a socialist harmonious society.

The basic goal of China's equal, unified and collaborative socialist national relations is the co-development for mutual prosperity among nationalities. The social requirement for accomplishing this basic goal is the establishment of the prerequisites for establishing a socialist harmonious society. The policy requirement for accomplishing this basic goal is persisting in and improving upon the regional national autonomy system.

2.2. Establishing a Socialist Harmonious Society and Regional National Autonomy System

One of the most important tasks of building a socialist harmonious society is to promote socialist democracy and implement the strategy of governance under law. The regional national autonomy system is one of China's foundational political policies, and is the fundamental means for China to promote the systematic and lawful national policy system. Persisting in and improving on the regional national autonomy system is the basic national policy of the Party and state in dealing with national issues, and is also an important task in building a socialist harmonious society. It has been proven that the national regional national autonomy system not only fits China's national circumstances of forming and developing a unified multinational nation, but its practice also helped to protect the equal rights of national minorities, maintain the unification of the nation, solidify the national coherence, promote collaboration between nationalities and enable the mutual prosperity of all nationalities over the last 500 years. Therefore, Comrade Xiaoping Deng pointed out: "This is an advantage of our socialist system, we cannot give it up" (Deng Xiaoping, 1993).

Persisting in and improving on the regional national autonomy system and fully implementing the *Law of Regional National Autonomy* is a part of building a civilized political environment. Just as building the material, political and spiritual comforts are tasks in the self-improvement of China's socialist society, persisting in the regional national autonomy system requires continual improvement to the system through practice of both the system and the law. Persistence is a prerequisite, improvement enables continual development, and the goal is to more effectively exert the advantages of the system. Although we have obtained significant achievements in the implementation of the regional national autonomy system, it does not mean that there are no more problems. Problems that still exist include those concerning the system itself, and those concerning the results of the implementation of the system. For example, the problem

Comrade Deng proposed more than 50 years ago has still not been effectively solved: "if we can't improve the economy, implementing regional national autonomy is useless" (Deng Xiaoping, 1994); another problem is that after 20 years since the *Law of Regional National Autonomy* was issued, five autonomous regions have yet to issue their own autonomous law. The existence of those problems is the reason why the Party and the state are putting a lot of effort into developing western China and prioritizing promoting the economic and cultural development of national minority regions in building a prosperous society; this is also the reason why the CPC has proposed the goal of "persisting in and improving on the regional national autonomy system and ensuring the autonomous regions are abiding by the law in their self-governance" as a part of building the governance power of the Central Party.

China's humanitarian concept, national equality policy and systems and laws in place for solving national issues are still in the course of development and improvement. Therefore, imperfections in those areas are not surprising at all. However, this does not support some western scholars' claim that China's regional national autonomy system is "fake". Basic beliefs of the western capitalist world including equality, freedom, compassion, democracy and human rights are integrated into their social system, legal system, policies and social mechanisms. But after hundreds of years since the beginning of capitalism, which capitalist countries can claim to have fully realized those beliefs? Why is that in certain of them that also practice the regional national autonomy system, there are still conflicts on nationalities rights, system setup and legal authority? Even the U.S., who claims to be the symbol for democracy, freedom and humanitarianism, while claiming to have escaped from "national conflicts and racial conflicts" and reached freedom, admits that "this freedom is a lot less free than what you hear in our national mythology" (Samuel Huntington, 2005, p. 53). China is at a preliminary stage in its socialist development, which places limitations on its material, political and spiritual development, as well as the implementation stage of the harmonious society. This is why we have to be persistent in adhering to and constantly improve on the basic principle of the regional national autonomy system, with the goal of achieving real equality and mutual prosperity among nationalities.

There are nearly 200 countries in the world, most of which are multi-national countries. In these countries, although national issues present themselves in different ways, it is the undeniable truth that they do exist. In western developed countries, there some where nationalities coexist in harmony, but there are also some that are faced with constant friction, persisting conflict, separationist movements and terrorist threats, the situation is the same with developing countries. This is determined by the prevalence, complexity and persistence of national issues. Therefore, highly developed capitalist states like the U.S. are troubled by the lack of "internal cohesion" achieved by "mutual understanding", causing worries that "the diversified U.S. society will become a breeding ground for national conflict" (Zbigniew Brzezinski, 2005, p. 218). While Chinese scholars consider that the U.S. has successfully managed national relations since the Human Rights Movement (Ma Rong, 2004), U.S. scholars consider there to be a national crisis around the national identity built on the white Anglo-Saxon as a the mainstream population caused by the rising Latino and immigrant population and the popularization of Spanish, and takes actions to rebuild that national identity.[2] Therefore, whether we view national issues in other countries or in China, we have to take into consideration the national history and reality, instead of making hasty conclusions and judgments on other countries' national policy systems, including regional national autonomy systems.

In persisting in and improving on the national policy system centered on regional national autonomy, we need to refer to and learn from successes and failures of other countries in this endeavor, but at the same time avoid copying their practices without change and making hasty assumptions. Learning the lessons of history, we all know that the tactics used by the former Soviet Union and eastern European countries to solve national issues all led to failure. The point is not to merely see failure, but to figure out its cause. On this topic, scholars from China and other countries have proposed various viewpoints, which can be summarized in two main ideas:

(1) While the former Soviet Union established policies, laws and mechanisms for solving national issues and promoting national equality, it failed to implement them. Its highly centralized government promoted big-Russian nationalist chauvinism, leading to a lack of cohesion with non-Russian nationalities.

(2) The Soviet Union dealt with ethnic issues using a "politicized" system setup and policy orientation, which not only fortified the power of each ethnic group, but even wrote freedom of secession into law; non-Russian

---

[2]This is the theme of Samuel Huntington's book: Who are we-challenges in the U.S. national characteristics.

ethnic groups were thus led to start separationist movements claiming "national independence" or "nationalism".

The second of these drew reference from the success the U.S. had in utilizing "acculturation" to solve ethnic issues; the inference was that China's national problems stemmed largely from the influence of the Russian "politicized" approach to ethnic issues (Ma Rong, 2004). The implication was that China's regional national autonomy system and national policy were products of a "Russian Model", and that China should, adopt a "new direction", following American recourse to "acculturation" as the guiding principle in national issues.

Adopting socialism on the "Russian Model" is something that almost all countries who have ever practiced, or currently still practice socialism have done, not to mention that the Russians, in promoting the Communist International, actively promoted this model, using power politics and even performing military attacks. Countries that, voluntarily or involuntarily, adopted socialism on the "Russian Model" inevitably, as practice has proven, adopted its malpractices in dealing with national issues, leading to separation and departure from socialism. Those countries, on the other hand, who realized early on the importance of taking their national circumstances into consideration and were not afraid to keep exploring their socialist paths in despite of outside pressures, were able to avoid these negative impacts. China is one of those countries.[3] We need not elaborate on the reasons why China is implementing regional national autonomy; this is not the focus of the issue at hand. In fact, the clash between the above two ideas on solving national issues is whether the latter should be resolved using a "politicized" system implementation or the "acculturation" approach.

National questions or ethnic problems, however labelled, exist in all multi-national countries. They manifest themselves in many aspects, including politics, economy, culture and social life, making it hard to sort them into the abstract categories of "politicization" and "acculturation". If we must make a judgment on the nature of national issues, we are talking in philosophical terms about the relationship between unification and diversification, or the issue of similarities versus differentiation. While

---

[3]As for Yugoslavia, they attempted to create a more superior "autonomous socialism" model than the Russian model, in criticizing the Russian collectivism they ventured to the extreme end of ethnic nationalism freedom, which led them to accompany the Soviet Union in destruction (see Hao, 1999).

the idea of "harmony in difference" is accepted under the traditional Chinese guiding principle of "unity of Heaven and Man", the goal is always to achieve "complete unity" in politics; the same goes for Chinese feudal leaders in dealing with national issues; while there were more open-minded policy-makers who adhered to the principle of "govern according to circumstances", the ultimate goal of governance was still to "educate and transform". This meant the assimilation of groups, and was both a policy to strengthen national powers and also a political measure — albeit less harsh than others — to eliminate differences and promote unity. Generally speaking, striving for assimilation and unification is the core cause for national conflict, and is the outcome of violent measures such as conquering, driving out, besieging and mass killing. Failures resulting from these policies and practices can be seen in both Chinese and international history; success stories are few. The same goes for the U.S. "melting pot" policy.

The U.S.A. is a nation of immigrants. Focusing on integrating nationalities, the "American Creed" has from the beginning been a basic guiding principle in handling national issues. In the 1960's, however, the scholars Glazer and Moynihan gained wide recognition for research arguing that the melting pot had proven a failure both theoretically and practically. The reason for this is that although the melting pot has the seal of the American Creed, the pot itself was built by the "first settlers," who brought with them Anglo-Saxon Protestant culture. The Anglo-Saxon Protestant culture Huntington refers to is a "value system for language, religion, society, politics, righteous[ness], and evil, and any mechanisms and norms that reflect those values systems" (Samuel Huntington, 2005, p. 27). This "melting pot" thus belongs not to the cultural arena but to the political, and is a machine by which the American Creed is manufactured. Doe the rise of the multiculturalism that replaced the "melting pot" theory mean that the American approach to non-political solution of domestic national issues has had "great success"? The answer is no. The reality is the opposite.

In comparison analyses of national issues and means to deal with them in the Soviet Union and the U.S., the ideas of "national identity" and "civil society" are in conflict with one another. Some research argues for the American approach of strengthening "citizenship awareness" while "weakening" or "eliminating" ethnic identity. In theoretical terms, the Soviet Union promoted collectivism; all nationalities had their own identities while being citizens of the Soviet Union; the U.S. promoted individualism, and strove to "bring people together" and "weaken" ethnic awareness. In practical terms, the Soviet Union faced a crisis over promoting "nationality" and its associated rights, eventually leading to separation; the U.S. "melting pot" policy led to the Human Rights Movement, multi-cultural policy, ethnic recognition[4] and a series of affirmative actions, such as bilingual education, that prompted strengthening ethnic awareness, all of which resulted in ethnic groups strengthening their identities, as well as promoting political activity (Zbigniew Brzezinski, 2005, p. 214). The two countries, while taking different paths, shared the same goal of achieving "unity". A simplified outline of why they both failed in their efforts is as follow:

Former Soviet Union:
Recognition of national identities and rights -> establishment of Russia -> failure -> higher levels of national recognition;[5]
U.S.A.
Americanization -> failure -> recognition of ethnic identities and rights -> reiterated Americanization.[6]

Without diving into the discussion of whether the U.S. multi-culture policy adheres to the "enculturation" orientation, the multi-culture policy's foundation of culture opposition is in direct conflict with the idea of individualism promoted by the U.S., as this policy is related to the entire foundation that the U.S. is built upon, which focuses on individual rights instead of collective rights. However, the multi-culture policy is focused on fulfilling the rights and political claims of individual ethnic groups. Under this circumstance, "how the U.S. society will evolve is a question that the new multi-culture advocates of the U.S. urgently need to know the answer during this transformational process".[7] 30 years after, Huntington proposed

---

[4] During the mid-1970s, Harvard University received funding from the "Ethnic Heritage Plan" of the U.S. government, and started to compile the Harvard American Ethnicity Encyclopedia, which was published in 1980. The encyclopedia categorized and described over 100 ethnic groups and ethnicities, it is a classic work in the American ethnic recognition effort, and is a guide to recognizing ethnic identities (see, Stephan Thernstrom, 1980).

[5] This refers to in the Russian Federation structure, the former Soviet Union autonomous national republic evolved into a national republic, national autonomous regions evolved into national autonomous republic countries.

[6] Opinions represented by Huntington and Brzezinski.

[7] *Idols of the Tribes*, Isaacs (U.S.), translated by Bochen Deng (Taiwan), Lixu Culture Affairs Company, 2004, p. 310. The author discussed the different types of tribes including race, nation, nationality, ethnic group, tribe and ethnicity, these all represent the abstract

an answer to the above question: "the emergence of the multi-culture theory and diversity theory has damaged the U.S. citizen identity and the core national characteristics, which are culture and the legal standings of the "American Creed", and the results of promoting those theories is "a series of movements that promotes collective rights over individual rights". These ethnic interest groups often "request to add the history of minority ethnic groups into the American history, or to replace the mainstream American history with the minority ethnic group histories. They demote the importance of the English language in American life, and promote the practice of bilingual education and the importance of language diversity. They advocate for the legal recognition of the rights of all groups and ethnicities, and propose that those rights should reign over the individual rights emphasized by the "American Creed". They proposed the multi-culture theory to provide support for their actions, and promoted the idea that the overarching American value system should be diversified instead of unified. All these actions put together led to the disintegration of the core characteristics of American that were built up over more than 300 years of history, and replaced them with minority ethnic group characteristics".[8] If we hypothesize that the multi-culture policy adheres to the "enculturation" policy, its implementation actually produced the politicization of ethnic group relations and challenges to national identity that were feared by Hungtinton and Brzezinski. Therefore, "enculturation" as a framework to describe the U.S. ethnic group policies and to evaluate its success in eliminating ethnic awareness and ethnic movements is clearly ineffective.

Multi-culture policy is not a universal solution for dealing with ethnic relations, nor is it a panacea for weakening ethnic awareness. Rather, it is a product of the crises faced by post-industrialization western countries, especially the democratization of immigrant countries, and is also a result of the transition from the orientation of "enculturation" to "political recognition", "differential politics" and "micropolitics" and the resulting fragmentation of the society. In reality, "for all ethnic behaviors relating to race, religion, origins and cultural differences, they are the same across all countries".[9] The U.S. is an immigrant country, and immigrants are

---

definition of group, so the translator translated all of them into zuqun, one of the most popular expressions in Taiwan at the time.

[8] *Who are we-challenges in the U.S. national characteristics*, Samuel Huntington (U.S.), translated by Kexiong Cheng, Xinhua Publications, 2005, p. 120.

[9] *Idols of the Tribes*, Isaacs (U.S.), translated by Bochen Deng (Taiwan), Lixu Culture Affairs Company, 2004, p. 282.

Diasporas, and their goal is to integrate into the society instead of separating out. But the so-called "colored" ethnic groups did not limit their demands and protests for equal rights to the methods of "enculturation" and depoliticization because of the implementation of the multi-culture policy, instead they just formed different political interest groups under the U.S. political framework, and these groups expressed their political demands and other demands through elections, litigations and lobbying. This practice is so common to the extent that "in 10 Americans, at least 7 belong to one or more political lobbying organizations".[10] From the perspective of ethnic politics, African-American, Jewish- and Latin-American interest groups exert the most political influence. The ethnic politics that arose out of the political practice of elections not only led to the practice of elite Americans to "utilize votes to bring together ethnic groups, increase the political functions of ethnic groups, and achieve the ultimate goals of ethnic unity", which also goes along with the ethnic group definition and theory of the U.S. immigrant society. Under the packaging of "cultural identity", the influence that dispersed to the entire world turned ethnic politics into a "higher purpose" that drove the disintegration of some countries and regions; an example would be Taiwan's "Four Big Ethnicities" and "ethnic politics" in the disintegration of the Chinese history and nation.[11] On this topic, something that Mr. Yiyuan Li said when he recommended the book *Idols of the Tribes* by Isaacs really provides food for thought: "as for the present-day Taiwan, it is still in a stage of political transformation, ethnic identities has begun to grow and form invisible walls under the catalyst of political competition, and the seed of disintegration has been sawn". The U.S. scholar Lucian W. Pye wrote a preface for this book, which offers some insights for us: "ethnic awareness can both build and break a country."[12] These opinions no doubt offer some answers to the "enculturation" of "ethnicities". If simply by changing the term for defining "ethnicities" various domestic ethnic conflicts and separationist forces will be resolved, that would be almost a fairytale that cannot be understood through modern science.

---

[10] *An analysis into the politics of U.S. interest groups*, Rong Tan, China Social Sciences Press, 2002, p. 14.

[11] Please see my work: An analysis into the ethnic groups and ethnic politics in Taiwan, *Social Science in China*, 2004, Issue 2.

[12] Read history as predictions, Yiyuan Li. *Idols of the Tribes*, Isaacs (U.S.), translated by Bochen Deng (Taiwan), Lixu Culture Affairs Company, 2004, p. 6.

A related controversy is "recognition of nationalities", which is one of the foundations for the implementation of the regional national autonomy policy. After the establishment of modern China, the CPC and the central government launched an nationalities investigation to identify the different nationalities, with the goals of establishing the political status of each nationality leader and to implement the regional national autonomy policy. This task was carried out over the stretch of 30 years, and helped secure the recognition of 56 nationalities in China. To this aspect, China's recognition of nationalities is different from the former Soviet Union's "categorization and ranking system for nationalities". Nationalities do not receive differential treatment based on size, length of history or development stage, but were recognized as a member of the Chinese Nation, this is a reflection of real national equality, and also constitutes the basic requirements for the implementation of the regional national autonomy policy. It goes without saying that different nationalities in China are at different stages of development, and there are a lot of disparities between the levels of integration. In the process of national recognition, various factors including historical relevance, language, similarities in culture and norms in grouping together nationalities, so as not to recognize all self-reported ethnic groups. This process is bound to have certain limitations, but I believe that this recognition process has achieved the best possible results under the historical and scientific circumstances at the time. Although there still exist nationalities that has not received recognition, as well as requests from certain national populations to transfer from one nationality to another, but these do not represent the majority of work in the process of national recognition, nor does it reflect the commonality of issues that exist. However, under the influence of some foreign scholars, some Chinese scholars have used the ethnic group theory as a framework and reference in looking at some nationalities, and as a result think that they have discovered various errors in the whole process of national recognition, or even started to preach ethnic awareness to assimilated groups, much like how some western scholars have attempted to teach historical norms to groups who have already lost that historical memory. What is the goal of ethnic group identification for the 56 nationalities (including the mainstream Han ethnic group)? Is the so-called "depoliticized" ethnic orientation and "enculturation" of nationalities in national identification aimed at solving national issues or to strengthen the national awareness of disintegration? Is the result beneficial to the integration of the Chinese nation, or will it lead to more conflicts between interest groups? These are all questions that require thought. In this aspect, when scholars criticize national recognition through the perspectives of ethnic discovery and ethnic establishment, a comment made by Steven Harrell is very insightful: "when western scholars criticize the Chinese for making mistakes in the ethnic group recognition process, they are essentially criticizing others on something that they have never done themselves."[13] The U.S. categorizes Spanish-speaking immigrants as Latin-Americans or Spanish, immigrants from Asia as Asians, and anyone associated with Africa as African-American as a method of ethnic categorization for the purposes of demographic descriptions, this is the U.S. national policy. But when we look at these ethnic groupings, aside from racial categorizations, how much of the grouping decision is based on ethnic culture? If there is any consideration for ethnic culture, then it proves that these ethnic groups do not identify with the "mainstream" U.S. culture.

In reality, some critical opinions of the national recognition process imply criticism for the region national autonomy system. However, if the regional national autonomy policy and other national policies employed by China are considered to be "politicized" means of solving national issues, then this means of handling national issues have become the mainstream option for many multi-national countries since the 1920s. The standards for solving racial, ethnic, religious, land ownership and language conflicts for the global society have been to lean towards the "political route". As for recognition for minority nationalities and autonomy of indigenous populations, these were implemented in some western countries including Canada, Spain, Belize, U.K., Switzerland, Norway and the Netherlands through forming federal systems, autonomous regions, national congress and regional congress systems. "These arrangements can accommodate the multi-culture policy, ethnic autonomy and the right to use the native ethnic language, and can also adopt the forms of agreements on rights, land distribution or legal immunity. Providing these rights to ethnic minority groups could help limit or mitigate the influence of national structures on minority groups".[14] The same goes for developing countries experiencing national conflicts, for example, the basis for the negotiation of the Tamil Issue in Sri Lanka was the establishment of the autonomous region, and the dissolution of the Movement in Muslim Mindanao in the Philippines was

---

[13]History and translation of some humanities terms, Steven Harrell, translated by Zhiming Yang, *World Ethno-National Studies*, 2001, Issue 4.

[14]*Multicultural citizenship: a liberal theory of minority rights*, Will Kymlicka (Canada), translated by Hongfeng Deng, Taipei Zuoan Culture Press, 2004, p. 2.

situated at an autonomous region. These "non-enculturation" systems of "political means of conflict resolution" were aimed at dissolving the ethnic nationalism. In fact, the "enculturation" of national issues is not a new idea, but is rather a remnant of the western theory of free evolution. The basic idea of the free evolution is to "separate national issue from the political arena, release them back into the civil society and cultural arena where they were produced, just like how the devil can be placed back into the bottle sealed with the God's name". Anthony D. Smith believes that ideas such as this are completely irrelevant hypotheses on cultural nationalism and political nationalism, and are misinterpretations of the core nature of nationalism. Therefore, "believing that it is possible to "return" nationalism to any arena including the cultural arena is both naïve and fundamentally wrong".[15] The complexity of national issues cannot be simplified solely through categorizing, redefining or renaming social arenas, but require the authenticity of the national equality policy. If we cannot obtain a good understanding of the national circumstances of the country that we are comparing to, it would be easy to fall into self-doubt due to one-sided arguments.

It is without doubt that in dealing with and resolving national (including racial and ethnic) issues, all multi-national countries are still exploring solutions. The same goes for China, who is still striving to improve its regional national autonomy policy and related laws through practice. The establishment and implementation of any policy cannot guarantee instant results; there will always be disparities between practice and results. Currently, the developmental goals targeted at resolving basic social conflicts and national issues is to provide a solid material foundation for maintaining the superiority of national political policies including the regional national autonomy policy, which is the prerequisite for development and improvement. The principle of economic foundation as the determining factor for superstructures demonstrated that the establishment, development and improvement of the superstructure cannot be separated from economic foundations. The establishment of a policy model incorporating advanced concepts does not mean that this model must have demonstrated the superiority that it should. Therefore, persisting in and improving on the regional national autonomy system is not only the internal requirement of the establishment of China's political civilization, but is also the concrete

---

[15] *Ethnic groups and nationalism in globalization*, Anthony D Smith (U.K.), translated by Weibin Gong, Jinyu Liang, Central Compilation & Translation Press, 2002, p. 14.

guarantee for all nationalities to share the fruits of the opening up of China and to implement national equality. Those who compare China's regional national autonomy system with the former Soviet Union's federal system and the regional autonomy model and its results are not being realistic. In China's 155 national autonomous regions of all levels, there is not one region that has demonstrated separationist intentions after the implementation of the regional national autonomy system, this is a fact. When we look at the Dalai clique, East Turkistan forces and the Eastern Mongolia Movement clamored by a small population of westerners, not a single one of these forces or movements were produced as a result of the implementation of the regional national autonomy system. All these forces and movements are aimed at slandering and attacking this system and achieving "a high level of autonomy" and "independence as a country", and the reason behind their attack is because the regional national autonomy system placed restrictions on the conspiracies of these extremist groups on compromising the integrity of the nation as a unified whole. Therefore, persisting in and improving on the regional national autonomy system and its legal backbone is an unshakeable principle, and also provides the fundamental guarantee for building a socialist harmonious society as well as consolidating and developing the socialist national relations.

2.3. Establishing a Socialist Harmonious Society and Protecting the "Two Resources"

No political party in the world besides the CPC shoulders such a heavy burden — that of modernizing 1.3 billion people, while also leading such a large population of national minorities and impoverished regions toward co-development and mutual prosperity. Heavy emphasis on dealing with national issues is thus an essential guarantee for modernizing socialism with Chinese characteristics, and is a formidable task in building a socialist harmonious society.

Speeding up development of national minority groups and the regions they occupy cannot be gauged by simple indices such as GDP. The cultural and environmental characteristics that are unique to nationalities impose unique requirements on the implementation of people-oriented and coordinated sustainable scientific development. "This is where developmental issues clash directly with cultural, civilization and environmental issues" (Edgar Morin and Anne Brigitte Kern, 1997, p. 60). This is not only reflected in China's economic and social modernization, but is also more prominently in the process of speeding up the development of national minority and the regions they occupy. National minority regions are precious sources of cultural diversity in China. A wealth of traditional knowledge and wisdom is embodied in its multiple languages, cultures, religions and modes of production. Modernizing of national minorities means the all-around modernization of politics, economy, culture and civil life, which on the cultural front manifests as the modernization requirement "mainly concerning their own ethnic culture" (Deng Xiaoping). Modernization can be an equalizing force in economic and lifestyle terms, closing gaps between how different people live, but it is not "a process of assimilation involving the destruction of cultures, but is implemented through recognizing and developing cultural diversity" (China Sustainable Development Strategy Research Report, 2004, p. 53). Under the impact of economic globalization, protecting cultural diversity is becoming a common vision of global society. In the natural world, the diversity of species is the foundation of maintaining ecological balance; for human societies, the diversity of culture should likewise be a foundation for maintaining peace. "In this world", therefore, "it is both right and absolutely essential to provide the equal legal recognition for the value structure behind different cultures. This makes it possible for mutual understanding and respect to exist between those cultures: this is the prerequisite for a diversified world to maintain peaceful coexistence" (Ervin Laszlo, 1997, p. 152). This is a new vision for humanity, one that was proposed by Karl Marx in earlier times. This vision is applicable to both international and domestic inter-national relations.

China, like all countries in the world, is in a process of nation-building. Only a handful of countries in the world — Japan, Portugal, Iceland, Denmark, North Korea and South Korea — fit into the traditional Western theory of one nation per country.[16] Most countries are what Anthony D. Smith described as "national states", (Anthony D Smith, 2002, p. 103) which is the same as what we call multi-national countries. In the western history of building nation-states, the following policy has almost always been enforced: "they encouraged, sometimes even coerced citizens in their jurisdiction to integrate into a public system in which a single language is used. To achieve linguistic and institutional unification, Western countries have implemented all kinds of policies, including the Nationality

---

[16]Not considering extremely small minority populations in these countries.

and Neutralization Act, the Education Law, the Language Law, Policy on Hiring Civil Servants, Military Service and National Communication Media, Etc." Furthermore, "these policies were often directed at ethnic minorities", (Will Kymlicka, 2004) with the goal of eliminating cultural diversity and promoting assimilation. These countries' idealized goals of unifying citizen and nation failed, however, to be achieved. Among member countries of the U.N., "most countries exhibit the characteristic of national diversity, and many of those countries have clearly defined ethnic categorization". Integrating different peoples into a unified nation has therefore been proven to lead to failure. The coexistence of citizenship and ethnic identity is a new concept: "in modern society, a country's success relies on such coexistence and its social foundations. One of the two types of social power can control the national institutions, and the other one can mobilize the citizens; their integration can be reflected through the coexistence of citizenship and ethnicity. At this point the people of the country will be viewed as both citizens and members of ethnic groups. When this coexistence is perfected and there are no more gaps between the components of citizenship and ethnicity, both culture and civil rights will be mutually strengthened and the nation will function fully. In contrast, when this coexistence is weakened or damaged... when one of the components gradually takes prominence over the other, national cohesion and national power will be weakened, lead to conflict between citizenship identity and ethnicity" (Anthony D. Smith, 2002, p. 103, 118). "The relationship between the ethnic community and the country" must, therefore "be brought together by an internalized and interdependent culture. This has become of the utmost importance" (Laszlo, 1997, p. 129). Adjusting and maintaining this interdependent cultural relations to maintain peace, is a test of multi-national nations' capacity to deal with and resolve national issues.

The cultural diversity between China's national minorities is a precious resource for the country and the nation, and need to be protected, uncovered and developed in the process of establishing a prosperous society, so as to become an organic component of the national culture. Establishing a socialist harmonious society requires a respect for knowledge and the ability to promote social creativity, and "real creativity would not create assimilation" (Anthony D. Smith, 2002, p. 121). The nation that we are building is an organic collective and innovation of 56 nationalities. Its backbone is the Han nationality. Its flesh and blood is made up of national minority, and the 56 nationalities make up the spirit of the nation. The idea of the nation as an "imaginary political community" (Benedict Anderson, 2003) simply reflects the reality that no multi-national country in the world has completed the nation building process of high integration and innovation. It doesn't seal off the possibility of progress of the human community. China's 56 nationalities have equal citizenship status, but each at the same time retains its own national identity. The coexistence of these two identities is one of equal, cohesive and collaborative socialist national relations. The "three must-haves" that are founded on equalizing basic rights are what tie this relationship together; their harmony is guaranteed by the national institutions, laws and policies. The relationship owes its capacity for adjusting in the interests of harmony reflects the executive power of the CPC in dealing with national issues. Solving national issues is a comprehensive task for multi-national nations, and is a *sina qua non* for promoting equality, humanitarianism and establishing a socialist harmonious society.

The harmony of man and nature is a foundation for establishing a socialist harmonious society; while implementing a prosperous society and meeting the goals of modernization, it influences and determines peoples' living environments, standards of living and virtuous cycles of between man and nature. Under the requirement of people-oriented, coordinated and sustainable scientific development, when we consider the requirements for the harmonious coexistence of man and nature in the establishment of establishing a socialist harmonious society, the national minority regions show some worrying signs. For example:

Regional ecology rankings are as follows: Ningxia (31)
Gansu (30)
Xinjiang (29)
Qinghai (28)
Inner Mongolia (26)
Sichuan (21)
Tibet (20)
Yunnan (18)
Guizhou (12)
Guangxi (10)
Hainan (4).
The regional environment ranking is as follows: Tibet (1)
Hainan (2)
Qinghai (3)

Xinjiang (4)
Gansu (5)
Yunnan (6)
Inner Mongolia (9)
Sichuan (11)
Guangxi (19)
Guizhou (22)
Ningxia (24).

These rankings clearly show that for ecological indicators such as ecological system strength, climate shifts and soil corrosion, national minority regions rank at China's lower end. They rank high on emissions and air pollution environmental indices. This is not to say, however, that these regions are environmentally sound: it simply reflects their low industrial capabilities. In addition, the ratings of regional environment resilience based on environmental and ecological protection indices show the fragility of ecosystems in those regions: Tibet (31)

Guizhou (30)
Sichuan (24)
Ningxia (22)
Yunnan (21)
Gansu (20)
Xinjiang (19)
Qinghai (17)
Guangxi (15)
Hainan (9)

Inner Mongolia (4) (China Sustainable Development Strategy Research Report, 2004, p. 410–425). For these low-resilience areas, the question of how to speed up industrialization and at the same time ensure the coordinated development of man and nature becomes a major conundrum in the establishing a prosperous and harmonious society in western China.

Early human society, we may say, was influenced by "environmental determinism," but this has surely been largely replaced by a of human and environmental model with "mankind's ever increasing power of changing the world around them" (Donald Hardesty, 2002). This model is centered on an interactive relationship between man and nature, and history has shown that the increase in mankind's power to intervene in nature and the increase in mankind's demand on resources go hand-in-hand with punishments nature gives back. Scholars describe this perverse interactive relationship between man and nature as a "techno-economic" developmental concept, and a reflection of human society as "extremely behind on the concept of development"(Edgar Morin and Anne Brigitte Kern, 1997, p. 78). A sustainable concept of development means, on the other hand, "ensuring the needs of the current generation are met while also preventing damage to later generations' ability to meet their needs" (Daniel A. Coleman, 2002, p. 121). A sustainable scientific development thus fundamentally means seeking a developmental model where man and nature interact in a virtuous cycle. This is a new quest for mankind, and implies rethinking and recreating on a serious of issues such as concepts, models and experiences of development. In addition, the influence ecological issues have on human societies is no longer restricted to critical environmental indices: it has spread to people's value systems, to social justice, social stability and even issues of national security. Related research has shown that the nature of security is "more and more related to factors — such as water resources, land cultivation, forestry, heritage resources and climate — rarely considered by experts and politicians". Wars over resources and environmental refugees are commonly seen in the world; environmental problems have also became a tool for the Dalai clique and the East Turkistan Forces in generating international public opinion and damaging inter-national relations. Therefore, in the strategic process of developing western China, the faithful implementation of the scientific development concept not only affects the fundamental interest of all national minority there, but also influences the establishment of a socialist harmonious society.

The severity of land desertification and grassland desertification caused by overloading, as well as the overall fragility of ecosystems in western China demand that we speed up the development of the economy and society under the direction of the scientific development concept. The concept of scientific development is "the result of many civilizations' experience, the complexity of the natural world, the deep understanding of the human history and many research findings" (Norman Myers, 2001). One of the most important lessons to be learned through the modernization process of the West its developmental concepts of "only looking at the world through economic and numerical viewpoints in disregard of tradition or cultural heritage. Much traditional wisdom has been lost before getting scientific recognition. Cultural diversity is a precious resource in the development of human society: "taking a look through history, all human cultures have been able to adapt well and effectively promote the stability and vitality of their surrounding environment" (Daniel A. Coleman, 2002, p. 117). Take China's national minority regions as an example, their practices of mountain agriculture, irrigation agriculture, grassland animal husbandry and forest hunting all included many region-specific production experiences and folk knowledge on how to maintain ecological balance. This was reflected even more prominently in the culture-diverse western China, where national cultures are infused with traditional knowledge on maintaining the virtuous interactive relationship between man and nature. These traditional wisdom and the values embedded in them are sources of knowledge for developing and implementing the scientific development concept that cannot be ignored, uncovering, organizing and summarizing these knowledge is not only a basic requirement for protecting and utilizing the "two resources" of cultural resources and natural resources, but is also a prerequisite for respecting knowledge, stimulating social vitality and promote creativity.

Building a socialist harmonious society poses higher requirements for promoting collaboration between nationalities and implementing the theme of mutual prosperity. We must be aware that with the development of China's economy and society, especially with the help of such factors as the improved market economy, speeding up of urbanization and the increased scale of population flow, the relationship and interaction between China's nationalities will become increasingly widespread and intimate. The movement of national relations into social and civil arenas will make them more intertwined with various social issues, and their influence in the whole social system is becoming more and more widespread and prominent. Dealing with national relations is in this sense no longer the responsibility of specialized institutes alone, but one shared by society as a whole. We are thus obliged to follow the requirements for establishing a socialist harmonious society and strengthen the power to influence national relations by innovating in the social management system and improving social mechanisms. National equality and the rejuvenation of the Chinese nation will be realized through speeding up the economic and cultural development of national minority groups, and the collaborative development of all nationalities to achieve mutual prosperity.

References

Anderson, Benedict (U.S.) (2003). *Imaginary Communities: Reflections on the Origin and Spread of Nationalism*, (trans. Wu Ruiren). Shanghai: Shanghai Century Publications Group.

Brzezinski, Zbigniew (2005). *The Big Choice: America at Crossroads.* Beijing: Xinhua Publications (Trans. Wang Zhenxi (2004). *The Choice: Global Domination or Global Leadership.* New York: Basic Books.)

China Sustainable Development Strategy Research Report (2004). The Sustainable Strategy Research Groups at the Chinese Academy of Science, Beijing: The Science Publication House.

Coleman, Daniel A. (2002). *Eco Politics: Building a Green Society* (trans. Mei Junjie). Shanghai: Shanghai Translation Publishing House.

Deng, Xiaoping (1993). All our endeavors are new ones, *Deng Xiaoping Collection*, Vol. 3, Beijing: People's Publishing House.

Deng, Xiaoping (1994). On the east-western national minority problems, *Deng Xiaoping Collected*, Vol. 1, Beijing: People's Publishing House.

Hao, Shiyuan (1999), *Imperial hegemony and Balkans "fire barrel"-looking at Kosovo through the history of Yugoslavia.* Beijing: Social Sciencces Academic Press.

Hao, Shiyuan (2000). For the five characteristics of national issues. The trend of growth and decline of the 20th century national issues and its influence on the new century. *World Ethno-National Studies*, No. 6.

Hardesty, Donald (2002). *Eco-Anthropology,* (trans. Fan Guo and Zou He) Beijing: Cultural Artifacts Press.

Hu, Jintao (2005). Establishing a socialist harmonious society. *People's Daily*, 26 May 2005 (English translation available online at http://english.people daily.com.cn/200506/27/eng20050627_192495.html).

Huntington, Samuel (U.S.) (2005). *Who are We-Challenges in the U.S. National Characteristics* (trans. Cheng Kexiong). Beijing: Xinhua Publications.

Kymlicka, Will (Canada) (2004). *Multicultural Citizenship: A Liberal Theory of Minority Right*, p. 1 (trans. Deng Hongfeng). Taipei: Zuoan Culture Press.

Laszlo, Ervin (U.S.) (1997). *The Choice of Fate,* (trans. Li Yinbo) Beijing: SDX Joint Publishing Company.

Ma, Rong (2004). A new perspective in guiding ethnic relations in the 21st century: "Depoliticising" ethnicity in China. *Beijing Daxue Xuebao [Journal of Peking University]*, issue 6.

Morin, Edgar and Kern, Anne Brigitte (France) (1997). *Homeland and Earth* (trans. Ma Shengli), Beijing: SDX Joint Publishing Company.

Myers, Norman (2001). *Ultimate Security: The Environmental Basis of Political Stability,* p. 20 (trans. Wang Zhengping and Jin Hui). Shanghai: Shanghai Translation Publishing House.

Smith, Anthony D (U.K.) (2002). *Nations and Nationalism in Globalisation* (trans. Gong Weibin and Liang Jinyu). Beijing: Central Compilation & Translation Press.

Thernstrom, Stephan ed. (1980). *Harvard Encyclopedia of American Ethnic Groups.* Cambridge: The Belknap Press of Harvard University.

Chapter 3

THE TWO REQUIRED PRINCIPLES FOR EVALUATING NATIONAL POLICIES FROM AN NATIONAL PERSPECTIVE

ZHOU DAMING

Department of Anthropology, Zhongshan University

National policy refers to a standard of action a country or society takes to resolve present and future problems in national development and ethnic relations, and is a reflection and practice of the government's basic method and principles in dealing with national and ethnic issues. Ethnic groups are population groups segregated by culture; each ethnic group has its own cultural heritage and history. If we evaluate the current national policy through cultural subjectivity and underlying political subjectivity, we need to take the following into consideration: satisfying the developmental needs of ethnic groups, and understanding the idea of choice. The coordination between these two principles creates the standards for evaluating national policies.

National policy refers to a standard of action a country or society takes to resolve present and future problems in national development and ethnic relations, and is a reflection and practice of the government's basic method and principles in dealing with national and ethnic issues. It is also an important area of study for ethnology and anthropology. From the perspective of ethnic studies, through the history and present of China's policies, we can gather the evolution of ethnic relations and predict its future development, which could be leveraged to assess whether the existing national policy can mitigate cultural and structural differences between ethnic groups, thereby ascertaining whether the government can guide ethnic relations to develop in the right direction.

In recent years, some scholars have studied China's current policy in terms of ethnic groups, leading to discussions of "depoliticization" and "enculturation" of ethnic groups. Do we need to "depoliticize" ethnic issues? This discussion clearly helps our grasp and evaluation of current policy and practices. Further discussion requires tackling issues in defining "depoliticization". This concept is infused with political ideology. Historically, widespread "depoliticizing trends" of various forms emerge after almost every political upheaval. The "politics" in "depoliticization" is less about national or international politics, their ever present power struggles, but political organizations, debates and battles, and social movements based on specific political values and its related interests, or in other words, interactions between political entities. Following this logic, the question being proposed is: are ethnic groups political entities? In other words, are they political groups or cultural groups?

Currently, the broad scholarly consensus is that ethnic groups are population groups segregated by culture, and have culture traditions and historical backgrounds. Ethnic groups have historically been viewed as cultural groups. During the early Qing Dynasty, the knowledge of different groups and cultures was the foundation for the formation of the Yixia concept. The *Book of Rites and Kingship* documented this in a clear and systematic way: "The people of those five regions — the Middle states, and the Rong, Yi, Di, Man — had all their several natures, which they cannot be made to alter. Those mediating in the east are called Ji, in the south, Ciang, in the west, Didi, and in the north, Yi. The people of the Middle states, and of those Man, Rong, and Di, all have dwellings in which they are comfortable; flavors they prefer; clothes suitable for them; implements they are suited to; and vessels that they prepare in abundance. These peoples of the five regions differ in words and languages, as well as in their predilections and desires." From the modern viewpoint, this paragraph summarized what we today consider cultural boundaries for ethnic groups, such as cultural differences between ethnic groups living in the east, south, west, and north and the mainstream Huaxia people. This Yixia concept became an important component of the "world concept" that developed later, greatly influencing the execution of ethnic relations and establishment of political systems for the three dynasties of Xia, Shang and Zhou.

We can see as well the regional difference in ethnic groups from the above paragraph. The "Middle States", "Rong", "Yi", "Di", "Man" in the paragraph refer to different ethnic groups living in various regions of China. From the early Qing dynasty, people started to use differences in material culture to categorize different ethnic groups. The question of how to learn about and coordinate the relationship between these groups became the main content of the theoretical framework of "unification" centered on the "emperor" as the central power structure. The categorization of ethnic groups and cultures changed a lot since the three dynasties of Xia, Shang and Zhou, but still strongly influenced how people categorized the different groups around them thereafter, such as coming up with names for certain groups, like "Si Yi", "Man Yi", and "Rong Yi".[1] Of course, these names changed with the rise and fall of dynasties, but mostly referred to groups who lived close to the capital city or groups residing in a heavily populated area.

This tradition has carried over to the present time, as we still associate different ethnic groups with specific geographic regions. Just as when Chapter 11 in *Detailed Annotations of the Book of History* (*Shang Shu quan jie*) explained the Wufu tributary relations as follows:

> Five hundred li (still beyond) formed the Peace-securing Domain. In the first three hundred, they cultivated the lessons of learning and moral duties; in the other two, they showed the energies of war and defense...

> In ancient times, in ruling the nation it was most important to distinguish Chinese from foreign. It was thus extremely important to draw national borders and fortify border defense. Areas adjacent to the kingdom were occupied by vassal states, connected states of various sizes and powers that were there to help the emperor protect his territory. The national border was fifteen kilometers from the borders of the vassal states, as remote lands lies outside of the vassal state borders; lands further away were still wilder. Hence, wild land was designated as the outer border of the national border. This was the border between China and foreign land.

Categorizing ethnic groups by region helped cement a certain ruling order. Different groups would have a certain autonomy within their habitat. This intricate historically formed relationship between people and regions means that we cannot deny or overlook the underlying political nature of ethnic groups.

---

[1]Where *yi* retains the ancient sense of "barbarian".

Evaluating current national policy in terms of cultural and underlying political subjectivity, we need to take the following principles into consideration: satisfying the developmental needs of ethnic groups, and understanding the idea of choice. The first of these, "development" refers, rather than to the widely accepted current definition, but to a developmental plan that does not go against the cultural heritage and psychological will of the locals, does not create threats to their natural environment, and follows the will of the locals. The second, "choice" is critical in establishing national policy. It requires that when evaluating policy, the compatibility between the policy and the value system and target dimensions of the ethnic groups must be evaluated. "Value systems" refers to how individual ethnic groups position themselves, the value orientation of ethnicity, the development trend of the ethnic group, and their self-evaluation of the current status and future development of their group. All this needs, further evaluation in the context of the national circumstances. The coordination between the two principles forms the standards for evaluating national policies.

Chapter 4

ESTABLISHING A MULTINATIONAL HARMONIOUS SOCIETY AND RESOLVING NATIONAL ISSUES — "DEPOLITICIZING" AND "CULTURIZING" NATIONAL ISSUES*

CHEN JIANYUE

Institute of Ethnology and Anthropology,
Chinese Academy of Social Science

Creating a unified and harmonious multi-national society presupposes inclusive and intermingled national relations. These, in turn, refer, fundamentally, to aligning policies with national circumstances, and secondarily, to the effectiveness of the policies and measures designed to protect national minority interests. Despite differences in viewpoints, both national studies and political science view national issues as political, as built upon national rights and interests. "Depoliticizing" or "culturizing" national issues is a fruitless endeavor. This paper deals with multi-national states, analyzing the institutional structures and policy approaches they apply to national issues. The discussion then turns to "depoliticizing" national issues as a scholarly theory.

In the view of political science, "all political theories take their starting point from the fact of human community" (Robert A. Dahl, 1987). This implies first of all that the human community is the environmental background of political development, and all political actions are centered

---

*This Chapter is based on an article originally published in *World Ethno-National Studies*, 2005, No. 5.

around the existence of such a community; secondly, politics refers to interest-based decisions that people make and implement in human communities (Jean Blondel, 1992); it is the process and result of the recognition of interests and the effective integration of diverse interests. Given the need to keep communities intact, politics naturally encompasses a culture of decision rules, legal regulations and policy formulation, encompassing the expression and integration of interests and collective movements. All human communities have unique economic statuses, historical heritages, cultural representations, national components, spatial and temporal backgrounds and interests. Establishing political civilizations aligned with such community features hence becomes an important topic for students of politics.

In terms of that human community, the state and its existence confirms the presence of an unsolvable paradox in society that forms inescapable opposition forces. There, a need arises for a power form, on the surface transcending the society, to ensure that these opposition forces do not fight to the destruction of themselves and the society. This power, meant to act as a buffer for conflicts and keep them within the boundaries of "order", is the state (Karl Marx and Friedrich Engels, 1972a, p. 166).

The state, more than any other community lays stress on the rational allocation of social resources, the distribution of power and the professional management of public affairs; only when it effectively manages public affairs can the state's existence can be sustained. Along these lines, Friedrich Engels pointed out that "political rule is everywhere based on the execution of some social functions, and it can be sustained only when it does so successfully" (Karl Marx and Friedrich Engels, 1972a, p. 219). Another distinction between the state and other communities is that the state power is public in that it is "separated from yet rises above the society". Marxists classically argued that "the core characteristic of the state is public power that is separated from the populace" (Karl Marx and Friedrich Engels, 1972a, p. 144). This separation of public power from the citizenry entails setting up mechanisms of interest aggregation, and of democratic supervision. The former entails citizens transferring certain individual rights to personnel in dedicated organizations of public affairs management, through voting procedures of some kind: for most modern states, in the form of representative voting. The latter entails citizens distributing public power through certain procedures to ensure mutual supervision and restrictions between each power entity, and enforcing supervision on the organizations and personnel that execute those powers through representative voting mechanisms — even influencing their recruitment decisions. Interest aggregation mechanisms to ensure the sustainability and long-term development of the state, and constitutional mechanisms built on the representative voting system and distribution of power are among the leading and typical representations of political civilization in modern states. The core of this political civilization is democracy, and democracy is "the nature of all national mechanisms, and is a socialized entity in the special form of national systems. The relationship between democracy and other forms of national systems is comparable to that between different races of people" (Karl Marx and Friederich Engels, 1972a, p. 281). It can be further said that the goal and direction of democracy is to form a diversified and inclusive harmonious society through the integration of multiple interests.

4.1. Policy Arrangements for Establishing a Multi-National Harmonious Society

Even in the pre-Qin era, Shi Bo and Yan Ying expounded a concept of "peace", and proposed the concept of lord and subject, of "keeping peace without intervening". Later, Confucian philosophers including Confucius, Mencius and Xunzi further developed this view of harmony and unity (Deng Honglei, 1987). The word "harmony" was first used in music and mathematics in Chinese books;[1] its first use in the political realm came

---

[1] The *Records of the Grand Historian*, Part II, Chapter of Music of (Vol. 24) records that, "The emperor went to the Mingtang Hall where political and religious announcements are made, to listen to music, enabling the masses to enjoy music and be cleansed of the evils of human nature, thereby taking on healthy and robust lives and mild temperaments. This is why we say that righteous and elegant music will build good folk customs, intense music will rally morale, while the bad music of Zheng and Wei will bring evil thoughts. When music and temperament are in harmony, even birds and animals will be touched, not to mention human beings holding the five constant virtues of benevolence, righteousness, propriety, wisdom and fidelity in their natures, as well as likes and dislikes! The propensity of people to be touched by music is thus quite natural. Inadequacies of governance, and the popularity of the bad music of Zheng made feudal and hereditary emperors compete with neighboring states in their proficiency of Zheng music. Since then Confucius found it impossible to coexist in the nation of Lu with female artists. Although after he withdrew from the political realm of Lu and compiled righteous and elegant music in an effort to guide people to the route of righteousness, as well as the satirical "Five Chapter" song to reflect reality, he was not able to convert people. As late as the Warring States period, emperors were still mesmerized by the bad music, making them negligent of progress and development, which ultimately resulted in their personal and national demise and destruction."

in volume 49 (Collected Biographies of Wang Chong, Wang Fu and Zhong Changtong No. 39) of the *Book of the Later Han Dynasty*:

> One man assigned to govern makes it his exclusive responsibility. Several people assigned to it become interdependent on each other and pass the buck. Inclusive rule will produce harmony, while passing the buck will result in disaster. Harmony is the source of world peace, while shirking responsibility is the cause of turmoil and disorder.

In such Chinese classics, it can be seen, the political meaning of the word "harmony" refers to an ideal state of political pluralism encompassing ideals of high-mindedness, interest aggregation and a realm at peace.

"Harmony" in western philosophy usually refers to a coordinated state of existence and development. Research on the harmonious characteristics of natural beings can be sourced back to the ancient Greek philosopher Pythagoras who expounded a notion of "beauty found in the harmony of numbers". After Heraclitus' philosophical research on harmony, Aristotle started to pay attention to the harmony of the multi-ethnic Greek society in his book *Politics* at the same time that he expounded the concept of "harmony is beauty". In *The Republic*, Plato further pointed out that within a nation with multiple interest parties, the integrity of national politics depends on the pursuit of harmony and unity, and the main means to achieve harmony and unity is through moderation; in addition, Plato made the early observation of the close relationship between the differences among interest parties within the nation and its fate. Both extreme prosperity and extreme poverty, he observed, are disturbing: "riches will lead to too much luxury, laziness and desire for revolution, poverty will lead to unruliness, inferiority, and also desire for revolution" (Plato, 1972).

The proposal of the concept of harmony itself means acceptance of a plurality of interests that naturally leads to the acceptance of the cultural diversity that is supported by multiple interests; within such a unified multi-national state, the acceptance of cultural diversity further implies the political acceptance of national diversity as a social phenomenon. The concept of harmony also means that the integration and adjustment of plural interests is no longer a pure theoretical issue for philosophy or culture: different interests also create different political civilizations and forms of the state. First of all, forms of state "cannot be understood on their own terms, nor as a general development of the human spirit, to the contrary, they are rooted in material life relationships", i.e., to production relations congruent with the developmental stage of human forces of material production. These relations of production together form the economic structure of the society on which superstructures, including legal and political structures as well as national forms are built, and also act as a foundation for production relationships (Karl Marx and Friedrich Engels, 1972b, p. 82). Secondly, forms of the state are determined by the specific conditions of different countries. Karl Marx argued that

> the "modern state" is an illusion, a standardized form of modern state that can be applied to all lands does not exist, the form changes with each state, it cannot be the same in Prussia, in the German Empire and in Switzerland, any more than it can be the same in England and America (Karl Marx and Friedrich Engels, 1975, p. 892).

Natural environments, national components, religion, culture and historical influences from the outside all exert influences on the form of the state, making it "possible to display endless variations and differences" (Karl Marx and Friedrich Engels, 1975, p. 892).

As one of the earliest forms of political organizations in human communities, "autonomy" evolved with the emergence of political phenomena in human society, the emergence of political action and the development of the state. This was proved during the political reality of ancient Greece in the fifth century BC, as well as documented in political classics authored by political theorists like Aristotle and Plato. The concept of "local self-government" was first proposed by Joshua Joulimin Smith, a British scholar, in his *Government by Commissions Illegal and Pernicious* (1849); he went on to publish *Local Self-Government and Centralization*. In *The Origin of the Family, Private Property and the State* (1884), Friedrich Engels' proposed "self-government" as a transitional form. Based on a study of the Attic tribe of Athens, Morgan had found that in tribal societies the trend was for self-government to develop into mature and comprehensive state institutions; it was an important stage in the transition from society to state (Yucheng Sang, 1994). As a structural form for political institutions of the modern state, it implies that "community representatives control the community's economy, society and political affairs; while not including security, legal matters and diplomatic affairs outside of order, this form of self-government allows members of multiple ethnic groups a large degree of control of public resources and social policies" (Smith, 1992). Self-government implied as well that after the horizontal separation of public powers in the modern state, there must be a vertical separation of public powers and formation of policy via the the interest aggregation of representative voting systems. This is a customary and important way of dividing power in modern state systems, whether unitary or federal. Most importantly, under the modern state political background of "created by society but rising above it, and becoming increasingly opposed to it", self-government functions to cultivate democracy, promote regional development, improve the governance effectiveness of the government and prevent extreme centralization of power:

> ...if all the power is held by the central government, and all the administrative functions are performed by the central government, then we are in danger of creating a super bureaucracy. Extreme centralization of power are generally results in delays in development, arbitrary ruling, corruption, low effectiveness and disregard of public opinions (Rarwal *et al.*, 1984).

Dividing into many forms, we may find regional, national minority regional, special administrative regional, overseas territory and indigenous reserve self-government; in China, regional, national minority regional, special administrative region (including Hong Kong and Macao), and villager self-government.

When it comes to the relationship between nationalities and the state, given the salience of common geographic location, common historical experiences and its socialization and cultural heritage is a major source of the sense of belonging to an nationality. This is also why many students of national politics agree, "a nationality always implies some degree of political self-rule" (Anthony H. Richmond); special occasions apart, the need for self-government in a multi-national state increases with the number of different opinions held, and the numbers holding them (Robert A. Dahl, 1999). Logically speaking, democratic political systems entail broad political participation, while self-government is a manifestation of the localization of political participation for multi-national states; "experience shows that participatory political systems are in general the best for peacefully resolving social conflicts, especially national conflicts" (Saad Eddin Ibrahim). More to the point, self-government should be viewed as essential for modern democracy, as it is the core of a specific political blueprint, whose basic prerequisite is "peoples' ability to choose, decide and defend their actions, shoulder responsibilities they choose to shoulder, and enjoy political freedom and equality" (David Held, 1998). Given the basic characteristics of political autonomy, caution is required in setting policies for a multi-national state, as any mistake could lead to national minorities challenging its legitimacy, which could further lead to intense inter-national conflict and even national disintegration. Given that each nationality groups within a multi-national state has different interests based on their languages, geographic locations, economic life, culture and psychological well-being, political models of self-government (including national self-government and federal systems) provide a policy solution for resolving such issues that accords with the historical experience of national self-government, and also guarantees national integrity. The core principle for both models is gaining national minority groups' acceptance of the legitimacy of the state thorough a variety of means to delegate power under the prerequisite of the acceptance of different interests and social development statuses of different nationalities, and on this basis keep conflicting interest within "order" so as to the maintain the multi-national state's authoritative position as "produced by the society but rising above it." National self-government emphasizes the autonomy of national minority groups, while national federal systems emphasize that of geographic regions. In general, the former is often used for multi-national states under centralized control, and the latter is often used for multi-national federal states. National self-government, however, may also be found in the latter. This institutional neutrality is evidence of a changing trend in political systems in modern states: "an interesting trend of this era is that while central governments are making the transition towards the federal government system, federal governments are also slowly progressing toward a more centralized system" (Michael Roskin and Robert Cord, 2001). The mutual neutralization of unitary and federal systems is reflected most prominently in the changes in the power relationship between the central and regional governments. It also implies the fulfilment of the political interests of both central and regional governments; the balance of these two interests is an emerging index of social stability and development, two essential areas of a nation's development: the transition from a federal to a central system shows the needs for political integration, while the transition from a unitary to a federal system portends fulfilling the political interests of regions and nationalities.

Given their different structures, multi-national states' methods of allocating autonomous power also differ: federal multi-national states often give regional governments a voice in deciding the powers of the central government, while unitary multi-national states often stress the absolute authority of the central government by allocating powers to regional governments. The institutional models adopted by a multi-national state to reduce tensions with nationalities, vary entirely with its politics, economy, history, culture and specific national issues. There is no distinction of East and West here, nor do ideological restrictions matter. In capitalist multi-national states such as the U.S., Canada, Australia and Spain, for example, the former three established autonomous reserves for indigenous people under a federal system, while the latter established 14 autonomous regions and 3 national self-governments under a centralized one; in socialist nations such as Russia, Yugoslavia, Czechoslovakia and China, the former three adopted a regional self-government model under a national federal system to solve domestic national issues, while China established a creative model of national regional autonomy system which incorporates national self-government and regional autonomy based on the national circumstances and characteristics of national issues.

The practice of many multi-national states in using a self-government model to solve domestic national issues substantiates Vladimir Ilyich Lenin's prediction in his 1916 paper "Concluding the debate on self determination":

> in order to achieve our common goals of absolute equality, intimacy and intermingling of nationalities, we must take different routes. Take the metaphor of reaching the center of a piece of paper, we can start from the left side and move to the right, or vice versa, as both methods will be able to take us to the destination (Vladimir Ilyich Lenin, 1958).

Both national autonomy and national federalism are options for national minority groups to take routes different from that of the national majority in order to achieve mutual development and common prosperity. Note that there is, in political science terms, close to zero correspondence between centralized power *vs.* regional self-government on the one hand, and state unity *vs.* division on the other: "the mutual incompatibility of centralized power and regional self-government is an overly-legalized concept and need not be considered too much" (Michio Muranatsu, 1989).

As a political model, national self-government creates an institutional platform for ensuring the equality, development and prosperity of the state's nationalities in. Actually achieving the system's goals depends on the specific policies and measures it is used to set up and carry out. In the case of a ruling party that sets up a multi-national state to sustain its ruling power, it must take into consideration the plurality of interests of the national majority and minority groups when planning the national self-government institutions and related legal regulations. If the self-government system cannot adequately reflect the plurality of interests, the state's integrity would be compromised, the political legality of the government would be placed under doubt, and its authority would be challenged.

In the selection of the structure of a modern state, classical Marxist authors display a special preference for the unitary model: "unitary states establish numerous government organizations according to systematic and rating principles of the separation of labor" (Karl Marx and Friedrich Engels, p. 434). At the same time, they also emphasize the importance of self-government, proposing the following statement when critiquing the self-government mechanism during the Paris Commune period:

> this self-government mechanism that is similar to the American federal states system is the most powerful lever in a revolution (Karl Marx and Friedrich Engels, pp. 390, 391).

As for the structural form used in building a socialist state, classic Marxist authors focus entirely on the individual circumstances of multi-national states in making institutional choices:

> ...when analyzing any social issue, the absolute requirement of the Marxist theory is to place the issue within a certain historical context. In addition, if we talk about a specific state (for example when we are talking about its national principles), we will need to consider the features that distinguish it from all other states in a given historical time (Vladimir Ilyich Lenin, 1972);

> ...an nationality's economic, political and cultural conditions form the key to finding the solution to solving that nationality's internal problems and determining what form the national constitution should take on in the future. In addition, it is entirely possible that each nationality requires unique means to resolve its problems. If there is ever a time when we have to propose questions through dialectics, it is here, when we are talking about national issues (Joseph Stalin, 1953).

4.2. Favorable Policies for National Minority Groups in the Establishment of a Socialist Harmonious Society for a Multi-National State

In its *2004 Human Development Report,* the UNDP (United Nations Development Programme) points out:

> States need to acknowledge cultural differences in their constitution, legal system and organization. They also need to establish various

policies to ensure that special groups — whether they be ethnic minority groups or marginalized majority groups — and their interests are not overlooked or overruled by the majority group or other mainstream populations (UNDP, 2004, p. 47).

As government action under an established system, public policy refers to codes of conduct laid down by a government, according to the goals of a specific time period, in the selection, integration, assignment and implementation of public interests (Chen Qingyun, 1996). Specifically for a unified multi-national state, its public policy needs to resolve are first and foremost problems of the aggregation of interests of various nationalities, and secondly the authoritative value distribution of scarce resources between them. In the view of Michael Hill, this kind of public policy and multi-national system arrangement designed to effectively integrate multiple interests, not only represents the establishment of a democratic system, but also means that a "democratic theory that is perhaps more advanced is in the process of formation", "this theory can explain the respect of politicians for minority interest groups...its sign is to achieve political consistency and ensure that the interests of minority groups are protected" (Michael Hill, 2003).

Public policies aimed at adjusting inter-national relations in multi-national states can be categorized into two types: one is community policies aimed at building the "state-nation", and the other is national preferential policies aimed at providing national minorities with preferential terms.

Community policies attempt to utilize a series of institutional arrangements and specific policies and measures to establish common historical views, mutual equality and collaboration, build a democratic inter-national interest mediation mechanism inductive to mutual prosperity, a public power sharing system that incorporates unification and self-government, a national education and social security system that is accommodating while cohesive, establish and strengthen the multi-national community awareness and culture that accommodates the cultural characteristics of all nationalities, so that the multi-national state can gradually become a community that accommodates multiple cultures and preserves national characteristics. The fundamental goal of community policies is to create the centripetal force that creates cohesion between nationalities in a multi-national state, promoting and consolidating the trust, communication, mutual aid and cohesion, thereby developing the identification and loyalty to the multi-national state, furthermore establish the unified "state-nation".

The UNDP made the following proposal based on case studies of multinational states including Spain and Belise: "successful strategies in building a "state-nation" can go, and have gone, through establishing of a comprehensive response policy for cultural recognition in order to constructively accommodate diversity. These are effective solutions to ensure the long-terms goals of political stability and social harmony" (UNDP, 2004, p. 49).

National preferential policies are based on frameworks for rational power distribution between central and regional governments; they ensure that national minority groups are treated favorably through the constitution and specific national affairs management legal systems. These policies also ensure that the regional power authorities in national minority regions established according to law are operating under the representative voting system in their exertion of the power and responsibility of the self-government of regional national affairs, that national minority groups and related regions enjoy preferential treatment in their politics, economy, culture, education, society and public health, and that the central government prioritizes the interests of national minority and national minority regions through implementing regional developmental strategies ad fiscal transfer payment systems that take national factors into full consideration.

National minority groups and regions are accorded preferential policies for the following reasons:

(1) They deal with market failure in domestic regional disparities and income differences between population groups;

(2) "Economic and social progress often overlook national minority groups or tribal groups" (UNDP, 2004, p. 16) is a market failure that needs to be resolved through government intervention, "the same policies will not produce the same opportunities for regions with special cultural needs or for regions that have gone through historical hardships, we need policies that differentiates between different regions" (UNDP, 2003, p. 38).

(3) Government intervention that features such a "differentiated policy path" will not only provide important public goods such as law and order, national defence and good currency, but others, like education, possible health and social security networks that can help alleviate poverty and improve the standards of living of vulnerable groups, thereby shrinking and equalizing regional differences within the multi-national state and realizing social harmony. "The more equally distributed income for residents, the better social welfare will be".

From this we can see that there is a close relationship between preferential policies for national minorities and the multi-national state's territory integrity, state-national identity, stable economic development, equality of regional development, development of culture and harmony in a diverse society.

However we want to evaluate social policies, they all represent a special interest protection for a specific region or group of people. National preferential policies in a multi-national state specifically emphasize protection and special treatment for specific national minority groups residing in specific regions, which is a common practice in both eastern and western nations.

Compared to national political arrangements that emphasize a constitutional system structure, preferential national minority policies are more flexible and easy to adjust, therefore are commonly used in various multi-national states. This, however, should not imply that they can be changed without restrictions: for recipient and state alike, preferential national minority policy is an adjustable but irrevocable strategic policy component. For a multi-national state in pursuit of stable development, the range of preferential policy should be restricted within the boundaries of effectively maintain the harmonious development of the state, so as to avoid bringing about persistent and severe feelings of unfairness and exploitation by other groups and regions that may cause debates on the nation's political legality. National minority preferential policies and other regional preferential policies must have a mutually-promoting and complementary relationship, policies that solely promote and consolidate any single party's interests must lead to the destruction of the internal national integration and regional development imbalances, leading to economic instability, social disintegration and cultural discrimination. The disintegration of the former Soviet Union and Yugoslavia are examples (Guo Hongshen, 1997; Chen Jianyue, 2004). For recipient national minority groups, the state's preferential policies are only measures to provide special assistance during a specific time and under a specific social background, the fundamental goal of which is provide fast-track development so as to become equal with other nationalities: over-reliance on preferential policies may not only create unfair exploitation of other nationalities, but also stall their own development.

4.3. The "Depoliticization" of National Issues: A Stigmatized National Study

Interests are what promote the development of nationalities, this was Vladimir Ilyich Lenin's basic observation of the driving force behind inter-national interactions in multi-national states, and is also a basic logical prerequisite of Marxist political theory of national issues, as well as a logical starting point for most political theories up to now. In other words, as long as we are talking about inter-national relations on a national state level and discussing the national policies of that multi-national state, the interests implicit in national interactions cannot be ignored or downplayed. It is also by this definition that all inter-national interactions are interactions between national interests; and all systematic arrangements and innovation on national relations by multi-national states are political solutions and arrangements of national interests.

"All that men fight for is related to their interests" (Karl Marx and Friedrich Engels, p. 82). From an individual point of view, interests are human considerations for the protection of their basic survival conditions and their development against competition, "the first principle of humanity is to protect the survival of the self, the first thing that humanity cares about is the care that the self should receive" (Jean-Jacques Rousseau, 1980). But in an environment of natural competition, efforts to maximize personal interests are obviously restricted by individual fitness and opportunity. Personal decisions to join one or more groups through consensus or acquiescence in order to more effectively maximize personal interests hence becomes the basic motivation behind the collective nature of the political life of humans. In other words, one group can only gain the value and validity of its existence through uncovering and showcasing its own power and eventually participate in the distribution of interests that cannot be obtained through individual efforts. As Mancur Olson states, "any collective or organization, no matter its size, serves the interests of a specific collective, and its nature is to help its members benefit" (Mancur Olson, 1995).

As a relatively stable collective form in human society, the nationality offers its members the prospect of a set of interests that no other group can provide: the continuity of a specific economic life, common cultural heritage and share of political power; this national interest orientation focus on the survival and development of each member and an "immutable" national identity means that nationality can provide a sense of mission, sense of intimacy and stability to its members that no others can, and at the same time "promote the life of the nationality" (Vladimir Ilyich Lenin, 1959) through national interests. In terms of aggregating interests internal to the nationality, due to the nationality's unique shared bloodline and fateful significances such as culture, history and economic life that exert the function of integration and show the potential for sharing benefits, making the internal integration function of nationalities seem more unique and intricate compared with other types of groups: in an environment where multiple cultures coexist and interact, the socialization process that is based on bloodline or similar cultures continuously cultivates a nationality's culture and spiritual characteristics. Enabling nationality boundaries to become clearer, this in turn leads to the creation of unique shared values that embody national cultures in which myths, religions, symbols and historical heritage are shared. The subtlety of this integration mechanism is its realization of political interests through non-political mechanisms.

Achieving political interests through non-political means is a hallmark of nationalities that different scholars interpret differently. Ma Rong, who since 2000 has used the "culturizing" approach to distil national identity and alleviate national issues, proposed his idea of "depoliticizing" national issues in a 2004 paper, branding it a "new idea for understanding ethnic relations" (Ma Rong, 2004). Putting aside related research achievements of overseas scholars on this topic, we can see from a series of studies Ma completed four years ago that "depoliticizing" and "culturizing" national issues are not new ideas (Ma Rong, 2000a, 2000b, 2000c). However, the attention that his paper received from academic journals, government internal journals and national academic conferences requires students of national issues to consider and respond to this not-so-new "new thought".

The best way to gain a systematic grasp of Ma Rong's personal views is to read and analyze his classic works in a systematic way. Reading Ma's works from 2000 and 2004, the ideas and Arguments in them seem to be presented in a continuous and systematic way, and "A Few Issues on Ethnic Research" and "New Thoughts in Understanding Ethnic Relations" appear to be his two most representative works. Hence for the purposes of this paper I confine myself to them.

> A national/ethnic group first and foremost has objective foundations of a (tangible) system and an (intangible) culture. In its interaction with other ethnic groups, "consensus" and "differentiation" of various levels are formed based on the degree of difference between these tangible and intangible aspects. In the social activities of ethnic group members, "collective awareness" will be formed naturally upon these objective foundations, and will be stabilized and disseminated through the process of interaction. This is how a "self-existing" national/ethnic group turns into a "self-aware" one (Ma Rong, 2000c).

This is the formula for the formation of national "self-awareness" through the differences in system and culture proposed by Ma, the core idea of which is that system and culture are foundational in forming a nationality and national awareness. They are, however, necessary but not sufficient for establishing national awareness: as of today no case of inter-national interaction that stemmed *only* from system and culture has been found. Without such a case, researchers cannot and should not crudely and arbitrarily categorize complex inter-national interactions as systemic or cultural: such a theoretical research that tries to linearly define nationalities and analyze national awareness through systematic and cultural differences, and furthermore to assert the nationality's changing from "self-existing" to "self-aware", obviously does not adopt an objective, rigorous and scientific attitude to research. There is nothing wrong with emphasizing the cultural features of nationalities in academic research, but to anchor the concept of nationality on culture and promote the "depoliticizing" and "culturizing" national issues, which should belong to a political realm, may be far off the mark. As far as branding the "culturizing" of national issues as a solution for those issues as a "new idea" and "guiding principle" to be offered to multi-national governments, and attempt to "lead China's ethnic relations in a new future direction", is still more unthinkable.

After concealing the interest motivations behind systematic and cultural differences, Ma Rong's research findings takes on an even more ridiculous turn: first, he simplifies national awareness as equivalent to the nationalism of "one country, one nation", arguing that "as soon as a group develops "ethnic awareness", the group boundary will be clarified and strengthened, promoting collective political, economic, cultural and even military activities of this ethnic". Secondly, he makes unqualified assertion that "to solidify or strengthen the relationship between an ethnic group and a region should be considered a form of regression", which obviously is confusing the essences of colonialism, big-nation chauvinism, chauvinism and national liberation movement. Third, when researching the inter-national relations of multi-national states, he once again relates nationalism in the sense of "one nation, one state" with national regional self-government system for the protection of national minorities' powers in managing local affairs, and predicts "when "regional self-government" has been solidified, under outside influences and certain domestic political and social conditions, separationist or independency trends may even appear". Lastly, under the banner of absolute equality, Ma argues that preferential policies for national minority groups aimed at integrating inter-national relations for multi-national states are "policies of inequality" that inflict "institutionalized discrimination" and "manifest inequity" on non-autonomous nationalities. Such paradoxical opinions are clearly a result of overlooking international experience in helping under-developed regions and disadvantaged national minority groups.

Hard pressed to make his case, Ma Rong calls on a number of so-called "international experiences" as supporting evidence. But on close inspection, we find to our surprise that they are all lacking in credibility. First, Ma claims that "the long-term effect of some "national regional self-government" or nations adopting similar systems (such as the Soviet Union, Yugoslavia and Czechoslovakia) are in need of further discussion". After which he quotes a paper by Chen Peng as supporting evidence, without realizing that Chen's research actually establishes that the dis-integration of the former Soviet Union was not due to national regional autonomy. Chen pointed out that "it might have worked out better for the Soviet Union to have adopted regional autonomy or a regional state system...both practically and theoretically, the federal system of the Soviet Union was unrealistic and flawed" (Chen Peng, 1993). Secondly, when talking about western states' experiences in striving to "culturize" ethnic and racial issues and avoid "politicization", Ma cites Japan as an example:

> Japan emphasized the cultural differences between the Ainu and the peo-ple of Okinawa, but avoided treating the two peoples as "nationalities" with clear group boundaries (Ma Rong, 2000c).

According to the research of Guo Hongshen, a researcher of the Institute of Ethnology and Anthropology at the China Academy of Social Sciences, and Jin Chunpei, a researcher who travelled to Japan, on the Ainu of Hokkaido, as well as research on Otsuka and Hei by the Japanese National Ethnic Studies Museum, the Ainu "are scattered indigenous people living among north-eastern pacific islands. They live by hunting, fishing and gathering, but while their production technologies are backward, they have formed their own unique economic and social life";

> from the exploitation of the Ainu people's territory and the wiping out of the Ainu national culture by Japan in recent times...the *Hokkaido Aboriginals Protection Law* was passed to implement the national assimilation policy...the Ainu policy viewed the Ainu group as a distinct "nationality" that "required assimilation";

Due to the Ainu's persistent resistance and the

"power sourced from prominent issues of global aboriginals and national minorities and the further development of international alliances...the [Japanese] government is considering the transition from the welfare policy to the national policy in its constitution" (Guo Hongshen and Jin Chunpei, 1990; Yokoyama Hiroko, 2004).

According to the research by an independent researcher from the UN Human Rights Committee conducted in 2005 on Japanese human rights, "(Japanese) national minority groups such as the Ainu group are under discrimination", but "a big problem is the lack of strong political desire to resolve this discrimination (by the Japanese government)" (*New Beijing Paper*, 2005). It can be seen that Ma's research is based on out-of-context quotes and the description of fake facts.

Ideas of absolute equality, complete ignorance of the reality of the existence of major inequalities in the development of nationalities, confusing internal national political arrangements and preferential policies for nationalities, replacing nationality *e pluribus unum* with its cultural equivalent, diluting national identity with citizen identity, using "culturizing" to downplay national issues, are threads of the logic running through Ma's research arguments. All stem from his failure at the starting point of his research to consider "interests" as a basic driver for national development. In his further arguments, Ma consciously or unconsciously inserts the nationalism of "one nation, one state" into national awareness, from which he made erroneous conclusions such as "self-government may lead to independence or disintegration", "the promotion of a common language is in fact forcing the utilization of Mandarin" and "national region self-government is a institutionalized discrimination".

While coming from different academic perspectives, both national theory and political science view national issues as a political affair established on the interests of nationalities: national issues refer to "various conflicts in various areas of social life from all historical periods from the formation and development to the destruction of the nationality between different nationalities and communities. National issues are social political issues, and belong to a certain historical category"; they are "in fact issues concerning the interests of different nationalities" (Encyclopaedia of China, 1986, 1992). As political, national issues must be solved through political systems and public policies. Attempts to "depoliticize" and "culturize" them are fruitless.

Equating and then separating the conceptions of "nation" and "ethnic group", with their very different internal and external meanings, is a practice that is seems to be favored by Ma and his followers, who also like working on nation in terms of "ethnic group." In his 2004 research, Ma utilized this practice to its full potential: firstly, he equated "nation" with "ethnic group", seeking to replace the former with the latter; secondly, he categorized "ethnic group" and "nation" as culture and politics respectively, which completes this replacement"; thirdly, he pointed out the cultural meanings in the concept of "ethnic group", arguing that national relations are cultural relations, and national issues are cultural issues; finally, he manufactured distinctions between the new concept "ethnic group" and the original concept "nation" and made them opposites, asserting that the self-government of national regions will definitely lead to "national independence" or "national disintegration" under certain conditions, and furthermore called for "depoliticizing" and "culturizing" national issues.

Using "nation" and "ethnic group" interchangeably is clearly a controversial issue in scholarly circles, and scholars can choose their own research direction based on their educational and personal preferences. Without making significant errors in the logical process, if the subject of study remains the same, then it should be common sense that whether a scholar adopts the concept of "nation" or "ethnic group" in approaching the subject makes no difference to the outcome of research; on the other hand, if the subject of study is not the same from the start, then no matter what the methods of study, they cannot obtain the same outcome. Let's look at several research efforts in nation *vs.* ethnic group terms. The United Nations Development Programme reached the same conclusions in their work on Spain, Belise, and India, which are

> promoting the trust, support and identification between all groups in building a democratic "state nation" ... the solution to national issues is to establish those systems and implement those policies that allow for both autonomy and centralized control. Autonomy brings a sense of belonging and pride to the people of an ethnic group, while centralized control brings people a set of common systems and symbols.

While the UNDP's research was also based on the ethnic perspective, it did not reach the same "depoliticization" conclusion like Ma Rong: "a form of replacement for nation-state is 'state-nation', in which various 'nations' — no matter based on race, religion, language and citizenship — can peacefully coexist in a unified national political system" (UNDP, 2004, p. 49).

By equating the concepts of ethnic group with nation, and concluding that nation are different from ethnic group and that national issues are not ethnic issues, these outrageous research findings by Ma resulted from critical errors in logic in his research process: firstly, after switching the two, he did not point out the identity between concept "nation" and concept "ethnic group", but on the contrary placed these two concepts that are originally used to describe the same things as "different points on a continuum"; secondly, he went on to make "nation" and "ethnic group" opposing concepts, arguing that "ethnic group as groups with certain cultural heritage and history, are very different from "nations" which are political entities connected to established lands"; thirdly, he made connections between the concept of nation and national self-determining, nation-states and nationalism to stigmatize the concept, asserting that it "is likely to be associated with a certain political entity and separationist movements that have the power to execute "national self-determining" and establish "nation-states"; lastly, he completely abandoned the stigmatized concept of "nation" in an attempt to establish the value and significance of "ethnic group" which he place on the same continuum; " The reason we distinguish between 'nation' and 'ethnic group' in the Chinese language is because the different use of these terms may actually imply varied orientations for viewing, understanding, and managing ethnic relations" (Ma Rong, 2004).

In addition, there are numerous erroneous uses of references in Ma Rong's research. After perusing the paper "A new perspective in guiding ethnic relations in the 21st century: 'Depoliticalization' of ethnicity in China", one of the most comprehensive references Ma uses is India's experience of ethnic integration. The Indian government, he states, strove to cultivate the common identity of "the Indian" among the entire population by creating a "common Indian culture" through historical articles and cultural heritages that could bring cohesion between different ethnic groups and religious groups...therefore while there are many different religions, languages, ethnic groups, political ideologies and a deeply rooted caste system in India, various ethnic groups in India are beginning to view "India" as a community with common culture and history, all groups cannot be separated from their cultural heritages, and the Indian film industry exerted significant forces in this effort to create a cultural-historical community" (Ma Rong, 2004). But is this the case? According to research carried out by the Southern Asian Research Institute at Sichuan University, India is far from being perfectly harmonious in its ethnic relations: under the rule of Nehru (1947–1964), fierce inter-ethnic conflicts emerged in the Andhra, Assam, Punjab and Nagaland regions due to the establishment and adjustment to the language system; in order to repress the anti-language discrimination movement of the Nagaland people who occupied a mere 6,370 square acres and had less than 350,000 in population, the Indian government even dispatched 100,000 soldiers, which is one-fifth of the national defence manpower, to carry out several repressive missions. Between 1964 and 1966 under the rule of Shastri, a language-related upheaval erupted in southern India with Madras as the center, and upheaval also erupted in the Tamil language region including actions such as destruction of railroads, burning down of government organizations, resignation of two central government officials and even bloodshed and violent actions involving the armed police. Between 1966 and 1977 as well as between 1980 and 1984 under the rule of Mrs Gandhi, an armed independence movement by the Mizo people erupted in 1966, in which 500 people died and 3,500 were arrested; in 1976 the Naxalbari rural armed Mizo forces in West Bengal which turned into the national "Naxalite Movement". In 1974 the "Narayan Movement" by Gujarat students caused a strike involving hundreds of thousands railroad workers, in which over 10,000 people were arrested. In 1987 Indian and Muslim racial killings erupted in Moradabad, the city of West India, the bloodshed spread to 10 other cities including Delhi as well as the Indian-occupied Kashmir region; in 1981 over 10,000 rebels joined the Islamic "Green Revolution" in Tamil Nadu, the state of Southern India, where Punjabi Sikhs occupied the golden temple in an armed confrontation with government forces. Through the 1980s, an average of 15,000 caste-related conflicts happened every year, and even Indira Gandhi, who was killed by Sikh guards in 1984, stated that India was under "a national atmosphere of violence and crime". Between 1984 and 1989 under the rule of Mrs Gandhi, the Punjab Sikhs continued with their terrorist activities after "Operation Thunderbolt" implemented by the Indian government, Assam was also plagued with upheavals due to their demands for independence. Between 1989 and 1990 under the rule of Vishwanath Pratap Singh, the fight over Ayodhya temples and the destruction of the Babri Mosque by over 100,000 Hindu fanatics led to religious conflicts which spread throughout the nation. In upheavals in Indian-occupied Jammu and Kashmir, Muslims raised political demands to secede from India and join Pakistan. In the high-caste student unrest in northern India caused by the "Dahlman report", 63 students burned themselves to death and 100,000 people marched out to the capital New Delhi. Under the rule of P. V. Narasimha Rao (1991–1996), the Ayodhya Babri Mosque was completely destroyed in 1992 by 500,000 Hindus, and more than 1,000 people were killed during a week-long ethnic conflict. In 1993 500 Muslims were killed within a week in Mumbai through organized attacks, the *Indian Times* commented that "during Mumbai's 300 year of history we have never seen such brutal violence". After Vajpayee gained control of the extremist "National Will Group" that originated in fundamentalist Hinduism in 1998, it carried out attacks on all religious national minorities under the slogan of "realizing genuine secularism"; while in north-eastern India upheavals caused by national minority groups demands for "independence" and "autonomy" were constant, punctuated by bloody clashes between guerrilla armies and the armed police (Yang Cuibo, 2004). Indian political expert A. H Sornjee once clearly stated "there exist surprising levels of diversity and disintegration in India, the extent of which has far surpassed Holland, Austria and Canada. When conflicts based on caste, rank, religion and region are put in the context of nationality, they no longer follow the route of power-sharing for the purpose of unification, but waver between conflict and compromise" (Howard Wiarda, 2004).

It is hard, in the face of all these bloody facts of inter-ethnic conflicts, to find traces of the "important success story of India after its establishment" of "at the same time of respecting the equal rights of all religions and ethnic groups, the government strives to establish the "national awareness" of all Indians, clearly placing national awareness above all ethnic groups and religious groups and striving to dilute ethnic group awareness" spoken of by Ma Rong (Ma Rong, 2004). The description of "facts" and errors in logic by the professor clearly went against the scientific attitude of "only a great amount of investigation and research, not merely common sense, can establish truth" that he promoted.

The UNDP report points out,

with India's attempt to force Hinduism on all groups, the contemporary Indian government is now facing serious challenges in its constitution's promise to honor multiple complementary identities. These challenges pose a threat to India's inclusiveness and also violate the rights of national minorities. The recent violence between ethnic groups brought concerns for the harmonious future of the human society, and formed a shadow over past accomplishment of the nation (UNDP, 2004, p. 49).

So different a conclusion by the UNDP on the same case and from the same perspective calls to mind the seemingly absurd question Wallerstein posed at the International Sociology Conference in New Delhi in 1986: "does India exist?!"(Immanuel Wallerstein, 2003).

Creating a national relations that consolidates the equality, cohesion and mutual-help between all nationalities, and establishing a society in which all nationalities coexist in a harmonious way requires the following from the government: first of all, it needs to accurately understand and evaluate the interests of each nationality in a scientific manner and steadily resolve conflicts between the ever-increasing material demands of the people and the under-developed social productivity using a scientific view of development. Secondly, the government needs to be persistent in its international political arrangements of national regional autonomy, improve and develop preferential policies for national minorities aimed at shrinking regional developmental differences, and achieve mutual development and prosperity of all nationalities in a cohesive nation. It is of the utmost importance for a respected expert and scholar to maintain an objective, fair, historical and scientific attitude. If not, the consequences could range from the loss of personal academic integrity and reputation to the more serious misguidance of academia and even the issue of using scholarship to kidnap politics with.

References

Blondel, Jean (1992). Politics. In *The Blackwell Encyclopaedia of Political Science* (trans. Institution of China Issues), David Miller and Vernon Bogdanor (eds.), p. 583. Beijing: China University of Political Science and Law Press.

Chen, Jianyue (2004). Unified diversity: National integration and legitimacy in a unified multi-national state. In *National Politics and the Modern Nation State*, Wang Jian'e and Chen Jianyue (eds.). Beijing: Social Sciences Academic Press.

Chen, Peng (1993). The federal state system of the Soviet Union. In *National Crisis and Disintegration of the Soviet Union*, Hao Shiyuan and Ruan Xihu (eds.), Chengdu: Sichuan Minzu Press.

Chen, Qingyun (1996). *Public Policy Analysis*, Beijing: China Economic Press.

Cuibo, Yang (2004). *Indian Politics and Law*, pp. 12–77. Chengdu: Bashu Book Agency.

Dahl, Robert A. (1987). *Modern Political Analysis* (trans. Wang Huning and Wang Feng), p. 129. Shanghai: Shanghai People's Publishing House.

Dahl, Robert A. (1999). *A Preface to Economic Democracy*, p. 109 (trans. Gu Xin and Zhu Dan), Hong Kong: SDX Joint Publishing Company, Oxford University Press.

Deng, Honglei (1987). Discussion on the innovative turn in Chinese traditional theory of harmony — a new view on the early Confucian concept of moderation. In *Philosophical Researches*, issue 1.

Encyclopaedia of China (*Volume on Ethnicity*), (1986), p. 314 and (*Volume on Politics*), (1992), p. 256. Beijing: Encyclopaedia of China Publishing House.

Guo, Hongshen and Jin, Chunpei (1990). *Japan Visit Report*, National Theories Research, issue 3.

Guo, Hongshen (ed.) (1997). *Comparative Analysis of National Issues between China and the Former Soviet Union.* Beijing: China Minzu University Press.

Held, David (1998). *Models of Democracy* (trans. Yan Jirong and Fang Xiangqin), p. 383. Beijing: Central Compilation & Translation Press.

Hill, Michael (2003). *Understanding Social Policy*, (U.K.), p. 95 (trans. Liu Shenhua). Beijing: The Commercial Press.

Hiroko, Yokoyama (2004). Issues in the independence movement of the modern Ainu people. In *Minzoku no bunka to shakai no doukuma — fujifu ka chino shi* (*50th Investigation Report of the State Ethnic Museum*), (Japan), p. 329–330. State Ethnic Museum.

Ibrahim, Saad Eddin. Ethnic issues in Arabic eyes (trans. Wu Qi). In *International Social Sciences Journal (Chinese version)*, Vol. 16, issue 2, p. 84.

Lenin, Vladimir Ilyich (1958). *Collected Works*, Vol. 22, p. 340. Beijing: People's Publishing House.

Lenin, Vladimir Ilyich (1972). *Collected Works*, 2nd Edition, p. 512. Beijing: People's Publishing House.

Lenin, Vladimir Ilyich (1959). *Collected Works*, Vol. 38, p. 86. Beijing: People's Publishing House.

Ma, Rong (2000a). On the definition of "Minzu", *Journal of Yunnan Nationalities University*, issue 1.

Ma, Rong (2000b). The emergence of national awareness, *Journal of Yunnan Nationalities University*, issue 2.

Ma, Rong (2000c). Several issues on ethnic study, *Journal of Peking University*, issue 4.

Ma, Rong (2004). New perspective in guiding ethnic relations on the 12st century: The "depoliticization" of ethnicity in China. *Journal of Peking University* issue 6.

Marx, Karl and Engels, Friedrich (1972a). *Collected Works of Marx and Friedrich Engels*, Vol. 4. Beijing: People's Publishng House.

Marx, Karl and Engels, Friedrich (1972b). *Collected Works of Marx and Friedrich Engels*, Vol. 2, p. 82. Beijing: People's Publishing House.

Marx, Karl and Engels, Friedrich (1975). *Collected Works of Marx and Friedrich Engels*, Vol. 25, p. 892. Beijing: People's Publishing House.

Marx, Karl and Engels, Friedrich, Vol. 1.

Michio, Muranatsu (Japan) (1989). Local power in the Japanese state. In *Modern Political Science Series*, Takashi Inoguchi (ed.), issue 15, (trans. Sun Xin) Beijing: The Economic Daily Press.

New Beijing Paper (2005). Japan accused of harbouring serious ethnic discrimination, A27, 12 July 2005.

N.N.A Rarwal, Vidya Bhushan, Vishnoo Bhagwan (1984). *Principles of Political Science*, p. 213. (New Delhi: Ram Chand & Co).

Olson, Mancur (1995). *The Logic of Collective Action* (trans. Yu Chen, Guo Yufeng and Li Chongxin), Shanghai: Shanghai People's Publishing House.

Plato (1972). *The Republic* (trans. Guo Binhe and Zhang Zhuming), Beijing: The Commercial Press.

Richmond Anthony H. *Nationalism of National Minorities and the Various Norms of Social Sciences*, trans. Feng Bingkum, *International Social Science Journal* (Chinese version), Vol. 5, issue 1.

Rousseau, Jean-Jacques (France) (1980). *The Social Contract* (trans. He Zhaowu), Beijing: The Commercial Press.

Roskin, Michael and Cord, Robert (2001). *Political Science*, 6th Edition (trans. Lin Zhen and Wang Feng), Beining: Huaxia Publishing House.

Sang, Yucheng (1994). *Self-government Politics*, p. 8–10. Hong Kong: SDX Joint Publishing Company.

Smith, Anthony D. (1992). Self-government, in *The Blackwell Encylopaedia of Political Science* (trans. the Institution of China Issues), pp. 163, 694. Beijing:
China University of Political Science and Law Press.

Stalin, Joseph (1953). *Stalin Collection*, 2nd Edition, p. 309. Beijing: People's Publishing House.

UNDP (2004). *Human Development Report*, (Chinese version), Beijing: China Financial and Economic Publishing House.

UNDP (2003). *Human Development Report* (Chinese version), Beijing: China Financial and Economic Publishing House.

Wallerstein, Immanuel (2003). *The Essential Wallerstein* (trans. Huang Guangyao and Hong Xia), Nanjing: Nanjing University Press.

Wiarda, Howard (2004). *Comparative Democracy and Democratisation* (trans. Rong Yuan), p. 128. Beijing: Peking University Press.

Chapter 5

EVALUATION ON THE "NATION BUILDING" OF INDIA BY THE UNITED NATIONS DEVELOPMENT PROGRAMME*

MA RONG

Department of Sociology, Peking University

From a certain perspective, India seems to have achieved some success in promoting the national consensus of "national unity", as a UNDP report states. While the report also expresses concern for some recent trends in India that threaten to disturb its harmony, we cannot take those concerns out of context, and mislead the reader to deny acknowledgement of the achievements of India in promoting national unity.

Our close neighbor India is an ancient civilization with a rich history and multiple coexisting religions, ethnicities, languages, and castes. Before it became a British colony, the Indian subcontinent had over 100 independent tribes of varying sizes, which the British colonial government integrated into a single political framework. With such a historical background, the Indian government started the process of nation-building after gaining independence, actively working to promote the common identity of "Indian" among the entire population, and creating a "common Indian culture" through historical articles and cultural heritages that would integrate all ethnicities and religious groups. Therefore, despite the existence of many

---

*This chapter is based on an article originally published in *Central Ethnic University Paper* (Philosophy and Social Sciences Section), 2006, No. 3.

religions (including Hinduism, Islam, Sikhism, Jainism, and Christianity), languages (with English being the common language), ethnic groups (including Bengalis, Tamils, Punjabis, and Biharis), political ideologies (even now there are still three states ruled by the Indian Republic Government) and the deep-rooted caste system, India is regarded as a harmonious community with a common culture and history.

In addition, after its independence, the Indian government strove to build a "state-nation" within its territory, and announced in its constitution: "We, the people of India , having solemnly resolved to constitute India into a sovereign democratic republic and to secure to all its citizens: justice, social, economic, and political; liberty of thought, expression, belief, faith, and worship; equality of status and of opportunity; and to promote among them all fraternity assuring the dignity of the individual and the unity of the nation" (*India Today*, 1997). Along with respecting and granting equal rights to all religious and ethnic groups, all the successive ruling Indian governments strove to establish the "national" awareness among all Indians, clearly putting national awareness above individual ethnic groups and religious groups, while downplaying ethnic awareness.

I gave affirmation for India's achievements in "nation-building" after its independence in a paper I published in the 6th issue of *Beijing Daxue Xuebao* in 2004. *World Nationalities* published a paper in 2005 (issue 5) which criticized my views in that paper. The author of the paper asserts that "time and time again we see erroneous arguments in Professor Ma's research. After reading the paper *New thoughts on understanding ethnic relations — depoliticizing ethnic issues*, I have found that one of the most comprehensive arguments offered by Professor Ma was the ethnic integration of India" (Chen Jianyue, 2005).

The *World Nationalities* essay's critique of my paper was mostly focused on two aspects. The first aspect was my affirmation of the achievements of India in its "nation-building" efforts, and referenced many incidences of conflicts in India that were related to caste, ethnicity and religion, thereby proposing the idea that "India's ethnic relations are not so harmonious and wonderful as described by Professor Ma" (Chen Jianyue, 2005).

However, I did not provide many arguments in my article on India's ethnic relations. While I gave affirmation for India's achievements in its "nation-building" efforts, I did not describe India's ethnic relations as "harmonious and wonderful". The point I tried to emphasize in my paper was "Nation-building is still in progress in India and there have been ethnic nationalist movements in India among the minority tribes and even guerrilla wars. But these issues have not been internationalized or become a serious threat to Indian unity" (Ma Rong, 2004).

The emergence of inter-ethnic violence indicates that there are issues between interest groups that remain to be solved. These types of inter-ethnic violence events have happened and are still happening in many countries including the U.S., the U.K., and France, but they do not mean that there are "separationist movements that pose serious threats to the integrity of the nation" in these countries or in India. The regional "independence" and "autonomy" movements in India have not been "globalized", the global community pays less attention to those movements compared to China's Tibet and Xinjiang issues. The Indian government rarely demands other governments to officially acknowledge India's territorial integrity, or to publicly announce non-support for regional separationist movements. From this perspective, in my opinion, the Indian government's efforts in promoting the unity of the nation has been relatively successful.

The second point in the critique of my paper is built around my citation of the UNDP's *2004 Human Development Report*. This report affirmed for India's achievements in "nation-building" in a "multicultural" system after the introduction of the concept. Below is the passage in entirety:

Case studies and analyses demonstrate that enduring democracies can be established in polities that are multicultural. Explicit efforts are required to end the cultural exclusion of diverse groups (as highlighted in the Spanish and Belgian cases) and to build multiple and complementary identities. Such responsive policies provide incentives to build a feeling of unity in diversity — a "we" feeling. Citizens can find the institutional and political space to identify with both their country and their other cultural identities, to build their trust in common institutions and to participate in and support democratic politics. All of these are key factors in consolidating and deepening democracies and building enduring "state-nations".

India's constitution incorporates this notion. Although India is culturally diverse, comparative surveys of long-standing democracies including India show that it has been very cohesive, despite its diversity. But modern India is facing a grave challenge to its constitutional commitment to multiple and complementary identities with the rise of groups that seek to impose a singular Hindu identity on the country. These threats undermine the sense of inclusion and violate the rights of minorities in India today. Recent communal violence raises serious concerns for the prospects for social harmony and threatens to undermine the country's earlier achievements.

These achievements have been considerable. Historically, India's constitutional design recognized and responded to distinct group claims and enabled the polity to hold together despite enormous regional, linguistic and cultural diversity. As evident from India's performance on indicators of identification, trust, and support (Fig. 1), its citizens are deeply committed to the country and to democracy, despite the country's diverse and highly stratified society. This performance is particularly impressive when compared with that of other long-standing — and wealthier — democracies. The challenge is in reinvigorating India's commitment to practices of pluralism, institutional accommodation

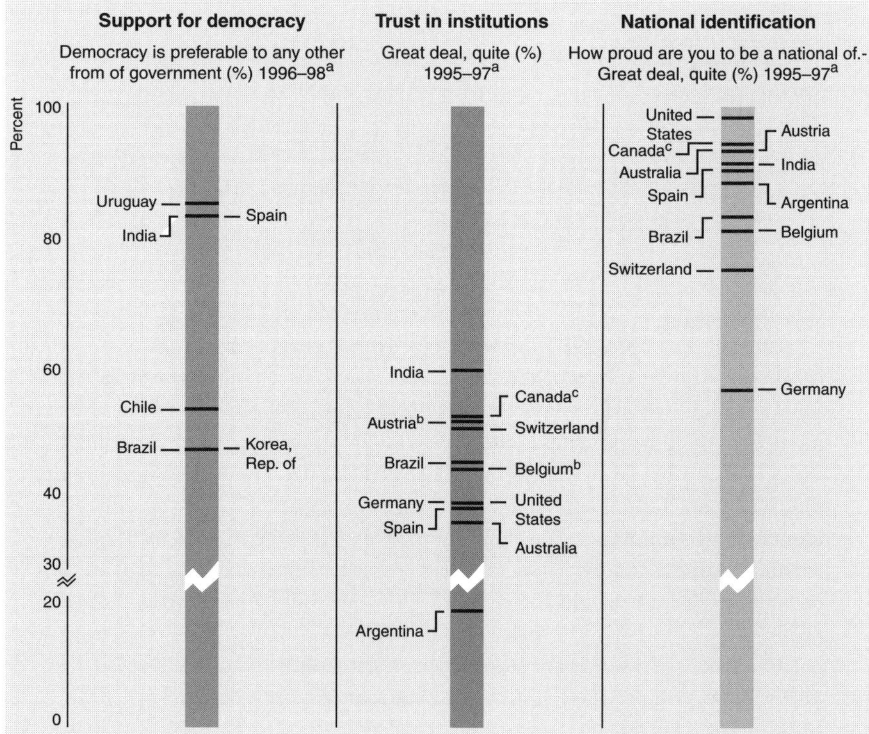

Fig. 1.   Trust support and identification: poor and diverse countries can do well with multicultural policies.

Note: Percentages exclude 'don't know/no answer' replies. a. The most recent year available during the period specified. b. Data refer to 1992. c. The most recent year during the period 1990–93.

and conflict resolution through democratic means (United Nations Development Programme, 2004).

This UN report provided a graphic representation of the "trust in institutions" of the mass public according to survey data gathered. India was at the top of the charts, placed above Canada, Austria, Switzerland, Brazil, Belize, and the U.S. As for the level of "national identification", while India was below the U.S., Austria, Canada and Australia, it was still above Spain, Argentina, Brazil, Belize, Switzerland, and Germany. Just as the quoted paragraphs from the report said, "its citizens are deeply committed to the country and to democracy, despite the country's diverse and highly stratified society. This performance is particularly impressive when compared with that of other long-standing — and wealthier — democracies". From this, we can see that the UNDP has explicitly affirmed India's achievements in "nation-building", which is in line with the opinions I expressed through my 2004 paper published in the *Beijing daxue xuebao*.

In order to prove that my opinion of India's nation-building efforts was wrong, The paper from World Nationalities singled out the sentences after the "but" in the quoted paragraphs from the United Nations Development Programme report: Modern India is facing a grave challenge to its constitutional commitment to multiple and complementary identities with the rise of groups that seek to impose a singular Hindu identity on the country. These threats undermine the sense of inclusion and violate the rights of minorities in India today. Recent communal violence raises serious concerns for the prospects for social harmony and threatens to undermine the country's earlier achievements. The paper then commented that "although the report from the United Nations Development Programme and Professor Ma's paper both took an ethnic studies approach to analyzing India's ethnic relations case, the two researches yielded such different conclusions..." (Chen Jianyue, 2005). The author of this paper seemed to think that just by quoting these few sentences, it would be sufficient to pursuade the readers that the United Nations report held a critical opinion of India's ethnic relations, and also to prove that my arguments on India's achievements in this aspect was totally the opposite with the UN report, thereby proving that my opinion was wrong.

It must be pointed out that the author of this paper only quoted a small portion of a paragraph from the United Nations Development Programme report, and largely ignored the paragraphs before and after that talked about India's achievements and relevant supporting graphs.

The author obviously misrepresented the basic arguments proposed by the United Nations report. I consider this method of taking citations out of context, misinterpreting the original article and misleading readers to be a wrongful practice.

The development and evolution of the human society are complex and diversified processes, due to multiple internal and external influencing factors, the process of "nation-building" of a modern nation and its internal group relations may take on many different trends, each country must both face its own history and national circumstance and also learn and borrow from the development of other countries. In ethnic relations, we very much need to learn about and study the theories, opinions, policies and practices of other countries. As for what endeavors of India on its "nation-building" can be considered successful or correctly directed, scholars are welcome to give their own opinions. Similarly, when it comes to the question of what issues remain to be solved in issues of ethnic relations, scholars are always invited to participate in open discussion. However, in conducing academic discussions, scholars need to uphold a rigorous attitude and always respect the original intention of the author when citing others' works, which also shows respect to readers.

References

Chen, Jianyue (2005). Establishment of a multi-national harmonious society and resolving national issues — "Depoliticizing" and "Culturizing" national issues. *World Ethno-National Studies*, Issue 5.

India Today (1997). *50th Anniversary of India's Independence*, Issue 49.

Ma, Rong (2004). New perspective in guiding ethnic relations on the 21st century: The "depoliticization" of ethnicity in China. *Journal of Peking University*, Issue 6.

United Nations Development Programme (2004). *Human Development Report.* Beijing: China Financial and Economic Publishing House.

Chapter 6

ON "AFTERTHOUGHTS" OF CHINA'S NATIONAL ISSUES AND "BEING PRACTICAL" — DEBATING MA RONG*

WANG XIEN

*Institute of Ethnology and Anthropology,
Chinese Academy of Social Sciences*

"Enculturation" and "politicization", it is argued, are inappropriate descriptors for classifying national policies. National recognition, regional autonomy and preferential policies were sensible choices to solve China's national issues; the focus need not be on preserving them or not, but rather on how to sustain, develop and improve them. There are traces of the Soviet model in China's national theories and policies, but they largely follow Marxist rather than Stalinist lines. Practice has proved that although there are many imperfections and complexities to China's model, we still made the right decision to create our own model of dealing with national issues with Chinese characteristics. Abandoning our existing national theories and policies and starting over is an option that we cannot afford to take. In theoretical research, we not only need to respect the work of others, but also need to stay focused on our own goals, and strive to enrich and build up on our own discourse and theoretical systems. If we do not do that, we will not be able to find a way out of our problems.

In recent years, Ma Rong has published a series of papers to promote "liberation of thinking", "being practical" and "rethinking" in the last

---

*This chapter is based on an article which was originally published in *Southwestern Ethnicity University Paper (Social Sciences Column)*, 2009. Here is the revised version.

50 years or so of China's national theories and policies. In addition, he proposed a "new idea" of replacing "politicizing" with "culturizing" in national policy. The frank words and strong opinions in these papers showed his powers of critical thinking and innovation, and also invoked widespread attention from scholars of national studies and concerned citizens. In this sense, Ma Rong has contributed to promoting China's national theory research and encouraged people to contemplate on national issues. However, as his "rethinking" process goes to the re-evaluation of the foundations and choices of national theories and policies, as well as methods of resolution, it obliges us to think about it seriously and responsibly.

The doubts Ma Rong cast over the national theories and policies of modern China were based on his analytical framework of "enculturation" and "politicization". He argues that:

Government policy plays an important role in guiding group identity and adjusting the boundaries of a political entity. Throughout the history of social development, governments have generally adopted two contrasting policies for regulating ethnic relations: one views ethnic groups mainly as political entities and the other views them primarily as cultural groups. The former policy emphasizes integrity, political power, and "territorial" conservation of ethnic groups. The later prefers to treat ethnic relations as cultural interactions, and to deal with the problems between people of different ethnic backgrounds as affairs among individuals rather than between groups as a whole, even though the common characteristics of the ethnic group membership are given recognition. By emphasizing the cultural characteristics of ethnic groups, their political interests are diluted. Furthermore, in processes of migration, the historical connection between ethnic groups and their traditional residence is gradually loosened (Ma Rong, 2004b).

The first approach related to "politicizing", while the second perspective concerns "enculturation". In Chinese history, the overall direction of development, despite brief, localized reversals, followed basic principles of "enculturation" and the culture-driven "natural integration" of ethnic groups. This process continued into the 1940s.

After the liberation of China, the Chinese government borrowed Soviet practices, adopting following measures to politicize and institutionalize ethnic issues.

1. 55 ethnic minority groups were identified through a large-scale process of "identification of nationalities" that delineated and solidified the "ethnic

component" of each individual and clarified national boundary, thereby solidified and strengthened people's "national awareness".

2. "regional autonomy" was given to all ethnic minorities in order to protect the "political rights" of each ethnic group.
3. ethnic preferential policies concerning politics, economy, education and culture were implemented in minority regions (Ma Rong, 2004b).

These "politicization" measures "will have the effect of pushing them away from being 'cultural groups' and towards the direction of becoming 'political groups' in the 'ethnicity-nation' continuum", "link each ethnic minority to a certain geographic area, provide these groups with a political status, administrative power in their 'autonomous territory'", allowing ethnic separationist forces to emerge and threaten the integrity of the nation (Ma Rong, 2004b).

Ma further argued that the Soviet Union was a classic example of "politicizing" ethnic issues, and that after the establishment of the New China, "we completely replicated the Soviet model in our ethnic theories and policies"; and "politicization of ethnic groups" was promoted in China for over half a century". Learning from the disintegration of the Soviet Union and the Yugoslavia, "Chinese scholars should rethink the Stalinist ethnic theories and Soviet ethnic policies that dominated China's academic field ever since the 1950s" (Ma Rong, 2007a).

National identification, regional autonomy and preferential policies are all "politicized" policy orientations replicating now-discredited Soviet practices. For Ma, "politicization" is a blanket term negating everything practiced in China, along with the relevant basic theories and research. But if this is justified, what is left of China's national practices, theories and all related achievements? It is clear that this attitude is nihilist, and far from "pragmatic".

"Enculturation" and "politicization" are, we should point out, inappropriate descriptors for classifying national policy orientations for several reasons. First of all, as Ma states, "national and ethnic issues are, at any time and in any country, bound to be political in nature" (Ma Rong, 2007b). Next, policies and institutions aimed at resolving such politicized national and ethnic issues are still political actions set up and carried out by the state. Thirdly, even where these policies were aimed at confining national and ethnic issues within the realm of "culture", their ultimate goal was still political stability. Hence, "enculturation" and "politicizing" cannot be used to categorize national policies; nor can they be used to evaluate their faults and merits. Opposition to Ma's views has appeared in the Scholarly literature;[1] here, we will further take up some of his major proposals.

6.1. Evaluating National Identification

National identification is the first national practice that Ma Rong criticized. He believes that "due to the 'national identification' process and the later 'national component' registration in the residence registration process implemented by the government, the boundary and national awareness between each ethnic group in China have become more clear and strong compared with the 1930s."(Ma Rong, 2007a). "The national identification" of those years cemented the basic framework of China's ethnic relations, to which many current problems may still be traced" (Ma Rong, 2007c).

Evaluating China's national identification should follow a logic of: Was it necessary? Was it scientific? and, What was the result?

Was national identification necessary? The question must first be answered, was it necessary to set national policies in place? For setting such policies, it is assumed that there are target groups on whom they are to be carried out. In the Chinese population, which groups are Han, and which are minorities? Within the latter, what is the breakdown? Without clarifying this, we cannot even start to talk about implementing policies or practices in terms of national equality and national cohesion. Fei Xiaotong states clearly in his paper *On the National Identification Issue in China*:

> China is a multi-national nation, but it is difficult to say how many nationalities there are. Before 1949, the Kuomintang government denied that China was a multi-national state, and even Sun Yat-sen's idea of a "Republic of Five Nationalities" came under attack. The government categorized many historically acknowledged nationalities into sub-branches of the Han nationality, which showed the blatant Han chauvinism that aimed to suppress and eliminate national minorities groups in China.

---

[1]Scholars have already conducted research on the fallacy of the categorization of "depoliticization" and "enculturation" (see Chen Jianyue, 2005; Chen Yuping, 2008). In addition, there are also scholars who have made commentaries on this categorization through the perspectives of theory versus reality, and history versus present (see Hao Shiyuan, 2005; Yang Jiancin, 2008; Ma Shoutu, 2008).

After 1949, under the Party's leadership, the People's Republic of China achieved the goal of national equality. Many national minorities groups that had been suppressed for a long time demanded their national traits be recognized and their names legalized. This was a victory for the national policies of the CPC as well as a sign of the minorities' self-awareness. In 1953, there were 400 registered national minorities. Of those self-titled groups, how many were exclusive entities? How many were referring to the same group? Many of those registered national minority names were names of the geographic area where they resided, many were names of sub-branches of other groups, some were different versions of the same name used by different people, and still others were Mandarin renditions of the original name. So to answer the question of how many national groups there are in China and list them, we will need to analyze the existing list. We call this task national identification, which is a scientific research project.

Post 1949, both Party and government gave great stress to national identification. This is because, in order to carry the Party's national policies fully, it was essential to first identify what groups there were. For example, in the interests of national equality at all levels of the state, we need to decide how many representatives from which nationalities we need to include in various levels of the People's Congress; and when establishing national autonomous regions, we need to figure out which regions have large minority populations, so on and so forth (Fei Xiaotong, 1980).

The quote above expressed clearly why China undertook the national identification process. Whether we replicated Soviet behavior, or whether other countries had similar procedures, need not concern us. The only standard applicable to our own conduct should relate to the demands of China's national practice, and on this basis we cannot find any reasons for questioning it.

In fact, national identification happened in countries other than China and the Soviet Union: it is an essential undertaking for any country implementing national policies, unless national breakdown there is so clear that it can be skipped. The U.S. is viewed as a nation that protects minority interests through the protection of citizen rights, but in reality, preferential "affirmative action" policies are in fact targeted at national minorities (we will elaborate on this later in the chapter). While there was no process of national identification, its target demographic was clearly

African-Americans, Native Americans and Latin Americans.[2] In India, the government only categorizes "tribes" within the country as "national minorities" in order to provide them with relevant supportive policies. The Indian Anthropological Bureau of Investigation once conducted national identification for its 461 tribal groups, providing clear boundaries and numbers for the concept of "national minorities". According to research, in 1991, there were 67,76 million members of tribes in India, taking up 8.08% of the national population (Xaxa Virginius, 2001). The U.S. and India exemplify what Ma calls ethnic policies of "enculturation" , but their experiences have proven that national identification are not unnecessary.

I wish to make three main points on the scientific nature of national identification:

First of all, we need to ascertain whether the criteria of "nation" are scientific. It is widely accepted that the question of what "nation" exactly are, is still unresolved. China utilized Joseph Stalin's definition of nation in a flexible way:

> Based on the actual circumstances of various nationalities in China, nation is defined as a stable community of people with prominent characteristics in economic life, language, culture or national awareness formed through history, regardless of size of population, size of occupied region, social development stage and economic or cultural development stage" (Huang Guangxue and Shi Lianzhu, 2005).

This is a scientific definition, as it stays true to the reality, and provides guidance in the national identification process. While the results of that process have not been without controversy, the standards have come to be accepted by the population at large.

Next, there is the question of whether the process of national identification was scientific. Given that the process started in 1950, when the central government sent visiting teams to national minority regions to get a first grounding in national identification; it ended in 1979 with the identification of the Jino people, nearly 30 years later. This in itself was a

---

[2]The examples here refer to countries that have not undergone national identification according to China's standards. In reality, the U.S. government sponsored *Harvard Encyclopedia of American Ethnic Groups* published in 1980 provided categorizations and description of over 100 ethnic groups in America, which, as "a classic work of American ethnic identification", can also be seen as a result of national identification (see Hao Shiyuan, 2005).

measure of how cautious the approach taken was, not to mention various in-depth research and investigations in that process. Between 1952 and 1953, regions including Yunnan, Guizhou, Guangxi, Guangdong, Hunan, Gansu, Qinghai and Fujian conducted surveys and research on local self-elected national minority groups. In 1953, the State Ethnic Affairs Commission began sending investigation teams to regions including Hunan, Hubei, Guangdong, Zhejiang, Fujian, Guizhou, Yunnan, Qinghai, Gansu, Xinjiang, Tibet and Inner Mongolia to conduct in-depth research on Tujia, She, Daur, Yi, Zhuang and Dai nationality in order to identify, screen and categorize them. There were complexities among the nationalities being identified, so much stress was laid on integrating knowledge from multiple disciplines in the national identification process, paying special attention to integrate the national minority language census and social history investigation conducted from the mid-1950s. These continual, detailed and large-scaled research and investigation efforts provided reliable backing for the national identification process (Huang Guangxue and Shi Lianzhu, 2005).

Finally, we need to discuss the level of acceptance and recognition of the result of the processes' outcomes. As well as conducting national identification according to objective characteristics, China also adhered to the principle of "following the will of the owner", which is to say, we must respect the will of the members of the nationality when making decision on national identity... issues of national identity cannot be outsourced to others, nor can our own wishes be forced on nationalities. The members of the nationality under investigation must have the last say (Fei Xiaotong, 1980). Therefore, members of most nationalities have been satisfied with the result of the national identification process, and the resulting 56 nationalities have gained acknowledgement from the entire country.

Needless to say, due to specific geographical and historical circum-stances, China's national identification process has been faced with a series of tough issues that are entangled with each other. In order to find solutions to these problems, we need to maintain a balance between drawing conclusions according to the research that has been done and respecting the people's wishes, between existing objective circumstances and inter-national and intra-national cohesion, as well as between current benefits and future effects. These complexities will no doubt lead to imperfections in the identification process, therefore, it is normal for a small number of the population to oppose the results and the failure to fulfill individual wishes. It is without a doubt that, overall, the national identification process adhered to the scientific principles and fulfilled the wishes of the majority of the population, as well as met the needs of China's national practices.

National identification, an action of state with unalienable political elements and implications, is not thereby made unscientific. In reality, government participation provided the necessary leadership and material backing for this nationwide task, and also provided a form of statutory ruling for the complex national reality. Hence I don't go along with reading national identification, or our understanding of the 56 nationalities, too politically. As communities of people formed naturally through the course of history, that is, they are no different from other nationalities in the world. Our identification process serves simply to confirm the existence of those communities, rather than "artificial", manufacturing nationalities by political means.

When we discuss the effects of this identification process on future national issues, we are in fact talking about whether these effects are positive or negative. Ma Rong argues, as noted above, that national identification "drew boundaries between China's nationalities, strengthening their national awareness compared to the 1930s", and this in turn stopped the "natural integration" process that had being going on through the history of China. This argument is also incorrect.

It is true that after 1949, and especially after the reforms, national awareness within the nationalities has grown steadily. National identification undeniably promoted the growth of national awareness and reinforced national identity, but was not the only or the most fundamental reason. Were it the case, we would have no way to explain how the same growth is happening in all the nations in the world today, including those that have not undertaken any national identification. The post-Cold War world is spoken of as undergoing a third wave of nationalism, the cause of which is the fact that national awareness supports nationalities at different levels, especially small nationalities or minority groups within newly independent nations. Therefore, we need to approach the issue of the growth of national awareness from the perspectives of the rules of national processes and their related social and historical backgrounds.

Humans congregate into different groups, each with its own rules. As a community formed naturally through the influence of certain historical circumstances, the formation and development of nationalities usually would go through the process from "self-present" to "self-aware".[3] From the overall process of the human history, we can see that the general awareness of nationalities is related to the emergence of capitalism in recent times, as well as the formation and development of nationalism. The emergence of this awareness went through three distinctive yet interconnected stages: The first stage was marked by the emergence of Western European nation states. The second stage was marked by the worldwide national liberation movements that lasted for over 200 years. The third stage was marked by the assertive display of nationality by nationalities within nation states. The first two stages were mainly about the self-awareness of large nationalities or mainstream nationalities, while the third stage was mainly about small nationalities or national minority groups, which is a natural and logical progression (Wang Xisi, 2005). People have generally become aware in recent years that, "with revolutionary developments in transport and communication, as well as the growing literacy and mobility of the population, it has become possible to rapidly overcome the barriers of culture. This developing trend not only allowed for individuals' understanding of other nationalities but also triggered members of a given nationality gaining self-awareness" (Walker Connor, 1973). Hence, from a high level, the occurrence and development of national awareness are products of history and cannot be altered by the will of people.

Modern China, while still riddled with poverty and underprivileged populations, is no longer closed off. "Nationalism" originating in the West has penetrated here; national awareness promoted by social reform and modernization is growing here just as in any other country. This self-awareness in the national democratic revolution aimed at warding off external powers, as well as in the Chinese nation on a national state level. It is also present throughout the modernization process of socialism as well as nationalities under the rule of the nation state. The presence of this self-awareness is beyond the question of whether there is national identification.

As to how we should face growing national awareness, there is a consensus in academia that as with nationalism, there are positive and

---

[3] "Nationalities" here refers to relatively organic and complete ethnic entities with geographic, historical and cultural backgrounds, in contrast to sub-branches or fragmented ethnic groups.

negative sides to it. In reality, recent world progress and the emergence of national awareness are closely related. When democratic thinkers of the 18th century were promoting the ideas of freedom, democracy and opposing autocracy, nationalist theories were on a high tide in various European nations. When Marxism carried out the theory of scientific socialism, with half the world adopting socialism, the world liberation movement was at its peak. The start of what western scholars called the "ethnic revival" in the 1960s, was when Martin Luther King's "I have a Dream" guided the Black Civil Rights Movement in the U.S. to make huge progress. From these, it can be seen that the growth of national awareness is a reflection of world progress — in national progress, we see reflections of advancements in eliminating social inequality, protection of dignity and promoting civilization.

More specifically on the effects of national identification within the country, we should see that on the one hand, growing national awareness did indeed produce undesired effects on national relations and social harmony. On the other hand, it also helped to promote the development of the groups themselves. The basic principle in China currently is "common prosperity" of all nationalities, and national awareness results from this. In promoting common prosperity then, we cannot hope to eliminate national awareness. What could be done is "controlling and adjusting" national awareness in order to promote the benefits and suppress the negative impacts.

In addition, we should see that while national awareness is growing in modern China, it never interrupted the national integration process that went on throughout history. Ma Rong's research findings provide proof here. He argued that inter-ethnic marriages resulted from harmonious relations between nationalities. But at the same time, inter-ethnic marriages can promote interaction and friendship between nationalities through interactions between the two families, further promoting the harmonious national relations in the future. This is also why people view inter-ethnic marriage as an important metric in evaluating ethnic relations and the level of integration (Ma Rong, 2004a, p. 437). After studying China's inter-ethnic marriage data in the 1950s, 1990 and 2000 and comparing them to the same periods in the former Soviet Union and the U.S., Ma Rong clearly states that: in spite of limitations in usable data and the fact that they came from slightly different time periods and, therefore, may cause some errors in comparison, the overall level of inter-ethnic marriage in China has been higher than in the Soviet Union in the 1970s, as well as the U.S. This means that China's ethnic relations are much more harmonious than in the latter two" (Ma Rong, 2004a, p. 454). Increase in ethnic awareness thus does not always mean ethnic segregation. Ma Rong states,

> Following general logic, increase in ethnic awareness and clarification of ethnic boundaries are clearly not beneficial to inter-ethnic marriage and ethnic integration. But, this is only a hypothesis that we are unable as yet to validate and prove with relevant survey data (Ma Rong, 2004a, p. 445)

This is, clearly, a rigorous research attitude. It nevertheless runs against Ma Rong's own argument on the interruption of China's ethnic integration process.

6.2. Evaluating National Regional Autonomy

National regional autonomy has been repeatedly emphasized as a basic policy in Chinese politics, and the reasons and implications for it have been stated and reinstated by many people, but if even well-known scholars such as Ma Rong retain doubts about it, it indicates a lack of understanding of some of the basic issues involved.

The first question is whether or not the policy should have been established in the first place. It is well known that China's national regional autonomy policy was first developed before the 20th century, and widely implemented in the mid-20th century. The theoretical basis for carrying this out was the national equality principle of Marxism. The CPC first acknowledged Marxism in the 1920s, when the Soviet Union was in the process of establishing the first communist state under the leadership of Vladimir Ilyich Lenin. Tsarist Russia before the October Revolution was a feudal Imperialistic country, and most of its nationalities were independent groups that suffered suppression for hundreds of years. In order to overturn the old system, Vladimir Ilyich Lenin promoted the idea of "national self-determinism", calling on suppressed nationalities to rebel against the Tsar. After the success of the Revolution, Vladimir Ilyich Lenin kept promoting "national self-determinism" and installed a federal system, creating the first socialist nation state in the world. The CPC elaborated on issues of national structure and nationalities for the first time at the 2nd National People's Congress, within which there were threads of national self-determination and a federal system: the autonomy of Inner Mongolia, Tibet and Southern Xinjiang was promoted, pushing these three areas to become "democratic self-governments",[4] which together with China proper would compose a "Federal Republic of China" (Central United Front Working Department, 1991a, p. 18). To the CPC, realizing national equality and acknowledging the self-determinism of various nationalities were two inseparable ideas. Therefore, in party-related documents of this period and even beyond to the 1930s and 1940s, we can see its support for national determinism of colonized and semi-colonized areas as well as the slogan of "recognizing the self-determinism of national minorities within China, as well as the rights of various disadvantaged nationalities to secede from China and become independent nations" (Central United Front Working Department, 1991b, p. 166). Later, national self-determinism and federal system implying independence were no longer emphasized; the former was replaced by "national regional autonomy". Given changing trends and in-depth understanding of the national circumstances, this was the correct theoretical and policy choice for the CPC on national issues. It is important to point out that it was the strategy or formal expression that was changed, not the stance and principle of giving each nationality equal rights.

In reality, giving national minority groups special political status enabling "rule according to customs" was a tradition followed over two millennia years of Chinese history. From the "subordinate nations" in the Qin dynasty, "subordinate lands" in the Han period, the "separated ruling of Hu and Han" in Wei and Jin, to the "Ji Mi Districts" of the Tang dynasty, and the "tribal chief" system in the Yuan, Ming and Qing dynasties, all were early forms of "autonomous rule" in different dynasties and eras. Apart from these official systems, many national minorities had their own political systems, such as the alliance, lineage, chief, village head, burke and *qianhu* systems, to name a few. These historical factors and national factors are historical legacies that the CPC can borrow from, as well as a historical grounds for national autonomy: if it was good enough for feudal state to respect unique cases and honor national minorities' right to self-govern, on what grounds would the CPC, for whom equality is the core of its national policy, ignore them?

In addition, "self-determinism" stemming from national awareness has been a common request from national minorities in recent times. After the 1911 Revolution, with a trend of "independence" from the Qing Imperial Court growing among the 17 provinces in the "main part" of China, political

---

[4] "Self-government" here has a different meaning to the present one; here it is closer to "self-determination".

powers in Mongolia, Tibet and Xinjiang were going through a process of segmentation and combination over the ideas of independence and autonomy. Outer Mongolia was the first to take steps towards independence, warlordism emerged in Xinjiang, and the "Tibet Issues" that have troubled China to this day also started to germinate. After this, and up to 1949, Outer Mongolia completed its independence process; Xinjiang witnessed the establishment of two separatist regimes related to the East Turkistan separatist movements[5]; and the "Tibet Issue" kept growing in complexity. The emergence of all these issues were related to the enforced intervention and penetration by external powers including Tsarist Russia (the Soviet Union), Japan, England and America, and were also supported by the emergence of national awareness influenced by nationalist theories at home and abroad. National awareness made autonomy an inevitable choice for eschewing separationist forces.

It was no coincidence that Inner Mongolia became the first autonomous province in China. Imperial aristocrats made proposals along these lines as early as Outer Mongolia's bid for independence. Under the instigation of the Japanese imperialism forces, Inner Mongolia started a string of "national independence" or "autonomy" movements, making various attempts to disintegrate the country. After the anti-Japanese war, these "independence" and "autonomy" movements reached a new high. Separationists were openly calling for an "Inner Mongolia Republic Interim Government", others calling for an "East Mongolia Autonomous Government", seeking integration of Eastern and Western Inner Mongolia first, to be followed by the integration of Inner and Outer Mongolia. In response, the Central Government pointed out that in Inner Mongolia, only "regional autonomy" was possible, "at most, Inner Mongolia can only request to become an independent province with a normal regional government: it cannot become a self-governed Republic in relation to China as a sovereign state" (Central United Front Working Department, 1991c, p. 1011). Instructed by the Central Government, communists such as Ulanhu took steps, staying close to the masses, and, using military power as a backup, brought all the previously mentioned autonomy movements together as the "Inner Mongolia Autonomy Federation" led by the CPC. They finally established the "Inner Mongolia Autonomous Government" on May 1st,

---

[5]Refers to the East Turkistan Islamic Republic that emerged in Kashgar in 1933 and the East Turkestan Republic that emerged in 1944 with the "Three District Revolution" in Xinjiang.

1947,[6] becoming a pilot for the CPC in promoting national regional autonomy to the entire nation.

From the establishment of the Inner Mongolia Autonomous Region, we can see that the CPC-led national regional autonomy movement was the sole rational choice in meeting the demands of self-aware nationalities. Such awareness can neither be curtailed nor given free rein: its growth can only be guided. Close examination of the CPC's documentation shows that the Party provided almost unqualified support for the "self-determination" of various nationalities, partly because it completely accepted Vladimir Ilyich Lenin's doctrine and the guidance of the Third International, and partly in order to integrate all forces to win the battle against the Northern warlord clique and Kuomintang rule. However, with the development of China's social conflicts and the deepening understanding of national issues, the CPC no longer associated "national self-determinism" with "independence", and the notion of "national autonomy" came into play. After 1949, "national self-determinism" and the related federal system were abandoned completely, and national regional autonomy became the fundamental national policy. This was in keeping with such a fundamental historical turning point. Practice shows that national regional autonomy is the result of the CPC's efforts to follow the development and changes in society and history, and prudently making choices in the practice of resolving national issues.

Secondly, there is the question of how to understand the nature of national regional autonomy. Does it lean more towards "separation" or "integration"? On this, Ma Rong expressed concerns that "ethnic regional autonomy officially linked each ethnic minority to a certain geographic area, provide these groups with a political status, administrative power in their 'autonomous territory'", therefore inevitably "politicizing" national issues, and to a certain extent promoting the growth of national awareness within some nationalities, as well as providing a more solid foundation for "national separationist movements" (Ma Rong, 2004b). The facts show, however, that China's national regional autonomy policy was not a "separationist" policy, but on the contrary, an "integrative" policy designed to prevent separation, protect integrity and promote inter-nationality cohesion and mutual prosperity.

---

[6]In March 1950, the Central People's Government officially gave the name "Inner Mongolia Autonomous Region" to the government of this region.

China's national regional autonomy gave national minorities ample room for self-governance. According to the different characteristics of congregation, one ethnic group can have its own autonomous territories in several different regions, another nationality can establish its own autonomous region or jointly establish an autonomous region with other nationalities, populous ethnic groups can establish autonomous regions, states or counties, while less populous nationalities can establish autonomous villages. "Not only closely congregated nationalities can enjoy the benefits of autonomy, those that coexist with other groups van also enjoy those benefits. From populous to less populous nationalities, from densely congregated to scattered nationalities, they are all viewed as equal autonomous units and can enjoy the same benefits of national autonomy. This policy is an innovation in history" (Zhou Enlai, 1994).

What we cannot forget is that China's national regional autonomy is not simply a "national autonomy" policy, but a form of "regional autonomy" in areas occupied by national minorities that integrates factors of economy, politics, nationality and regions. As early as December 1951, Li Weihan stated:

> The regional autonomy of nationalities is a regional autonomy policy on the basis of national minority settlement areas (this should not be established on the basis of the ratio of national minority populations within a region, which is an erroneous methods that is against the common programme) established within the territory of the People's Republic of China, under the leadership of the Central Government, and following the common programme of the Chinese People's Political Consultative Conference. This is a pillar principle and pre-requisite, and cannot be violated in any way (Li Weihan, 1981).

Here, "national regional autonomy" is emphasized, and the principle of "not depending on the ratio of national minority populations within a region" crushed the expectations of attempting to establish an autonomous system based on individual nationality, and also distinguished China's model with the Soviet Union's single-nationality autonomy model. This was adhered to in the establishment and implementation of China's various national policies and laws in the following years. Therefore, China's national regional autonomy is fundamentally an "integrative" policy that is aimed at protecting the integrity of the nation and the cohesion between nationalities.

In order to embody this "integrative" idea, for the establishment of the Tibet autonomous region, the Central Government did not take the suggestion to integrate all Tibetan regions of congregation into a single autonomous unit, but rather established autonomous counties in Qinghai, Gansu, Yunnan and Sichuan apart from the autonomous region in Tibet, as these regions have closer economic ties with the province they are a part of, and this arrangement would benefit collaboration. Similarly, during the establishment of the Guangxi Zhuang autonomous region, the Central Government did not take the suggestion to establish the autonomous region in Guixi, where the Zhuang nationality is more densely congregated, and keep the Guangxi province intact, as by doing this, the Zhuang autonomous region would stand alone, which would not be beneficial to its economic development. If the railroads need to be separated from the Han region in Guangxi and the manufacturing and mining industries need to be separated between the east side and west side, it would be destructive to mutual development compared to if the two regions were integrated. Therefore, the Guangxi Zhuang autonomous region is also a cooperative autonomous region (Ma Rong, 2004b, p. 173).

Also, in order to showcase this "integrative" policy, "during the establishment of the Xinjiang Uygur Autonomous Region, we did not approve of naming it Uighuristan. Xinjiang not only has the Uygur nationality, but there are also a dozen other nationalities, and we cannot establish 13 different autonomous regions for these different groups. The Central Government and Party finally decided on establishing the Xinjiang Uygur Autonomous Region, with the consent of Xinjiang residents. By naming it the Xinjiang Uygur Autonomous Region, the region wears the "hat" of the Uygur nationality, as it is the biggest nationality in Xinjiang, taking up over 70% of the population, the other nationalities will also wear this hat ... Xinjiang and Inner Mongolia in the title have two layers of meanings, one refers to the region, and the other refers to the nationality. On the surface, the naming of regions seems less important, but it is of the utmost importance when it comes to the issue of national regional autonomy in China, where these is an implied sense of inter-national cooperation" (Ma Rong, 2004b, p. 175).

Students of China's national policies will all be familiar with Zhou Enlai's speech in 1957 at the Qingdao National Practice Seminar, from which the above quotes are drawn. Zhou, of all the Party's founders, gave the most complete and focused account of national regional autonomy, and the notion he stated repeatedly and maintained throughout was the spirit of "national cooperation". He said the following on this topic:

> Within China's big family of nationalities, the reason why we are adopting the national regional autonomy policy is to achieve mutual development and prosperity through inter-national cooperation and mutual support. China's nationalities are better integrated than separated. We should stress national cooperation and mutual assistance, and oppose national separationist and independence. The national regional autonomy policy adopted by our big family of nationalities is beneficial to the prevalent implementation of national autonomy, as well as conducive to the promotion of inter-national cooperation and mutual support. We do not want national separation, nor do we want national independence. The only way to establish a truly equal and friendly family of nationalities according to the requirements of the constitution is on the basis of mutual development and prosperity (Zhon Enlai, 1994, p. 177).

This thoughtful speech laid the truth about the national regional autonomy policy. According to this, our policy is different from the federal system which is based on the congregation of single nationality and where nationalities can easily separate from each other, and is also different from the "reserved region" policy which provide "protection" on the surface but in reality segregates national minorities to distant and under-developed regions away from modern civilization and development, but rather it builds a political foundation for all nationalities to come together and strive for mutual prosperity. This policy is beneficial to "integration" as opposed to "separation".

In reality, both federalism and national regional autonomy register the existence of nationalities and national awareness, and both arise from efforts to resolve national issues according to different national circumstances and guiding principles. The policies adopted have no causal relation to the latter, nor to the existence of separationist forces. "East Turkistan" and "Tibet Independence", the national separationist forces that pose the greatest threat to China, both were formed long before 1949, and their rise and fall were connected to the great background of world history. The rise of national separationist forces influenced by global nationalist trends, and international anti-China forces' exploitation of national/religious issues to penetrate and put pressure on China, are unrelated to national regional autonomy policies, successful or otherwise. If there is any linkage between these, it would not be that China's national regional autonomy provided the geographic foundation for their "national independence": to the contrary, it would be that multiple "integrative" factors of the national regional autonomy policy denied the separationist forces any success. This is why hostile forces both home and abroad, as well as separationists, put so much effort into attacking this policy. The current request from "Tibet Independence" advocates to "integrate all Tibetan regions and obtain complete self-governance powers" provides ample evidence that our current autonomy policy does not meet their separationist needs.

When the limitations of the theory of national self-determinism and the related danger of disintegration of multi-national states have been acknowledged by all nation states in the world, the option of resolving national issues through "autonomy" will receive more and more attention from other nations and become the first option for more and more underprivileged or minority groups in order to obtain their rights. Apart from the well-known examples of autonomy in Spain and Italy, there have been many "national autonomy" movements by national minority groups in countries ranging from Greenland and the Aland Islands in Europe, to Nigeria and Ethiopia in Africa, to Indonesia and Bangladesh in Asia, and to Taiwan in China. The trend even reached India, which Ma Rong promoted as a success case of the "enculturation" of ethnic policies and "nation-building".[7] Of course, for any state, dealing with issues of national autonomy will always be tough, and practice shows that "acknowledging the autonomous rights of national minority groups is conducive rather than detrimental to political stability". "Governments denying or even revoking existing national autonomous rights, will lead to political instability, not acknowledging them" (Will Kymlicka, 2005, p. 26). The choice to carry out national regional autonomy was a wise one: not only did it achieve the intended political effect, it protected the integrity of the nation and promoted the cooperation, development and mutual prosperity of all nationalities.

Thirdly, there is the question of whether national regional auton-omy can be revoked at this stage. According to Ma Rong's theory of

---

[7]During early colonial times, the British Indian government established ruling systems in India's tribal regions that are different from other regions. After the end of the colony, the Indian government inherited these systems and gave these regions certain autonomous powers. However, these powers were not executed. Ever since the 20th century, increasingly marginalized tribal regions started to fight for their own rights, and the battle to "fight for autonomy" was initiated, exemplified by the Jharkhand region in mainland India and tribes in North Eastern India (see Xaxa Virginius, 2001).

"culturizing", national regional autonomy was a mistake in the first place; now that it has already been established, we should in due course end it. Ma wrote an article about this, arguing that we should learn from the example of Joseph Stalin missing the opportunity to unify the federal system into a single nation during the late 1940s, which lay the foundation for the disintegration of the Soviet Union (Ma Rong, 2007d).

Vladimir Ilyich Lenin viewed the federal systems as a transitional stage towards an integrated nation, and ethnic regional autonomy too was a form of "transition", as it only applied to certain national statuses. As for whether the former Soviet Union missed its opportunity to end the federal system, we can delve deeper into that topic. But arguing from this that China's national regional autonomy should end too is premature. There are three prerequisites for national regional autonomy: first, a certain level of congregation of national minority groups; second, the unique traits that accompany this congregation; and third, the need for self-management based on those unique traits. Given these, we can see that the ethnic regional autonomy policy needs to be continued in the long run.

We can't deny that the establishment of China's socialist economic system made national distribution characteristics more prominent than the mixed distribution from before, especially with the rapid modernization following the reforms. Many minority populations left their regions and came to Eastern China from the west, and from rural to urban areas. At the same time, large numbers of Han migrated to regions previously dominated by minorities. The national minority population in western China dropped from 77.64% of the total Chinese population in 1982 to 71.27% in 2000, and within that same period the percentage of national minority people living in the 8 settlement provinces dropped from 69.59% of the total Chinese population to 63.16%. Furthermore, the percentage of national minorities in western China among the local population increased from 17.93% in 1982 to 21.31% in 2000, and within that same period the percentage of national minorities living in the 8 settlement provinces increased from 33.13% of the local population to 37.46% in 2000 (Hao Shiyuan and Wu Xingwang, 2006, p. 225). These contradictory sets of numbers do not present a paradox, as the first set reflects the increasing trend of national co-existence, while the second reflects the fact that ethnic settlements still exist.[8]

---

[8]Between 1982 and 2000, the increase in the ration of national minorities in western China and the eight national minority settlement provinces was due to the fact that there were less national minorities migrating to central and eastern China in proportion

The existence of national settlements determines the uniqueness of national regions. This includes cultural uniqueness. National minority cultures are important components of the Chinese national culture. In the present world, focus on the protection of cultural diversity has stepped up, and nationalities have become increasingly protective of their historical and cultural heritage. Therefore, maintaining and promoting these different cultures through national regional autonomy is not only crucial to the existence and dignity of nationalities — it is key to the overall prosperity of China's national culture. There are also economic aspects to this uniqueness. The breathtaking natural beauty of national settlement regions is at one with their underdevelopment and poverty. Over half a century was spent trying to change our underdeveloped status, and while the results we achieved cannot be overlooked, it is difficult to close the huge gap in such a short span of time. It is beneficial to utilize the policy advantages and cooperative advantages of national regional autonomy to promote the enthusiasm of nationalities, in order to speed up development, close in on the economic gap and realize mutual prosperity.

Self-governance is an extension of the theory of self-determination; its practical foundation is national awareness. In various countries in the world, including China, national awareness has been steadily growing instead of decreasing. The growth in the demand and protection of national rights is a manifestation of this, which will be a long-term presence. Therefore, national regional autonomy is still a basic and unalienable prerequisite for meeting national minority groups' request to realize their rights.

No matter how this is approached, national regional autonomy is both feasible to set up and necessary to continue. Given this, the point is not about keeping or discarding it, but rather how to persevere in and develop it. At the end of the day, this policy is far from perfect, and we still have a long way to go to improve it and discover its full potential.

6.3. On National Preferential Policy

Ma Rong does not agree with the principle of the national preferential policy, as this is a "politicization" of national policies. He argues as well

---

to Han people, as well as the higher increase in national minority population due to family planning policies. This showed the existence of the congregation of national minorities, but cannot be viewed as the intensification of this congregation. This is because as national minorities are migrating to predominantly Han areas, between 1982 and 2000, national minority populations in central and eastern China increased from 2.07% to 3.36% (see Hao Shiyuan and Wu Xingwang, 2006).

that during a certain period in history and under certain circumstances, preferential policies may help ameliorate national barriers and conflicts, but they will not decrease national awareness, nor prevent increased national awareness as a result of institutionalization in a fundamental way. Hence, preferential policies can only contribute to increasing international cooperation and ameliorating conflict, but cannot truly promote inter-national harmony (Ma Rong, 2004b).

Here, we should first lay out one point of disagreement with Ma Rong: we believe that the goal for national policy in present China should be the equality, cohesion and mutual prosperity of all nationalities, instead of "national integration". This is in line with the CPC's description of national policies and the understanding among mainstream academia in the field of national theory. If ethnic integration is not our policy goal, then we should not maintain the related expectations and requirements.

Secondly, even if we make ethnic integration as our goal or starting point, preferential policies are not in opposition of this goal, as the inequality or discrepancy between ethnic groups is the fundamental barrier for national integration. When the inequality or gap is great, the dominant or more advanced nationality will not discard its own culture in order to acknowledge disadvantaged or underdeveloped nationalities, while disadvantaged or underdeveloped nationalities may give up their own culture and national identity. However, this is assimilation and not integration. Assimilation can be a form of progression under many circumstances, but it still differs drastically from natural integration on the basis of equality. The fundamental step to achieve national integration, then, is to eliminate national inequality or discrepancy. From this perspective, carrying out preferential policies in order to promote the development of disadvantaged or underdeveloped nationalities cannot be viewed as only an effort to "increase inter-national cooperation and ameliorate inter-national conflict"; national integration is also naturally included.

Ma Rong does not completely negate national preferential policies, but only disagrees with "overall preferential policies directed at national minorities", calling for an "individual supportive policy" that is based on the principle of citizenship rights. Using the U.S. as an example, in daily life or social events, members of minority groups are officially treated as individual cases rather than collectives of an independent political group. Problems (such as inadequacy of the English language or lower levels of education) faced by disadvantaged groups are not perceived as "political interests" and regulated through government policies. Rather, these problems are resolved through assistance from public or semi-public social welfare programs (Ma Rong, 2004b). Whether this is social or government behavior, and whether it is a general welfare policy or an ethnic policy are still questions awaiting answers. Even if we view it as an "national (or group) preferential policy", it is not the only national preferential policy in the U.S., the biggest of which is the controversial "Affirmative Action".

"Affirmative Action", sometimes translated as "sponsored action", "equal rights measure" or "preferential policy", is a compensatory social policy implemented since the 1960s by the U.S. government. It aims at improving the disadvantaged situation of domestic national minorities and women and strives to give effect to laws that eliminate racial and gender discrimination in employment and education (Zhang Aiming, 2000). Carrying this out is clearly a form of government action, as it is legally backed by the 1964 Civil Rights Law. The landmark document of the issuance of this policy was the 11246 Administrative Order signed by President Johnson on September 24th, 1965, and the implementation of the policy was made possible by the orders of the U.S. Department of Labor and other agencies. The target audience of this policy was clearly focused on a few groups: national minority groups and women. For the former, the Presidential orders issued in 1965 clearly mandated that quota restrictions would be implemented for employment based on race, ensuring that black people would enjoy employment opportunities. Later, the Federal Office of Contract Management at the U.S. Department of Labor further clarified the target of the policy in 1970 and 1971 through administrative orders as "blacks", "Asians", "American-Indians" and "Latin Americans" (Zhang Aiming, 2000).

Therefore, the national preferential policy of the U.S. that is mainly composed of the "Affirmative Action" is neither a "cultural" civil action nor an "individual supportive policy" unrelated to national minority groups. Preferential treatment through individual support is not what the U.S. practices. This, however, is not to deny the existence of such policy measures, only that if these policies are not targeted at minority groups or ethnic groups, then it cannot be viewed as a "national preferential policy". Ma Rong proposed that "with the development of the society and the historical progress of ethnic integration, developmental discrepancies between ethnic groups caused by historical issues will gradually decrease; hence, we need to consider how to move from striving for "equal distribution of interests between ethnic groups" to "equal competitive opportunities between individuals", "gradual transition from supporting disadvantaged groups through group-wide policies to supporting needy individuals through social support" (Ma Rong, 2007a). However, national preferential policy without targeted groups simply does not exist. Therefore, the shift from "group-wide supportive policy" to "individual supportive policy" is not a "transition" of national preferential policy, but the elimination of such policies.

The necessity of group-wide preferential policies comes from the existence of inequality or discrepancies between groups, or "ethnic stratification" in the words of Ma Rong. "Ethnic stratification refers to structural discrepancies between ethnic groups in their social stratification, relating to overall differences among different population groups in levels of education, industrial and occupational distribution, and income distribution" (Ma Rong, 2007a).

The development of national minorities in China is at the same pace as the nation-state and unprecedented progress has been made in both their political status and social economic standard. However, there are still considerable gaps when compared with the development of the Han nationality. Based on this reality, it was a correct choice for the CPC and the central government to take speeding up the development of nationalities and national settlements as the main goal for current and future national practices. Given that national minority groups are less developed overall compared with the Han nationality, and national minority groups are restricted in their education, employment and development due to their uniqueness in language and culture, preferential policies are still essential; the time is not right to discuss revoking this policy. However, we should also acknowledge that there are many differences between each nationality and national region, and it is necessary to make adjustments to the policy according to different circumstances. More specifically, for those nationalities that have little or no developmental gaps with the Han nationality, or for those who have surpassed the Han group, the preferential policies could be held back accordingly. For those underdeveloped regions where there are little differences among local nationalities in educational level and living standards, regional preferential policies could replace national preferential policies.[9] If we don't do that, then real inequality

---

[9]Here, we need to be clear on the differences between national "preferential policies" and "special policies", the former is a compensatory measure based on the inequality or unbalances development between nationalities, and the latter is a form of special treatment based on the respect for ethnic cultural differences. The former can be revoked after the elimination of inequality or unbalanced development, but the latter needs to be preserved for a long time due to cultural diversity.

will be created. Of course, these policy adjustments are of the utmost importance and, therefore, should be handled with extreme caution; we must firstly conduct thorough research and investigation, and secondly be prepared to explain our decisions and persuade people to buy in. In issues of national policies, any mishaps and hastiness will result in unsalvageable consequences.

In his promotion of preferential policies and critique of group preferential policies, Ma Rong actually built upon the controversy in the U.S. society on this issue. After the implementation of the Affirmative Action, discussion about this issue started to spread throughout various levels of the American society. Proponents of the action believe that the Affirmative Action is a continuation of the Civil Rights Movement in the national legislation; it is a form of compensation for the inequalities caused by the institutionalized racist policies of the past, and is a policy guarantee for the elimination of racism and the true realization of the fair and equal distribution of social resources. Opponents of the action argue that the Affirmative Action in reality will lead the movement to gain equal rights between nationalities onto a slippery path by going against the principle of "equal opportunities", which is unfair to the other groups not included in the action. The implementation of public policies according to racial and national identity distribution have deepened the barrier and opposition between racial and nationalities (Shi Yi, 2000, pp. 94–98).

These discussions relate to important theoretical issues including equal opportunity, equality of results and the means to realize citizen rights and, therefore, are very relevant to China's national theory and policy, and thus have gained the attention of Chinese scholars. However, when it comes to how to evaluate these discussions and the lessons China can learn from them, we not only need to look at theoretical descriptions of each viewpoint, but more importantly should look at the objective reality.

National minorities in the U.S., especially blacks, have gained considerable social status since the 1970s. In 1964, there were less than 100 black government officials. The number increased to 1469 in 1979, and to 5434 in 1980. In 1960, around 22,700 black students enrolled in undergraduate education, that number increased to 1,080,000 in 1981. In 1959, the average annual income of a black family was 3,079 dollars, that figure increased to 26,522 dollars in 1996 (Shi Yi, 2000, pp. 94–98). These progresses are all directly or indirectly related to the Affirmative Action implemented by the U.S. government. However, it is commonly accepted that there have been no fundamental changes in the disadvantaged status and discrimination of black people in the U.S. society. Opponents of Affirmative Action argue that it fostered the complacency of black people, which was determined by black culture and due to their own deep-rooted shortcomings. Whether black people's current status was caused by "negative roots" of their culture, or shortcomings of the policy still requires further research; Affirmative Action was carried out through waves of controversy, and the extensiveness and thoroughness of implementation should come under doubt. In reality, Affirmative Action started to wind down with the Reagan and Bush administrations of the 1980s. In 1994, a Republican-controlled Congress forced President Clinton to amend various equal rights measures. In 1996, the state of California passed the Civil Rights Motion, banning discrimination or preferential treatment for any individuals or groups based on racial or gender differences, thereby nullifying Affirmative Action. Two years later, another 13 states proposed similar motions (Shi Yi, 2000, p. 100). A major important policy should thus be evaluated both on its content and its implementation: we cannot mix implementation issues with policy issues.

Preferential treatment and assistance for national minorities have always been closely tied together with China's national policies, and their implementation started much earlier and had much wider coverage. National preferential policy was highly effective in helping national minority groups overturn the status quo of underdevelopment and close the gap with Han social development. It was celebrated by national minorities as well as supported by Han populations. Of course, we cannot deny that there are some issues to these policies, such as the "one-size-fit-all" approach and some unfairness. It has caused some discussions and dissatisfaction, but China has never wavered on its choice to establish and implement preferential policies. This difference between China and the U.S. is based not only on different national circumstances, but more importantly on our determination to eliminate national inequality and developmental gaps completely. In "rethinking" them, being different from others should not lead to them being seen as wrong.

6.4. On the "Soviet Model" of China's National Theory and Policy

Ma Rong may have been implicit and polite in his criticism of the national regional autonomy policy and national preferential policy. His critique of

China's national theory and policy in that they follow the "Soviet model" was on the other hand quite blunt. He stated:

> In the 1950s, China almost completely accepted Joseph Stalin's national theory and related basic concepts of the Soviet Union, carrying out a series of systems and policies related to ethnic issues modelled after the Soviet Union. China's national theory and research on national issues still largely follow Soviet traditions to this very day, and carried forward the Soviet Union's national theory and policies of Joseph Stalin's time in the basic principles, theoretical framework, analysis model and terminology. If we ask ourselves honestly, compared with 50 years ago, can we find any new theoretical conclusions and systematic analysis on the new developments in global trends and national issues in this past half century in current text books on national theories in our universities or related government documents? Have we proposed any truly creative ideas in the basic concepts, theoretical frameworks and analysis models for national issues? The policies and systems borrowed from the Soviet Union in the 1950s have been practiced in China for over half a century, and fortunately there have not been any huge issues. But we must see that the basic ideologies, political systems, economic systems, social structures and national relations formed in Joseph Stalin's Soviet Union have undergone huge changes in present Russia. Joseph Stalin's theories (including his national theories) and the various practices led by him and the Soviet leadership after him are in need of re-evaluation and re-thinking. His halo as great proletarian revolutionary political leader and author of Marxist classics has faded, and his historical contribution is up for scrutiny. An issue we are considering today is the need to change our mindset of holding Joseph Stalin's national theories as unshakable over the last few decades, and in order to do that we must liberate our thoughts and be very practical; we need to re-analyze and rethink both Joseph Stalin's national theories and policies according to the Soviet Union's 70 years of practice in national issues, and also the CPC's national theories and policies modeled after Joseph Stalin's national theory according to over half a century's practice since the establishment of the New China (Ma Rong, 2008).

Ma Rong makes many points in the above paragraph, from the theoretical model guiding national practice, practical measures taken to resolve national issues under its guidance, to national research, all the while connecting everything back to the "Soviet model" or "Joseph Stalin's theory". However, after close examination, these critiques are mostly made on their face value instead of following the principle of "being practical".

First of all, Soviet traces are to be found in China's national theories, this is the indubitable fact. This was due to the fact that when Marxism was taken as a guiding principle for the CPC, it was at the outset transmitted to China from the Soviet Union; at that time, only the latter could tailor socialist theories and practical models for national issues, and it was inevitable for the CPC to be influenced. But one thing that we need to be clear on is that the basis of China's national theory belongs with Marxism and not "Joseph Stalin's theory".

Here, it is necessary for us to trace the source of a few basic arguments established as the principles for China's national theory ever since the 1950s.

Let's first look at the argument that "nation" is a historical concept. The historical materialism argument that the nature of the human society is a "natural historical process" that guides its development patterns have been consistent throughout the observations and descriptions of classic Marxist authors on ethnic phenomena. Karl Marx and Friedrich Engels repeatedly touch on this in *The German Ideology* and *The Communist Manifesto*, and Vladimir Ilyich Lenin further pointed out that "homeland and nationalities — these are both historical concepts" (Vladimir Ilyich Lenin, 1987a).

We now turn to the argument that national issues are social in nature. While Karl Marx and Friedrich Engels did not explicitly state this in their works, it was obvious that they embraced the thought (Vladimir Ilyich Lenin, 1958a). As Vladimir Ilyich Lenin said, "individual requests of the democratic movement, including ethnic self-determinism, are not absolute, but are a small part of the democratic movement of the entire world (or the entire socialist movement)" (Vladimir Ilyich Lenin, 1958b).

As to the principle of national equality, classic Marxist authors respected the independence and uniqueness of nationalities, and consistently emphasized national equality. Karl Marx and Friedrich Engels said, "in all of history, each nationality has had some superior characteristics over others" (Karl Marx and Friedrich Engels, 1987). Vladimir Ilyich Lenin said that "those who do not recognize and persevere in national equality and language equality, and those who do not fight against national suppression or inequality, are not followers of Marxism, or even democracy" (Vladimir Ilyich Lenin, 1987b, p. 230). "We demand the absolute equality of all nationalities in the country, and the unconditional protection of national minority rights" (Vladimir Ilyich Lenin, 1958c).

Moving on to the opposition to nationalism, Karl Marx and Friedrich Engels made little direct comment on it, but provided a great deal of indirect discussion. In contrast, Vladimir Ilyich Lenin directly criticized a variety of nationalism theories (including "Big Russia nationalism" and "local nationalism"). It can be said that Vladimir Ilyich Lenin's nationalism was created on the basis of debating and critiquing nationalism, as well as the basic arguments on nationalism by the classic authors of Marxism.

Next, let's talk about the relationship between national issues and class issues. In the Marxist theoretical framework, nationality and class are important concepts. Vladimir Ilyich Lenin said that "we should say to socialists in all nationalities: within every modern nationality, there are two nationalities" (Ma Rong, 2007b, p. 235). Here, the "two nationalities" within one is an emphasis on the internal class factors in nationalities. This is because all classic Marxist authors argued that in a class society, the interest of class is higher than that of nationalities, and the lines between classes are more prominent and more important than those between nationalities. "Whenever any serious and important political issues occur, cliques form based on class instead of nationality" (Ma Rong, 2007b, p. 238).

We shall now talk about the issue of the socialist era as a time of mutual prosperity for all nationalities. In general, classic authors of Marxism view the demise of nationalities as something of the communist era, but as for how nationalities fit into the socialist era, there was no socialist practice on the part of Karl Marx and Friedrich Engels, nor were there any detailed predictions of the status of ethnicity. Vladimir Ilyich Lenin and Joseph Stalin made comments regarding this, and their basic idea for the development of national issues in a socialist society was as follows: socialism can be divided into the two stages of "victory in one country" and "victory in the whole world". The ultimate resolution of national issues in these two stages will be national integration.[10] In the first stage, however, that of "victory in one country" or "the period of proletariat

---

[10]Before the October Revolution, Vladimir Ilyich Lenin discussed the "integration" or "unification" of nationalities, such as talking about how the working class political party "not only needs to persevere in the fight against opposition forces and national capitalist nationalism forces in order to unify the working class of all nationalities, but also need to integrate them" (see Vladimir Ilyich Lenin, 1958d). However, here, the terms "integrate" or "unify" are different from the "integration" implying the demise of nationalities. Because, when criticizing the idea of "getting rid of nationalities", he clearly stated that "of course this is something great, and it will be accomplished, but only during another stage in the development of communism" (see Vladimir Ilyich Lenin, 1958e). He also said: "just as humans will only accomplish the elimination of class after the transition period of suppression by dictatorship, humans will only be able to achieve the integration of nationalities after experiencing the transition period of complete freedom and liberty to separation obtained by suppressed nationalities" (see Vladimir Ilyich Lenin, 1958f).

dictatorship and the construction of socialism", is also the stage of the "renaissance" and "prosperity" for various nationalities. During this stage, national issues mainly present themselves as the "real inequality" caused by the unequal development of various nationalities, as well as distrust between nationalities due to "the two nationalism". Therefore, the main task in resolving the issues of this stage is to strive to develop the economy of those national regions that are behind and promote national culture infused with socialism, in order to enable the nationalities of these regions to catch up with the other nationalities who are developing at a faster pace so as to realize the mutual prosperity of various nationalities (Vladimir Ilyich Lenin, 1987c; Joseph Stalin, 1990c).

Lastly, let's discuss the issue of national autonomy. Classical Marxist authors, especially Vladimir Ilyich Lenin, discussed federalism at length, as well as paying much attention to national autonomy. For example, Vladimir Ilyich Lenin said in 1913: "all countries that divide their regions according to the different living habits or national components of the inhabitants should allow them ample self-determination and autonomy" (Vladimir Ilyich Lenin, 1958g), and "it is apparent that if the autonomy of these regions with prominent economic or lifestyle characteristics and ethnic components cannot be guaranteed, then we cannot even begin to envision a democratic country in the true sense" (Vladimir Ilyich Lenin, 1987b, p. 248).

These positions were promoted in the CPC's documents and national research after 1949, and are still being stated today. A look through the expression of the basic arguments of national issues by party leaders and in government documents since the reforms clearly proves that. We have quoted the "earliest versions" of these arguments in order to show that the basic principles of the CPC on national theory all originated from classic Marxist authors.[11] Some elements from Joseph Stalin were included, but the core remains the reinstatement, emphasis and development of Marxist principles, and not "Joseph Stalin's theory".

Joseph Stalin should be given historical responsibility for the Soviet Union's national issues. They applied methods of class struggle to the resolution of national issues, enforced exile and repression on over 10 national minority groups, connived at a "Greater Russia", and made unrealistic assumptions on the resolution of national issues. These factors

---

[11]Due to Joseph Stalin's mistake, currently Joseph Stalin is not listed as an "author of classic Marxism", but due to his great contributions and influence on Marxism national theories, the academic field in national studies still view him as a "classic author".

all contributed to the intensification of national issues in the Soviet Union, resulting in its disintegration. All these originated, however, from discrepancies between theory and practice. Joseph Stalin's national theories, especially his accounts of national issues during and in few years after his early years, are all precious legacies of Marxist national theory. For example, *Marxism and the National Questions* is the landmark work of Joseph Stalin's national theory. This work was accomplished after Joseph Stalin accepted some of Vladimir Ilyich Lenin's suggestions following numerous discussions in 1912 on the national theories of the Russian Party. The paper systematically laid out Joseph Stalin's ideas on the concept of ethnicity and trends in the development of national movements; it criticized erroneous arguments that endangered the revolution including "national cultural autonomy", the "alliance model" and the "cancellation party". After its publication in 1913, Vladimir Ilyich Lenin praised it as one of the few Marxist articles of the time that embodied the national creed of the Russian Party. "Almost all of the content of the article except from the parts on the definition of nationalities had been repeatedly demonstrated by Vladimir Ilyich Lenin in his many articles, some of which were titled after Joseph Stalin's thoughts, including *Corrupting the Workers with Refined Nationalism* (May 1914)" (Hua Cunzhi and Chen Dongsi, 2002). Aside from this, other major works of Joseph Stalin on national issues include *The October Revolution and National Issues, Discussion on the Party's Current Tasks in National Issues, National Issues in the Construction of the Party and the Nation*, and *National Issues and Leninism*. These are all explanations and extensions of Vladimir Ilyich Lenin's national theories, and should be considered representative articles of the Marxist nationalism. Therefore, no matter if we are talking about China or foreign countries and no matter if we are looking at the times before or after Joseph Stalin, we cannot omit Joseph Stalin from the discussion of the Marxist nationalism.

Because of the great contributions Joseph Stalin made to the Marxist nationalism theories, as well as his prominent status in the entire international communist movement, the Chinese Communist Party referenced his articles and arguments in the description of its nationalism theories from its early establishment to the establishment of the New China. This is also the reason why China's theoretical framework exhibits traces of the Soviet Union or the "Joseph Stalin model". However, as the theoretical principles upheld by China were already established by Karl Marx, Friedrich Engels and Vladimir Ilyich Lenin long before Joseph Stalin, and also because most of Joseph Stalin's works, concepts and terminology we referred to originally were based on Marxism, therefore, it is incorrect to say that China "almost completely accepted the Soviet Union or Joseph Stalin's nationalism theories and basic concepts". The nationalism principles the CPC accepts and upholds belong to Marxism, not Joseph Stalin's theory. Calling these theories and principles wrong, is to point the finger at Marxism, not Joseph Stalin. On this, we should assume a fair stance.

Secondly, it is true that the CPC learned from the Soviet Union, and there are many similarities in China's national theories and policies with the Soviet. But we cannot say that China adopted a "Soviet model" completely. In reality, ever since the establishment of the New China, we have taken an approach to resolving national issues that exhibits Chinese characteristics.

China learned from the Soviet Union that the CPC chose to adopt the Soviet Union's "national self-determinism" and federal system as the theoretical framework and policy approach from its establishment until 1949, at which time this approach was abandoned. From that time China, like the Soviet Union, implemented various economic and cultural policies in order to assist the development of national minorities, focused on training and electing national minority officials, implemented the fight against the Big Nationalism (especially Han Chauvinism) and regional nationalism and provided special care and preferential treatment to national minorities. These similar policy guidelines formed through learning were based on certain similarities between the two countries in their national issues:

1. Both were guided by Marxism and Leninism, placing emphasis on respecting and protecting the equal rights of national minorities and maintaining national cohesion.
2. Both had a dominant nationality and many smaller nationalities in their national makeup. Nationality Russians made up 54% of the national population at the establishment of the Soviet Union[12]; Nationality Han made up 94% of the entire Chinese population at the time of the first national census in China, with the rest 6% being national minorities. These ratios largely confine ethnic relations in both countries to the dominant nationality's relations with the smaller ones.
3. Both had nationalities with similar discrepancies in developmental terms. National Russians were more "advanced" in their group's

---

[12]In 1921, the Soviet population was 140 million, of which non-Russian population was 65 million, taking up 46% of the entire population, and the Russian population was 75 million, taking up the other 54% (see Joseph Stalin, 1990a).

development compared with the underdeveloped national minorities congregated around the national border. The similarities between the 65 million non-nationality Russians at the time was, according to Joseph Stalin, that they were lagged behind the development of central Russia. The 25 million people of Turkic nationality "had not experienced capitalism"; the six million "nomads" clung to a "clan lifestyle" (Joseph Stalin, 1990b). China's national minorities were similarly generally less developed than the Han. Before the democratic reform, all nationalities were in a pre-capitalist stage of society, featuring feudal lords, slavery and the clan system.

Given these similarities, especially the common distribution of Marxism ideologies, China learned from the "advanced" form of Soviet national theories and policies. Inevitably therefore, there were many similarities and commonalities.

Learning from the Soviet Union was confined to a certain historical phase, however, and the "model" formed was somewhat superficial. According to basic Marxist principles, the fundamental solution to China's national theories and policy is to tailor them to Chinese characteristics. First and foremost, the setup of the national structure was a big differentiator between China and the Soviet Union. In the Soviet federal system, each Union Republic was a "self-determined" national unit, constitutionally sovereign countries with the right to secede. In China, national regional autonomy was implemented within a unitary national system, one in which national minority settlements were allowed regional autonomy under the unitary rule of the state. Each autonomous region was both an autonomous unit as well as an administrative region of the country. Nationalities in the Soviet Union were divided into different levels according to population, politics and historical or developmental status, enjoying different levels of political rights. In China, they were treated the same regardless of population and developmental status, and were given the same political rights. We are all familiar with these differences.

Also deserving attention is that while some policies seem to be similar with the Soviet Union's, they have mostly been adapted to suit Chinese characteristics. For example, the idea of "nationalization" has been consistent in China's national practices, and this idea originally came from Joseph Stalin. At the establishment of the Soviet Union, in order to expedite cultivating national minority officials and enable non-Russian national minority officials, Joseph Stalin called for "nationalizing government organ officials". However, when he extended this idea to the Party, government, industry, committee and cooperative levels, it brought about negative effects, stimulating regional nationalism. China also proposed "nationalizing autonomous organs" in the 1950s, but it was quite different from Joseph Stalin's.

First of all, the scope of nationalization was different. The Soviet Union included all organs within ethnic settlement regions, but China restricted the score to only include "self-governed nationalities", which only included government and NPC Committee organs and not the Party Committee and other non-government organs.

Secondly, the content of nationalization was different. The Soviet Union's nationalization pertained to economics, politics, culture and education, but China's nationalization included the following three aspects:

1. A certain ratio of officials of national origin needs to be maintained in self-governed organs, those officials need to hold actual power;
2. One or more commonly used languages used by local nationalities must be utilized;
3. National forms must be adopted.

Thirdly, when China proposed "nationalizing national autonomous organs", the notion of converting officials of national minority origin into Party members was proposed. The idea of cultivating officials of national minority origin who were also Party members was first invented by the CPC. It was thought that only by converting those officials into CPC members could the negative effects of "nationalizing organ officials" be counteracted. Only if communism were viewed as the highest value, could officials from all national origins come together and serve the entire nation with a unified goal or purpose.

Lastly, according to the population structure of national autonomous regions, the officials at self-governed organs was switched from predominantly of local national minority origin to the same proportion as the ratio of nationalities in the population, corrected the erroneous concept of "nationalization" as the local nationality "taking over" everything, and promoted mutual trust and cohesion between various nationalities. Currently, government documents as well as national legislation of China's Party and government make specific provisions on nationalization, without using the concept of "nationalization" (Guo Hongsheng, 1997). This is not a unique case.

In fact, China's national theories and policies are not only infused with Chinese characteristics, but stay abreast of social innovation and development. From the four descriptions of the basic concepts of China's national theories and policies by the central government after the reforms, we can see that the content has grown in its richness, comprehensiveness and practicality. As Jiang Zemin's explanation on "national issues" at the 1992 Central National Working Conference, which was reiterated recently in the "12 rules":

> National issues include those of national self-development, and also includes relations between nationalities, between nationalities and social classes, and between nationalities and states. Therefore, placing "national self-development" within the scope of "national issues" is not only in conformity with Marxist principles, but is also a theoretical innovation based on the reality of national issues in China and focusing on the resolution of existing issues.

The "12 rules" state that

> ...the socialist era is one of mutual prosperity of various nationalities, during which commonalities between nationalities are increasing; national characteristics, differences and disparities in economic and cultural development will nonetheless always exist.

This statement, underlining the principle that the socialist era is a time of national prosperity, also summarized the rule of the coexistence of commonalities and differences. In addition, the Central Government stipulated that the basic characteristics of national relations in China's socialist society are equality, cohesion, mutual help and harmony, which is related to the reality of the modernization of socialism with Chinese characteristics. These are all modern and innovative ideas in national relations theory. They depart from Soviet national theory in terms both of terminology and content, and it is unreasonable to say they still conform to the "Joseph Stalin model".

Facts show that China's national theory and current policies under its guidance do not follow this model, but one of continual localization of Marxism and blazing a trail of resolving national issues with Chinese characteristics.

The evaluation of the merits and downfalls of the methods to resolve national issues should include both "horizontal" and "vertical" comparison. Vertically, it is clear that national relations, the development of each nationalities' economy and culture as well as national cohesion is at the highest standard since 1949. Horizontally, the existence of national separationist forces creates some imperfection. We cannot view this as a "national issue", but others may not see things the same way, and the existence of separationist forces does in fact influence China's national relations and cohesion. However, using the existence of these forces as a measure of the quality of methods to resolve national issues may not be reasonable, depending on different national circumstances. Ma Rong often compares the U.S. with China, arguing that in the U.S., despite residual, historical racial discrimination and prejudice, and occasional racial and national conflicts, the integrity of the nation has not come under serious threat since the Civil War. ... we should acknowledge that the U.S. has achieved considerable success in mediating national relations since the "Civil Rights Movement" (Ma Rong, 2004b).

Why are there no separationist forces that threatened the integrity of the U.S.? The political reasons behind this cannot be ignored, but more importantly, the U.S. is an immigrant country with little over two centuries of history. After immigrants came to the U.S., ethnic groups or nations were rapidly disintegrated and swallowed by industrialization and urbanization. The biggest issue faced by immigrants in their new social environment was immersing themselves and be accepted in the local society as fast as possible; it was that they did not have the opportunity to create their own "nationality" and conspire to gain independence. In other words, the immigrant identities of the majority of ethnic groups and racial groups in the U.S. meant that there were no historical and regional bases for them to engage in national separationist activities. Without this identity, it cannot be guaranteed that there would not be separationist issues. In fact, some aboriginal Indians in the U.S. have long engaged in "separationist" activities, claiming to be the "first nation", and have been making continual efforts in "independence" and "nation-building", although the impact has been minimal.[13] Didn't Ma Rong state that

---

[13] A recent example of this: a self-entitled "Hawaii Kingdom Government" organization peacefully "occupied" the Iolani Palace of the former monarchs of the Hawaii Islands, declaring an interim government. A century ago, the monarchy of the Hawaiian Kingdom was overturned by the U.S. government, and the islands became the 50th state of the U.S. This was long ago, but the aboriginal residents of Hawaii have not given up the idea of gaining independence. They established various organizations and demanded ending "occupation" by the U.S. and gain independence. In addition, since 1974, the aboriginal Lakotas of western United States have also fought for their independence, and

"even in the U.S., with its developed economy and military might, there are still some ethnic minority groups (such as blacks and native Indians) and organizations given to engaging in "ethnic autonomy" and setting up independent nations" (Ma Rong, 2004a, p. 609)? Not to mention that apart from the issue of separation, neither the U.S. nor India can say that they have resolved all their national issues, as ethnic conflicts, caste oppositions and religious conflicts that are related to their national circumstances have been incessant. Comparing China with these two countries produces no convincing evidence of the failure of China's national policies.

In today's world, separationist trends and movements are explicitly or implicitly present. They are caused by national awareness induced by the theory of "one nation, one state", and the maximized utilization of this awareness by various social forces and interest parties. "In the past, the long-term stability of many multi-national nations in the West was taken for granted, but more instability seems to have crept in nowadays. ... Flemish, Scottish and Quebecois, despite living in prosperous and liberal nations where basic citizen rights and political rights are protected, have very prominent independence movements. This shows that the threat of national separationist forces are everywhere, whether the nation be capitalist or socialist, a democratic or military regime, rich or poor" (Will Kymlicka, 2005, p. 90).

Fairly speaking, from a worldwide perspective, the Tibet and Xinjiang issues in China are no more serious than similar issues in other nations. Then why do they receive so much attention? There is only one answer, and that is the long-term support, connivance and speculation by international opposition forces. Looking at the worldwide activities of "Tibet Independence" forces behind the "March 14th Lhasa Incidence" in 2008, as well as the congregation and inflammation of "East Turkistan" forces in European and American nations, these in both cases were supported

---

drafted their own Declaration of Independence based on the one drafted during America's independence from the British. On December 17th, 2007, the Lakota representative wrote to the U.S. Department of State and declared the unilateral withdrawal from all contracts with the U.S. government, some of which has over 150 years of history. Lakota leader Russell Means said on the press release in Washington D.C. on the 19th: "The people of Lakota are no longer American Citizens, and any individuals from our surrounding five states can join us". Representatives from the "Country of Lakota" visited consulates of Bolivia, Chile, Venezuela and South Africa to inform them of its independence. In the months that followed, they continued to conduct their own diplomatic affaires, establish diplomatic relations with some countries and establishing diplomatic offices (see The China Daily website).

by Western anti-China forces. Socialist China has always been a target for international opposing forces in their attempt to initiate disintegration and penetration, and China's gradual rise in status has made it a central focal point for the global society. Therefore, it is nothing strange that sensitive national issues are being exploited and amplified. The point is that we cannot ourselves be ignorant of these facts and stumble into confusion.

As a huge multi-national state, China has inherited from its history elements of cohesion and harmony, as well as disagreement and hatred. Since the establishment of the New China, we have made huge efforts to promote national equality, cohesion and prosperity, and we have all witnessed the achievements. It is unfair to negate them due to the existence of separationist forces nurtured and supported by international opposition forces. Many countries, including the U.S., provide fine examples of how to resolve national issues, and it is important to respect and learn from these examples, but we cannot engage in "copycat" actions that neglect our own characteristics. Practice has shown that although we are faced with many imperfections and complexities in our methods, the decision to adopt a method to resolve national issues infused with Chinese characteristics has been a successful one. To abandon the current theories and policies due to certain issues, and start over, is not a practical attitude, and the price that we have to pay in order to do this is one that we cannot afford.

Thirdly, there are faults and shortcomings to China's national theory research, but we have been making progress, and it is unreasonable to say that the discourse accumulated over decades all belong to the "Soviet model". We need to follow in our own steps in theoretical research and strive to enrich and improve our own discourse and theoretical system, which is our only option.

There are actually two layers of meaning for China's national theory: the first relates to Party and state guidelines on national issues which act as a guiding ideology, and the other layer relates to theoretical research on these issues. The interdependent relationship between the two means that the status of China's national theory research to a certain extent can be reflected in the development of the Party's national theory and its practice in resolving national issues. It was because of this that Ma Rong heavily criticized China's "national theory research" or "national issues research" as well as posing questions to the national theories and policies that acted as the guiding ideology. He argued that

China replicated the Soviet national theories and policies of Joseph Stalin's period in basic concepts, theoretical framework, analysis model and terminology. If we ask ourselves honestly, compared with 50 years ago, can we find any new theoretical conclusions and systematic analysis on the new developments in global trends and national issues in this past half century in current text books on national theories in our universities or related government documents? Have we proposed any truly creative ideas in the basic concepts, theoretical frameworks and analysis models for national issues?

These words are painful to hear. But of course, there are some merits to Ma Rong's arguments in that he posed a series research ideas and topics for how to innovate in our research of national issues (Ma Rong, 2007a).

We admire Ma Rong's courage, vision and methodology in his theoretical research, and we must acknowledge that there are many limitations and shortcomings in China's ethnic studies, especially relating to the discipline of national theory. As in our analysis of the Party's national theories and policies, however, we need to analyze in detail whether China's current national theory research still follows the "Soviet model" without "innovation".

From a disciplinary perspective, China's national theory research is different from other national research, as it is not born from the "national study" that came into China in the early 20th century, but originated from the Party's study of the "Hui" and Mongolian nationalities during the anti-Japanese war. The goal was to reveal the Japanese imperialist attempt to disintegrate China's national relations, and to promote cohesion among national minorities in order to fight against the Japanese. The theoretical foundation utilized was Marxist national theory. After the establishment of the People's Republic of China, research on domestic national issues and Marxist national theory intensified. Central and regional nationality institutions were established in the early 1950s, and one of the main academic courses was national theory and policy. Hence, the earliest batch of leaders in national practices received Marxist national education and policy training. After this, both Party and state placed heavy emphasis on national theory due to the explicit nature of Marxism and close ties with practical issues. It became one of the pillar disciplines in China's ethnic research.

It is apparent that from its birth to development, there have been inseparable relations between China's ethnic theory and Marxism. It was then unavoidably tainted with "Stalinist theory". But we should be aware that there are some merits to China's ethnic theory research, which has been progressing and developing.

The prime feature of Joseph Stalin's national theory is his definition of "nation". This definition has been queried by Chinese scholars ever since the 1950s, and discussion of it has never ceased. These were and could be no conclusions to these discussions, but the spirit of challenging Joseph Stalin's concept of "nation" and its theoretical framework has been consistent. Thinking about the flexible application of the definition of nation in China's national identification process as well as the practice of referring to all nationalities as such instead of following the "tribe" theory — don't these prove that China's national research has already surpassed the "Joseph Stalin model"?

In reality, after relation between China and the Soviet Union disintegrated in the 1960s, the two countries have diverged ideologically. China had identified its own approach in academia, including national theory. The lack of marked change was due to the negative influence of the "leftists". After the reforms, this situation improved drastically with the improvement of the overall academia environment. Let's look at a few examples of research on specific topics:

1. *National and class issues.* On July 15th, 1980, *People's Daily* published special commentator's paper titled *Discussion on the argument "national issues are fundamentally class issues"*. This paper and later related papers clarified the confusion created by the idea that "national issues are fundamentally class issues", therefore, exerted important effects on correcting national practices, as well as liberating national theories from ideological restraints.

2. *Differences and commonalities of nationalities, or the relationship between diversity and unity.* In the few years after the Third Plenary Session, the national theory academic field carefully summarized historical experiences and came to the shared realization that national characteristics or national differences have been present for a long time, their demise will come long after the entire world has turned to communism. The increase in national integration factors was a natural process in the development of nationalities instead of manufactured by human beings. Promoting "national integration" through administrative means will only result in the contrary. People also talked about how each nationality in China has its own characteristics as well as similarities with other nationalities. Those commonalities and common interests are inseparable with national characteristics and unique interests. In promoting common interests, we need to take into consideration the unique characteristics of nationalities, as only by protecting the unique interest of nationalities

can we better promote the common interest of all nationalities. In the construction of a socialist society, only by appropriately treating national characteristics and the relationship between commonalities can we promote the development of the construction of socialism and the prosperity of all nationalities, as well as improve the national relations in a socialist society (Sun Qin, 1984). From the late 1980s, with the promotion of the theory of diversity and unity by Fei Xiaotong and the introduction of multiple foreign multicultural theories, the discussion in academia on the uniqueness and commonalities in national issues have become integrated.

3. *National awareness and national identity.* National awareness was originally viewed as the "common psychological characteristics" as described by Joseph Stalin to a great extent, but at least since the late 1980s, the academic world in China's national studies placed much attention on "national awareness" as an independent but also important issue, which resulted in many research findings and formed a research focus point. These research efforts were a theoretical reflection of the increase in various nationalities' national awareness with the promotion of the modernization of socialism and the influence of the worldwide nationalism trend. The significance of this is to remind people to face the existence of this phenomenon, grasp the opportunity and make relevant efforts. Therefore, although the discussion this issue was the most active in the 1990s, but is did not cease after that period. The related issue of "identity" quickly became the focus point after the turn of the century, showing that China's academic field is connected with the global trend.

4. *National political theory.* National politics is an important aspect of national theory research, but before the reforms there were no substantial national political research in China. In 1993, China Social Sciences Press published Zhou Xing's book *National Politics*, which became a trailblazer in this area in China. In 1995, Beijing University Press published Ning Sao's book *Nation and the State — International Comparisons between National Relations and National Policies.* After this, in 2001, China Social Sciences Press published Zhou Ping's book *Introduction to National Politics.* In that year, Zhu Lun proposed the topic of "joint rule of nationalities" based on his observations of the inter-national politics in many modern multi-national states. In 2004, Social Sciences Academic Press published a collection by Wang Jiane and Chen Jianyue titled *Inter-national Politics and the Modern National State,* in 2007, Guan Kaize published his book *National Politics* (Central

Ethnicity University Press), in 2008, Gao Yongjiu published *Introduction to National Politics*. These works broke new grounds in China's national politics research from different angles and perspectives, becoming shining stars in national theory research.

5. *Debate on national issues.* "Ethnicity" was a concept introduced to China from the West. The mainland scholarly world started to use it during the 1980s and 1990s, but with no consensus on its meaning. Translation and comprehension of the term are crucial to how China's relevant research can adhere to international standards as well as to China's diplomatic affairs and the understanding and resolution of existing national issues, hence debate on the issue has continued ever since the 1990s. Ma Rong also took part in this discussion, arguing for his own influential viewpoint. In 2001 and 2002, Hao Shiyuan published a series of papers on ethnicity, not only expressing his ideas on the issue, but also on the relationship between foreign and existing Chinese scholarly terms (Hao Shiyuan, 2002a, 2002b, 2002c). This lent his work considerable influence. Currently, there remains much controversy on the meaning and utilization of this term, but it is important to promoting national theory research, and national, and even diplomatic work.

6. *Establishing a discipline.* One prominent feature of research in national theory in the 1980s was the focus on setting up a discipline. There was great deal of discussion of its status, nature and scope. Even naming the discipline was debated, with supporters of "national theory", "theoretic nationalism", "political national studies", "national issues studies" and "national issues theory". In 1994, Jin Binggao published a *General Treatise on National Theory*, which was amended in 2007. Focused on delineating national theory as a discipline, the book became very influential as a landmark work in the pedagogy of national theory.

In addition, research on classic Marxist national theory, the Party's national theory, nationalism theory and ideology, national processes, spirit and cohesion, the relationship between globalization and nationality, basic status and patterns in current national issues all underwent new development or gained new perspectives after the reforms. The achievements should not be dismissed or slighted.

As in any other field, scholarship on national theory in China has formed a discourse of its own. Including some components originally introduced from the Soviet Union, traditions from China's history, as well as western factors, this endeavor adheres to Marxist concepts of nation and the definition of "nation" influenced by Joseph Stalin. Now, however, it leans towards diversification, but is widely recognized for its objectivity, tradition and history. "National equality", "national cohesion", "national issues", "national development", "national patterns" and "mutual prosperity of all nationalities" are still commonly used key terms, with the more recent additions of "nation-state", "nation-building", "diversity and unity" and "diversity". Hence, despite some lingering Soviet influence, a discourse system has grown up as scholars reflect Chinese characteristics, that has left the "Soviet model" far behind.

We cannot cut ourselves off from history; it is difficult to change historically formed discursive habits. For example, the concept of "ethnic" might be distinguished from "nation", but to apply this change to China would be difficult and awkward, such as trying to replace "national minorities" with "ethnic minority", "national policies" with "ethnic policies", or "national theories" with "ethnic theories". The difficulty is that in China, terms such as "national minority", "national policies" and "national theories" are so ingrained in people's minds that they are not just widely used as policy terms and social language, but have also been accepted among scholars. Given that the objects described can be expressed clearly, they do not need to be replaced.

What are the criteria for evaluating a theoretical system? The first criterion should be practice, not whether it conforms to a "norm" of some kind. It is fine to learn from others' strong points, but we cannot demean ourselves and throw away things that have been proven through practice to be effective. There are currently many shortcomings in China's national theory research, including its lack of openness, concentration and a set of widely accepted ideas of theoretical scope, research methods and discipline. These, however, are signs of the immaturity of the discipline, issues in the "developing" stage, not issues rooted in Joseph Stalin's theory. Therefore, in national theory research we need to focus on our own approach, strive to enrich and improve our own discursive and theoretical systems. Attempting to start over and depart from the national circumstances will surely result in failure.

References

Chen, Jianyue (2005). Establishing a multi-national harmonious society and resolving national issues — "Depoliticizing" and "culturizing" national issues. *World Ethno-National* Studies, Issue 5.

Chen, Yuping (2008). My views on "depoliticizing" national issues, *Journal of Southwest University for Nationalities*, Issue 7.

Connor, Walker (1973). The politics of ethnonationalism. *Journal of International Affairs*, 27.

Fei, Xiaotong (1980). Issue in China's national identification. *China Social Science*, Issue 1.

Guo, Hongsheng (ed.), (1997). *Comparing National Issues in China and the Former Soviet Union*, p. 156–157. Beijing: China Minzu University Press.

Huang, Guangxue and Shi Lianzhu (ed.), (2005). *China's National Identification — Origins of the 56 Nationalities*, Beijing: Minzu Publications.

Hao, Shiyuan and Wu Xingwang (2006). The development and review of China's national minority populations. In *China National Development Report* (2001–2006), Hao Shiyuan and Wu Xingwang, (eds.). Beijing: Social Sciences Academic Press.

Hao, Shiyuan (2002a). Early meanings and application of the terms "Ethnos" and "Ethnic Group", *Ethno-National Studies*, Issue 4.

Hao, Shiyuan (2002b). Identity group and ethnic group in the social fission of western nations including the U.S. *World Ethno-National Studies*, Issue 4.

Hao, Shiyuan (2002c). Discussion about the definition of ethnic group in the Western Academic Field. *Journal of Guanxi University for Nationalities*, Issue 4.

Hao, Shiyuan (2005). Establishing a socialist harmonious society and national relations. *Ethno-National Studies*, Issue 3.

Hua, Cunzhi and Chen, Dongsi (2002). *Stalin on National Issues*, p. 6. Beijing: China Minzu University Press.

Kymlicka, Will (2005). (Canada), *Minority Rights: Nationalism, multiculturalism and citizenship*, translated by Deng Hongfeng. Shanghai: Shanghai Century Press.

Lenin, Vladimir Ilyich (1987a). An open letter to Boris Souvarine. In *Lenin on National Issues (Part II)*, The Institute of Ethnology and Anthropology, Chinese Academy of Social Sciences (ed.), Beijing: Minzu Press.

Lenin, Vladimir Ilyich (1987b). On the critique of national issues. In *Lenin on National Issues*, Vol. 1, The Institute of Ethnology and Anthropology, Chinese Academy of Social Sciences (ed.).

Lenin, Vladimir Ilyich (1987c). Socialist revolution and national self-determination. In *Lenin on National Issues*, Vol. 2, The Institute of Ethnology and Anthropology, Chinese Academy of Social Sciences (ed.), p. 503.

Lenin, Vladimir Ilyich (1958a). On national self-determinism. In *Collected Works of Lenin*, Vol. 20, p. 437. Beijing: People's Publishing House.

Lenin, Vladimir Ilyich (1958b). On the debate and summary of the self-determination issue. In *Collected Works of Lenin*, Vol. 22, p. 335. Beijing: People's Publishing House.

Lenin, Vladimir Ilyich (1958c). Draft programme of the fourth congress of the social democratic party of the Latvian border region. In *Collected Works of Lenin*, Vol. 19, p. 100. Beijing: People's Publishing House.

Lenin, Vladimir Ilyich (1958d). Another discussion on division according to nationality. In *Collected Works of Lenin*, Vol. 19, p. 553. Beijing: People's Publishing House.

Lenin, Vladimir Ilyich (1958e). Eighth congress of the Russian (Bolshevik) communist party. In *Collected Works of Lenin*, Vol. 29, p. 166. Beijing: People's Publishing House.

Lenin, Vladimir Ilyich (1958f). Socialist revolution and national self-determination. In *Lenin Collections*, Vol. 22, p. 141. Beijing: People's Publishing House.

Lenin, Vladimir Ilyich (1958g). Introduction to national issue. In *Collected Works of Lenin*, Vol. 19, p. 239. People's Publishing House.

Li, Weihan (1984). *On Several Issues in National Policies, Unified Front and National Issues*, p. 464. Beijing: People's Publishing House.

Ma, Rong (2008). Field research and open mind are the condition for developing ethnic study in China. *Northwest Journal of Ethnology*, Issue 1.

Ma, Rong (2007a). The subjects and approaches of current ethnic affairs study in China. *Journal of Central University for Nationalities*, Issue 3.

Ma, Rong (2007b). The 'enculturation' of ethnic relations. *China Reading Weekly*, p. 235. 24 October.

Ma, Rong (2007c). Afterthoughts on ethnic studies — Theory and practice (part I). *China Ethnic News*, 2 March.

Ma, Rong (2007d). Influences of the federal system on the disintegration of the Soviet Union. *China Ethnic News*, 2 November.

Ma, Rong (2004a). *Ethnic Sociology — A Sociological Study of Ethnic Relations*. Beijing: Peking University Press.

Ma, Rong (2004b). A new perspective in guiding ethnic relations in the 21st century: "Depoliticizing" ethnicity in China. *Journal of Peking University*, Issue 6.

Marx and Engels (1987). The holy family, or critique of critical criticism. In *Marx and Engels on Ethnic Issues*, Vol. 1. The Institute of Enthology and Anthropology, Chinese Academy of Social Sciences (ed.).

Ma, Shoutu (2008). The unification of logic and history: A basic principle of social sciences research. *Ethnic Practices Research*, Issue 2.

Shi, Yi (2000). From patriarchy to liberation — the U.S. government's ethnic policies, Central Ethnicity University Doctoral Dissertation, p. 94–98.

Sun, Qin (1984). 35 years in the discipline of national theories. *Ethno-National Research Dynamics*, Issue 3.

Stalin, Joseph (1990a). Discussions on the current tasks of the party in national issues. In *Stalin on National Issues*, The Institute of Ethnology and Anthropology, Chinese Academy of Social Sciences (ed.), p. 175.

Stalin, Joseph (1990b). The 10th Representative Conf. Russian Communist Party (Bolshevik), The Institute of Ethnology and Anthropology, Chinese Academy of Social Sciences.

Stalin, Joseph (1990c). The political report of the alliance (Bolshevik) central committee to the 16th representative conference. In *Stalin on Ethnic Issues*,

The Institute of Ethnology and Anthropology, Chinese Academy of Social Sciences (ed.).

The China Daily website, 22 December 2007.

The United Front Work Department of CPC Central Committee (ed.), (1991a). Manifesto of the National People's Congress of the CPC, 1992. In *National Issues Collection*, Beijing: Party School of the Central Committee of CPC Press.

The United Front Work Department of CPC Central Committee (ed.), (1991b). Outline of the Constitution of the China Soviet Republic, 1931. In *National Issues Collection*.

The United Front Work Department of CPC Central Committee (ed.), (1991c). CPC Directives on the disadvantages in establishing an East Mongolian autonomous government, 1946. *National Issues Collection*.

Wang, Xisi (2005). Ethnicity and assertive ethnicity — current phenomena in world ethnicities and the analysis of ethnic processes. *World Ethno-National Studies*, Issue 4.

Virginius, Xaxa (2001). *Articulation of Autonomy among Ethnic Minorities in India*, published in the Int. Conf. ethnic regional autonomy (Sponsored by the State Ethnic Affairs Commission and the Hong Kong University of Science and Technology) article collection, p. 289.

Yang, Jianxin (2008). Some thoughts on theories of China's national relations. *China Ethnology Collection*, Vol. 1.

Zhang, Aiming (2000). The evaluation of the "Affirmative Action" of the U.S., *Journal of Nankai University*, Issue 3.

Zhou Enlai (1994). On a few issues in China's national policies. In *Comments from main CPC leaders on National Issues*, The Office of Policy Research, State Ethnic Affairs Commission (ed.), Beijing: Minzu Press.

Chapter 7

MY VIEWS ON "DEPOLITICIZING" NATIONAL ISSUES*

CHEN YUPING

Southwestern Nationalities University

Neither "ethnic group" nor "nation" are easy terms to define. But the question of whether national issues can be *depoliticized* is a major question concerning Marxist national theory as well as understanding and evaluating the CPC's post-1949 national policies. Issues concerning nationalities and national relations are "political" in nature, and "depoliticizing" them is a distinctly political action with no theoretical backing and should not be put into practice. Due to China's national composition, there is a need for the establishment of a national policy platform to resolve national issues. "National integration", an ancient Chinese idea, should be reviewed: the main methods of resolving national issues in ancient times were "non-forced" or "forced assimilation". The view that the national policy of the PRC has "broken thousands of years of traditional national integration" is unfounded.

Over recent years, the debate over national issues whether it can be "depoliticized" has arisen out of the proposals for the "depoliticization" and "enculturation" of national issues. This is a major question for the Marxist national theory, and for understanding and evaluating the CPC's post-1949 national policies.

---

*This chapter is based on an article which was originally published in *Southwest Ethnic University Paper* (*Humanities and Social Sciences Section*), No. 7 (2008). Here is the revised version.

Debate on the definition of an "ethnic group" is heated, with many scholars publishing papers to voice their opinions on it. Discussion of whether national issues can be depoliticized — a topic closely related to implementing national policies — seems, however, to be avoided in journal publications. Meanwhile, heated "under the table" discussions go on in non-public journals. Depoliticizing ethnic groups issues is, needless to say, a highly sensitive topic, closely related to the political situation. It is ill-advised, however, to limit the discussion of theoretical issues of this kind, whose evaluation holds important implications for current policy, to a small group. An honest and practical attitude should be adopted, with discussions out in the open. Everyone's proposals should first thoroughly consider the suggestions of others, and so reaching mutual understanding on what is best for the public welfare is easier. Such an approach is, I believe, more aligned with the central government's basic principles of "emancipating the mind, driving innovation and promoting philosophy and the social sciences." With this in mind, I set out to place my personal views on the table.

7.1. The Debate Over "Ethnic Group"

The original question proposed was based on the "depoliticization of ethnic groups", like the "nation" and "nationalism", which are difficult terms to define. From the beginning of the 20th century, renowned scholars including Alfred Weber, Ernest Gellner, Benidict Anderson, Kedourie, and Eric Hobsbawm have struggled to define correctly the term "nation." Anderson proposed that nation are "imagined communities". There are even more different opinions on the definition of "nationalism". Professors Mingde Cui and Luchao Cao summarized in their paper *Review and Evaluation of the Research on Chinese Nationalism over the Past Decade*: "there are over 200 different definitions for nationalism in academia" (Cui Mingde and Cao Luchao, 2006). After the establishment of the People's Republic of China 1949, Chinese scholars have used Joseph Stalin's idea of the four components of nation as the standard definition of "nation". When we look at it now, although there are significant scientific backing for the four components of nation, it still does not accurately define the term. Knowledge in the field of philosophy and social sciences is different from that of the natural sciences. In the field of natural sciences, definitions, and theorems are usually exclusive and can be accurately expressed. This is not the case in the fields of philosophy and social sciences. For example, what is "benevolence"? In *The Analects*, the term "benevolence" was used

109 times, each time described from a different angle. What is "Taoism"? How can Taoism be defined in simple words to obtain agreement from all groups of people? But whenever we use the term "Taoism", it will invoke some meaning in our minds, but to clearly and accurately describe the term is very difficult. Therefore, the question of whether we can give an accurate definition to the term "nation" is a hard one to answer. There are so many different countries and regions in the world, each with its unique living environment, lifestyle, cultural heritage, and social norms; would it be possible to succinctly summarize the common characteristics of all these groups and have everyone agree with these? I believe that the answer is no. The 6 + 1 method of defining "nation" agreed upon after the 2005 Working Conference of the CPC Central Committee is only a descriptive term for "nation" that is more scientific, but not far from the only definition. Therefore, based on the understanding of "nation", scholars will continue to propose different opinions, and we will venture closer to the truth through these long-term discussions and debates.

The heated debate on "ethnic groups" in recent years is similar to the issue of defining "nationality", which is impossible to accurately define. In different countries and regions, the term "ethnic group" is used to describe different kinds of groups. The term is "constantly evolving with the academic research of western scholars and political manipulations" (Hao Shiyuan, 2002). Thus, there are different scholarly conceptions of the term. Therefore, presently, we try not to accurately define the term. Instead, we should focus on the relations between different definitions, which would be more conducive to furthering research on the matter.

In reality, the more important question in this debate is whether "ethnic groups" can be "depoliticized". Proponents of this argument, lead by Ma Rong, a professor of Beijing University, have encountered much opposition from other scholars. Ma Rong later conceived the concepts of "national politicization" and "politicizing national issues" (see Ma Rong). These ideas are essentially the same as his earlier idea of "depoliticizing ethnic groups" (see Ma Rong). For the sake of simplicity, we will use the terms "politicization" and "depoliticization" of national issues from now on in this article.

7.2. On the Question of Whether National Issues Can Be "Depoliticized"

In recent years, there have been heated discussions in academia over the definition of "ethnic groups", but rarely has anyone conducted an in-depth analysis and discussion on the definition of "depoliticization". What is "depoliticization"? What does the prefix "de-" mean? The *Shuowen Jiezi* (an analytical dictionary of characters) offers the following explanation for *qu*, the Chinese character rendered as "de-": "*qu* means the contrary". Duan Yucai notes: "*qu*, means to depart from". The ancient Chinese reference book *Jingji Zuangu* defines "*qu*" as "get rid of", "abandon", "take off", "destroy", and "kill", in all, of which departure is the common element. In recent years, "de- something or other" is often used as a political term, drawing on the meanings of "departing from" or "contrary to". Strictly then, "depoliticizing national issues" is to rid them of political elements. In Ma Rong's usage of "depoliticizing", he repeatedly stresses the notion of removing national issues from the political realm in favor of "culturizing", implying that politics and culture are opposite and mutually exclusive realms. Therefore, whether the term of "depoliticization" is considered in its historical or contemporary meaning, its strict definition should be "departing from politics". Otherwise, the term is being misused.

Ma is the main voice in China advocating "depoliticizing" national issues. In works including *Ethnic Sociology* (Ma Rong, 2004), *New Perspective to Understand Ethnic Relations — Depoliticizing Ethnic Issues* and *Current Topics and Thoughts in the Research on China's Ethnic Issues*, he repeatedly makes his case for "depoliticizing" national issues, more frequently, with reference to "ethnic groups". Thorough study of these works shows that Ma had reasons for advocating this argument.

Ma clearly agrees with Josef Rothschild's statement, which he quoted in his works:

> In modern and transitional societies — unlike traditional ones — politicized ethnicity has become the crucial principle of political legitimation and de-legitimation of systems, states, regimes, and governments and at the same time has also become an effective instrument for pressing mundane interests in society's competition for power, status, and wealth, both dominant and subordinate groups come to view the state as the gatekeeper of contradictions, and the controller of the conflict. Hence, either exclusive or participant power over the state apparatus becomes a crucial need and goal for them. Their most convenient, feasible, and productive ideology for this quest is politicized ethnicity, which can readily be mobilized along the fault lines of the contradictions and the conflicts (Joseph Rothschild, 1981).

With the third wave of ethnic movements seen towards the end of the 20th century, the phenomenon described by Rothschild is indeed a common one, and its prevalence in the world cannot be denied.

One of the main reasons for Ma supporting the "depoliticizing" of national issues is related to the lessons learnt from the former Soviet Union. He believes that the former Soviet Union inherited the concept of the "politicizing" ethnic issues from Europe:

> Various groups were linked together under the Federation or the Union, while maintaining their own republics or autonomous regions and a full range of political rights. It was exactly this type of institution that later provided legal grounds for these groups to separate themselves from the USSR and to 1 establish their own independent states.... In handling ethnic relations, the Soviet government emphasized the political power of minority groups, either consciously or unconsciously and institutionalized such power... in the 1930s, a "nationality recognition" campaign was implemented, and every resident's "nationality status" was identified and formally registered in his/her internal passport. The internal passport system that lists the owner's nationality "has had a negative impact on integration", because it has created a "legal — psychological deterrent" (Ma Rong, 2004).

Ma cites such policies stating, "once internal and external factors developed to a certain point, the Soviet Union would face the possibility of disintegration" (see Ma Rong). This foreshadows his account of the disintegration of the Soviet Union and the independence of the ethnic groups. The reasons for the disintegration of the former Soviet Union are extremely complex, and there are many different opinions among scholars. It stemmed, in my view, from many combined factors, but negative effects of the federal system and issues of inter-national relations pointed out by Ma were indeed among them. Ma also points out that "the ideas, systems, and policies of the former Soviet Union in dealing with national issues influenced the policies of the People's Republic of China significantly" (see Ma Rong). After the disintegration of the Soviet Union, many scholars spoke of "differences" between its national policies and China's. Many Chinese policies, such as national identification, were carried out under Soviet influence, and deviated from traditional Chinese practice. While we admit that some of our practices were borrowed from the Soviet Union, we were also selective in adapting their policies. In addition, the Soviet Union's failure in its attempt to build a socialist society does not mean that all the measures it ever implemented were wrong and not worthy of borrowing. In evaluating the national policies of the former Soviet Union based on the fate of the nation, it neither conforms to the principle of being realistic and practical, nor the ancient maxims of China.

After a comprehensive review of Ma's works, I believe that he emphasizes the severe social effects resulting from the propagation of nationalism in the late 20th century that accompanied the third wave of national movements. There are certainly negative influences from the former Soviet Union on China's policies related to national relations. While his case for "depoliticizing" national issues has been widely criticized by national theorists, there is no doubt that he put forth his argument in good faith. When faced with complex domestic and international national issues stemming from the propagation of nationalism, Ma is searching for means to:

1. eliminate centrifugal tendencies,
2. crush "separatist" conspiracies among opposition forces,
3. foster national harmony, and
4. protect stability of the nation state.

Agreeing with him about negative influences in society due to the "politicizing" of national issues, I also view Ma's devotion to this as the exercise of his scholarly responsibility. Nonetheless, I disagree with "depoliticizing" of national issues — the idea lacks theoretical support, hence, cannot and should not be implemented.

What is politics? Here is another ambiguous social science term. The noun *politics* cannot be found in the *Britannica Concise Encyclopedia*, but the entry for *political philosophy* states, "one may characterize as political all those practices and institutions that are concerned with government" (Britannica Concise Encyclopaedia, 1985). In the *Great China Encyclopedia*, the term "politics" is explained as follows:

> Specific actions and resulting specific relationships of power entities of the superstructure for the protection of their own rights. It is an important social phenomenon in a certain stage of the historical development of humanity; this social phenomenon is very complex; politicians and political scientist of different ages have attempted to discuss it from different angles and with different points of emphasis,

but we have not arrived at an accurate definition to this day (Great China Encyclopedia, 1992, p. 481).

In the *Great China Encyclopedia* entry, there are also several references to different schools of thoughts on "politics". Two references should be pointed out,

First, in China, Sun Yat-sen's saying "politics refers to anything that involves managing people" has gained much influence. Some politicians believe that politics means managing civil affairs using a public mandatory power (Great China Encyclopedia, 1992, p. 482).

Second, As a way for the ruling party to protect its own rights, politics mainly manifests as various hegemonic actions relying on state power and various anti-hegemonic actions relying on restrictive powers over the state (Great China Encyclopedia, 1992, p. 482).

We have seen changes in the definition of "politics" in different periods since 1949. However, no matter how modified, national relations will always belong to the politics. In his account of "politicizing" and "culturizing" national issues, Ma used the term "policy-oriented" (Ma Rong, 2004, p. 609) frequently. Who orients the direction of policies? It is "the state", of course. What does "orientation" mean? Orientation is a form of government intervention, or actions to allocate resources "with the power of the nation". These methods themselves are "political" in nature. There are different ways to conduct government intervention in national issues. Some focus on emphasizing the differences between nationalities, while others focus on national awareness and to downplay the prominence of national characteristics. However, they are all political actions taken by the "state", so why should the former be called "politicization" and the latter "depoliticization"? Ma heavily promoted the "depoliticization of ethnic groups" adopted by the U.S., but he also stated,

"in the U.S., where the economy is developed and the military power is strong, there still exist forces of ethnic self-governance and independence within some underprivileged ethnic minorities including African–Americans and indigenous Indians and their organizations. Understandably, these forces are closely monitored and suppressed by the U.S. government" (Ma Rong, 2004, p. 609).

Thus, "depoliticizing ethnic groups" in the U.S. is a political measure. "Depoliticization" itself is a form of "political" action in "allocating state power". Issues of ethnic relations always belonged to the "political" realm, so the proposal to "depoliticize" politics lacks theoretical validity.

Had Ma summarized his idea not as "depoliticizing" national issues, but as "national policies oriented toward downplaying national characteristics and national awareness", would it have been more viable? I do not believe so, at least not in China's contemporary context.

The Chinese have long known of how different living environments shape the philosophies of different population groups. In a chapter on "Kingly institutions", the *Book of Rites* says:

> In all their settlements, the bodily capacities of the people were bound to accord with heavenly and earthly influences — cold or hot, dry or moist. Where valleys are wide and rivers large, the land was differently laid out; and the people born there had different customs. Their temperaments, as hard or soft, light or grave, slow or rapid, were made uniform by different measures; the flavors they preferred differently harmonized; their tools differently made; their clothes differently fashioned, but always suitable. Their training was varied, without changing their customs; and the governmental arrangements were uniform, without changing the suitability, in each case. The people of those five regions — the Middle states, and the Rong, Yi, and other wild tribes round them — all had their own different characteristics, which they could not be made to alter. The tribes on the East were called Yi. They had their hair unbound, and tattooed their bodies. Some of them ate raw food. Those on the south were called Man. They tattooed their foreheads, and had their feet turned in towards each other. Some of them also ate their food raw. Those on the West were called Rong. They had their hair unbound, and wore animal skins. Some of them did not eat grain-food. Those on the North were called Di. They wore skins of animals and birds, and dwelt in caves. Some of them did not eat cereals. The people of the Middle states, and of those Man, Rong, and Di, all had their dwellings where they lived at ease; their preferred flavors; the clothes suitable for them; their proper implements for use; and their vessels which they prepared in abundance. In those five regions, the languages of the people were mutually unintelligible, and their likings and desires were different. To make their thoughts understood, and communicate their likings and desires, there were officers who act as intermediators, otherwise known as the transmitters in the East; representatives in the South; Di-dis in the West; and interpreters in the North (The Thirteen Classics, 1980).

This passage from The Kingly Institutions makes this point repeatedly: "The people of those five regions — the Middle states, the Rong and Yi and other wild tribes round them — all had their different characteristics, which they could not be altered. The languages of the people in the five regions are mutually unintelligible, and their values different". This shows, that the ancient Chinese people had a clear understanding of the differences between nationalities and the reasons for their evolution. Conflicts arising from those differences have existed since that time. According to this conception, the treatment of "us" and "them" cannot be the same, even under the same political ruling system. Therefore, this division represents how the power of national state adopted different "political orientations" or "hegemonic actions" in dealing with "us" and "them". The pre-Qin idea of "distinguishing *hua* (Chinese) from foreigner" outlines the differential treatment between China and its surrounding nations. We will not go into detail here, but it also talked about the different political treatment of different nationalities under its rule. The earliest example of this occurs in the *Collected biographies of Man in the South and Yi* in the *Southwest* in the *Hou Han Shu*:

> The "Ban Man" people, an ethnic minority located near the border were barbarians. During the Reign of Emperor Zhao Xiang of Qin, there was a white tiger that often followed other tigers to the lands of Qin, Shu, Ba, and Han, and had injured thousands of people, there was a man from the Yi ethnicity in Bajunyan who made bows and arrows out of white bamboo, climbed up to a high building and shot down tigers. The Shao emperor awarded him for his bravery, but because he was a member of the Yi ethnic group, the emperor, not wanting to promote him, carved an agreement in stone giving the Yi people preferential treatment, including waiving the fee for the usage of land, by a hectare of land per household, waiving the fee for having even ten wives; if an Yi person committed homicide, the death penalty could be revoked by paying a fee. The two parties agreed that "if Qin were to invade Yi, Qin will give Yi a pair of yellow dragon, and if Yi were to invade Qin, Yi will give Qing a container of wine" The Yi people adhered to the agreement peacefully (Fan Ye, 1965).

Carving covenants into stone in reality is an act of "legislation", and embodies the "dominating action" of the state. This reflects the principle of "merit-based reward" of the Qin system, not any special treatment for the Yi people. What exactly a "yellow dragon" was is now obscure; it very likely referred to a dragon-shaped piece of jewelry made of precious jade, clearly costing more than a container of wine. Clearly a measure to give the Yi people more power in the event of conflict between the Yi and Qin people, this is a representation of a measure to protect the disadvantaged, using *de lego* inequality to compensate for the *de facto* inequality between Qin and Yi.

What does this example teach us about national policies? Where there are nationalitis, there will be differences between nationalities, and where there are differences, there will be conflict. Can the latter be resolved and eliminated naturally in everyday life? The answer is negative. As with class conflict, the state power must step in to alleviate and resolve it, maintaining it within the boundaries of "order" (Friedrich Engels, 1972). These conflicts emerge out of national differences; hence the state must intervene to deal with national issues in reality. Marxism firmly upholds national equality, but in a multi-national state this cannot be realized without state intervention. Even in socialist societies that have eliminated exploitation, equality cannot exist naturally. If we know clearly that issues are caused by national differences, but out of other considerations try to resolve them by downplaying national characteristics and awareness, we will surely fall into a paradox and be incapable of effective intervention.

If this is so, why would some Western multi-national states apply hegemonic action to downplaying national characteristics? I believe this is out of a need to strengthen citizen awareness. The transition from traditional empire states to modern democratic nations was a lengthy process. It has lasted for hundreds of years, but can we claim that it has been completed? I would argue no. As long as there are numbers of citizens with stronger "ethnic awareness" than "citizenship awareness", the transition is incomplete. The reason western nations had policy orientations of strengthening "citizenship awareness" and downplaying national charac-teristics was to alleviate conflicts rooted in national issues and safeguard social stability. Of those nations, the U.S. has its own unique reasons for adopting such a policy orientation. The U.S. is a new immigrant nation with many ethnic groups among the population, without a single ethnic group that dominates others significantly both in number and political, economic, and cultural power. In such an immigrant society, any awareness and actions based on ethnicity will create serious centrifugal forces and damages the society. The only solution was to create a "United States of America" and build citizenship awareness. For a long period after the establishment of the U.S., the only differentiation among the population was between the white and the black people, but not between ethnic groups. For almost half a century, racial differences have not been discussed openly; instead, the so-called "culturizing" hegemonic action was used to downplay existing racial issues and racial inequalities. In 2000, a female African–American vice Minister of the New York State Department of Education said to our education representative group, "I made three times the effort compared to others in order to get to where I am." By "others" she clearly meant Caucasians. Nobody openly objected to her promotion, but she knew clearly that for racial reasons she was forced to work harder to get a promotion. From this example we can see that "ethnic culturizing" implemented in the U.S. whose real political function was to hide ethnic inequality.

Without going too far, in comparison with the U.S. in terms of "culturizing" national issues to cover up complex issues of ethnic conflicts, the point holds that China is very different to the U.S. in national circumstances. At the establishment of the new China, the Han nationality made up 94% of the total population, and numerous other nationalities only made up the remaining 6%. After 50 years of government policy-led development, Han still makes up 92% of the total population, giving them an absolute numerical advantage over other nationalities. In addition, for historical reasons, the Han gained clear advantage over others in economic and cultural development, as well as power in the state system, which was unavoidable. We should also point out that counteracting Han chauvinism, formed through long-term economic and cultural dominance, can be neither easy nor fast. Faced with such national circumstances, if we do not emphasize national issues and do not take issues of national equality, national emancipation, national coherence and mutual development, and prosperity in the consideration of the basic strategy of the state, national minorities in China would face an unavoidable fate of marginalization. Such a developmental trend is clearly against basic Marxist principles and the nature of socialism, and will bring about severe damages to China.

We need to resolve existing issues of nationality and national relations, and to do that, we must first admit to the nature of those issues, carry out targeted policies and measures to establish regulations and policy platforms, and use them to resolve issues in an appropriate way. In implementing policies, if we try to downplay or reframe national issues and try to resolve them outside of the national policy platform, we will surely run into the problem of not knowing where to start, leading to many unresolved issues. For e.g., since 1949, the government has given policy support to some national minority groups in order to promote national equality and coherence; the state gives them material and financial support to help them overcome difficulties and develop their productivity, as well as implementing favorable college admission policies in areas with under-developed educational systems. If we were to follow the principle of "depoliticization", we will need to unlink the above policies with national policies in order to avoid negative influences. Under what name should they be implemented? Would "supporting underprivileged areas and populations" work? When the nation was first established, there were many "underprivileged" areas and populations within the Han nationality and under-developed educational systems with limited national financial power and educational resources — it was impossible to help all in need. What should the solution have been? This was the reality of the national circumstances, and a priority system was needed to determine whose problems would be resolved first. This is where the state had to make a decision. National equality and national coherence were in relative terms more important and urgent in the big picture, and had to be given priority. The nation hence chose to first resolve urgent "national" issues rather than urgent "citizen" issues. This is why formulating the *National Regional Autonomous Law* and several other national policies in order to build an appropriate platform for resolving national issues was the right choice for adhering to Marxism and the principles of the People's Republic of China, as well as staying grounded in the national conditions.

China is still in the process of transition to a modern state, and there is indeed a process for each nationality to transition from their "national awareness" to "citizenship awareness", an identity shared with other members of the Chinese nation. This transition is time-consuming, and there are complex issues to be resolved and difficult tasks to be completed, during the process. The basic principles of the CPC, guided by Marxism and upholding the mission of the CPC is to face the existence of different nationalities, admit their traits, differences and existing conflicts, strive to realize national equality through "state hegemonic action" and promote the ideal of "common unity, common prosperity, and development". Focusing on China's national conditions, the issues discussed above can only be understood and resolved on the "national" political platform, and while some policies and measures may produce negative effects such as Ma pointing out, the scientific and unshakable evaluation of those policies and measures should be mainly positive. The negative impact and social consequences of not implementing them would be much greater and more serious. In building a political platform for "national issues" to resolve the issue of national equality and "two commons" is an unavoidable and necessary stage, and is also a long course of history. Within this course of history, various nationalities will integrate together and gradually eliminate their "national awareness" and fortify their "citizenship awareness" on the basis of "sufficient development", (Li Weihan, 1981, p. 596), ultimately fortify the ethnic awareness of Greater China. The elimination of "national awareness" is the product of natural integration and development of different nationalities in their politics, economy, and culture. Trying to interrupt the natural course of history, to "depoliticize" national issues and weaken people's "national awareness" through "state hegemonic action" will do much damage to China's national practice. This is the lesson learned in the national practice since the establishment of the nation.

7.3. Afterthoughts on the "National Integration" Process in China's History

Ma Rong published the paper "The Subject and Approaches of Current Ethnic Affairs Study in China" in the April 2007 issue of *Ethnic Sociology Research Communications*, restating his views on "depoliticizing" of national issues. He states:

> China undertook "national identification" in the 1950s to clarify each citizen's "national makeup" and institutionalized it, establishing national autonomous regions and implementing favorable national policies for certain nationalities. These actions enabled the 55 national minorities in China to become "nationalities" with certain political status and political coloring, discontinuing the national integration process that had been going on for thousands of years. China's history proves that the "culturizing" of ethnic groups is an effective way to promote the spread and development of civilization without compromising political unity (see Ma Rong).

Ma's opinions led to my in-depth afterthought on what is the accurate definition of "national integration"? I have used the term "national integration of ancient China" extensively in my own scholarly work, publishing a well-known work on *Issues of National Integration in Ancient China* (Chen Yuping, 2003). But do I know the real meaning of "national integration"? That is hard to say. Comrade Li Weihan once said of "national integration".

> National integration is about eliminating nation and national differences. Hence it is not something that will happen today or tomorrow, but in the distant future. It will only be gradually realized after the full implementation of socialism (Li Weihan, 1981, p. 597).

This account of the historical stages for realizing national integration is very clear and completely in conformity with Marxism. Li Weihai later spoke of "national assimilation" when talking about national integration:

> Some pose the question of how to use the terms "national assimilation" and "national integration". I believe that the former is a term to describe some kind of national relations in the course of history. It is suitable for describing the actions of enforcing assimilation on another nation or being assimilated by another nation in a society with existing class and national oppositions. This is how we have used the term in the past. Of course, for "national assimilation" in our history, there is one type of assimilation that happened more naturally. In the sense that this type of assimilation was not accomplished by violence or oppression makes is somewhat similar to national integration. Another type of assimilation was coerced assimilation through applying national oppression. The results of coercive assimilation in some respects promoted the progress of civilization for some nationalities, but at the cost of great pain and sacrifice for others. It inevitably around their resistance, leading to international conflict and hatred, and obstructing or slowing down the process of integration (Li Weihan, 1981, p. 602).

Realistically speaking, the last sentence of this quote can lead to a misunderstanding, that the process of national integration was stretched out to the class society period. Many scholars and educators, including myself, in the spirit of promoting national coherence, usually call non-enforced assimilation in the national relations in ancient China "national integration".

What is "national integration" in the strict sense? It should be equal mutual integration and recognition on the basis of the elimination of exploitation and the development of each nationality. It is impossible to have national integration in this strict sense in class societies. Personally, I highly value the Confucian national view established under the guiding principles of the Confucian core of "benevolence" from ancient China, and the widespread influence it had on national relations. I am also clearly aware however of the fact that this kind of liberal thought was only superior in comparison with the mindset and policies for national relations of other counties and regions of the same time period especially the white-centric mindset of Europe, and has no place as a criterion for evaluating modern societies. Thorough research on national interaction in ancient Chinese history reveals that many national minority groups integrated into the majority Han nationality, the majority of which were not due to coercive administrative measures. But behind the face of non-enforced integration, was there a plethora of hidden unwillingness and forced compliance? The answer is affirmative. Mencius promoted "influencing national minorities" and opposed the idea of "assimilation" (Great China Encyclopaedia, 1992, p. 2706), which was the basic principle followed by later generations. Ever since Confucianism gained dominance, it became the guiding principle for the ruling of various dynasties as well as some national minorities in the central plains, and Confucian studies became essential for entering high society and elites. Especially after the imperial examination system was implemented in the Sui and Tang dynasties, the only way for a common citizen to enter the political realm was by taking the imperial examination, and the content of the examination was mainly on the Han culture and Confucianism. On the surface, the dynasty did not inhibit non-Han from taking part in the imperial examinations, but national culture was excluded from the subject matter examined. The Han utilized their superior position in material, system and spiritual culture, which both attracted and also encouraged assimilation from other nationalities: do you want development, acceptance and acknowledgement? The price is to let go of your own culture and conform to my rules and customs. This is an undeniable fact in China's history, following the notion of "influencing national minorities". If observe only the absence of overt administrative coercion, but fail to see its covert aspects, then it fails to measure up to "national integration". The traditional practice described above should be termed "non-coercive assimilation" or to be more precise, "assimilation with covert coercive elements", as "influencing national minorities" had to a great extent to be carried out through state hegemonic action.

"Non-administrative coercive assimilation" became the main reason for the snowballing of the Han in China's history. This method is indeed superior to the methods taken by other countries and regions in national interaction, which is why the Han make up more than 90% of the national population. Non-recognition that the method of "non-administrative coercive assimilation" was a great policy deserving to be acknowledged in its historical background would be going against the "absolute requirement" of historical materialism that emphasizes "seeing issues within a certain historical context" (Vladimir Ilyich Lenin, 1960). However, the success of this kind of "non-administrative coercive assimilation" has one prerequisite, namely that the Han needs to hold actual cultural advantage in China, Asia and any other scope that people can see. Only by fulfilling this requirement would it be possible to attract other nationalities, gain their respect and willingness to give up their own culture and assimilate into your culture for the sake of development. However, if the Han nationality loses its position, would other nationalities still be willing to do this? China's backwardness in recent times was in fact the inevitable result of an agricultural civilization centered on traditional Han culture falling behind the industrial civilization of Europe. Once the superiority of the Han culture was lost, respect of other ethnic groups will deteriorate. A classic example of this is Japan, which modeled itself after China for a long time, but decided to adopt the "European" model and depart from the Asian model, and even attacked and humiliated China, its former role model and teacher. With the spread of western nationalism ideologies, the strengthening of national self-awareness is a worldwide trend, and there would be no exception for various nationalities in China. Given these new historical terms, the "national integration process carried on from thousands of years of Chinese history" cannot be continued. The CPC established a set of national policies with Chinese socialist characteristics based on basic principles of Marxism and the Chinese national circumstances, in hopes of realizing national equality and coherence, as well as promoting mutual prosperity and development. This is the correct "state hegemonic action" to take with the mindset of advancing with the times. The saying "breaking the process of integration" is clearly against dialectics.

References

Britannica Concise Encyclopaedia (1985). Vol. 11, p. 346. Beijing: Encyclopedia of China Publishing House.

Cui, Mingde and Cao, Luchao (2006). Literature review and analysis of Chinese nationalism research in the recent ten years, Issue 1, *Journal of Yantai University*.

Chen, Yuping (ed.) (2003). *Research on Problems of National Integration in Ancient China*. Chengdu: Sichuan Nationalities Publishing House.

Engels, Friedrich (1972). *The Origin of the Family, Private Property and the State*, Beijing: People's Publishing House.

Fan, Ye (1965). *Later Han: Biographies of the South Barbarians and Southwest Minorities*, Vol. 86, p. 2842. Beijing: Zhonghua Book Company.

Great China Encyclopedia-Politics Volume (1992). Beijing: Encyclopedia of China Publishing House.

Hao, Shiyuan (2002). Discussion about the definition of ethnic group in the Western Academic Field, *Journal of Guangxi University for Nationalities*, issue 4.

Lenin, Vladimir Ilyich (1960). On the subject of national self-determination. In *Selected Works of Lenin*, Vol. 2, p. 512. Beijing: People's Publishing House.

Li, Weihan (1981). *Issues of Unified Front and Nationality.* Beijing: People's Publishing House.

Ma, Rong (2007). The subjects and approaches of current ethnic affairs study in China, *Ethnic Sociology Research and Communication*, Issue 42.

Ma, Rong (2004). A new perspective in guiding ethnic relations in the 21st century: "Depoliticising" ethnicity in China, *Ethnic Sociology Research and Communication*, Issue 34.

Ma, Rong (ed.) (2004). *Sociology of Ethnicity — Research on Ethnic Relations from a Sociology Perspective.* Beijing: Peking University Press.

Rothschild, Joseph (1981). *Ethnopolitics: A Conceptual Framework*, pp. 2–5, New York: Columbia University Press.

The Thirteen Classics (1980). Beijing: Zhonghua Book Company, p. 1338.

Chapter 8

CURRENT CRUX AND SOLUTIONS TO CURRENT ETHNIC ISSUES IN CHINA*

MA RONG

Department of Sociology, Peking University

Prior to 2008, most Chinese people had little understanding and concern for existing "national issues" in China. However, after the incidents such as the March 14th Lhasa riots, the protests overseas during the Olympics Torch Relay and the violence in Xinjiang, people began to realize that China indeed has "national issues", and that they are closely connected to the "Tibet Separationist" and "Xinjiang Separationist" movements. These events not only made Tibet and Xinjiang appear as centers of instability, but also considered Beijing and other major metropolises as possible targets for terrorist attacks. This affected China's global image and diplomatic relations. It can be stated that to this day, China's national issues have gained enough importance to obtain attention and concern from the central government as well as the nation as a whole, and are directly connected to the core interests of the Chinese nation.

The question remains, what is the crux of national issues in China? How can we make sense out of complex national conflicts that currently exist? Only when we have found the source of the problem, we can go in search of the solution. This article will start by discussing some of the most basic concepts, and integrate the history of China's "national" phenomenon with the most prominent issues of the present days, in the analysis of the crux of China's ethnic issues in the new century, and also probe into possible future solutions.

---

*This chapter is based on a Chinese article originally published in *Leaders*, No. 26 (Feb 2009). Here is the revised version in English.

8.1. On the Origin and Meaning of the Concept of *Minzu*

Given that we are considering "ethnic issues", we should start the discussion from the origin and meaning of the key-word *minzu*.

The interpretation of *minzu* offered in the Great China Encyclopedia (Nationality Volume) runs:

> the term "group (zu)" has been used widely in ancient Chinese writings, as well as the terms *min* (people), *ren* (population), *zhong* (race), *bu* (tribe), *lei* (kind), as well as *minren* (ethnic people), *minzhong* (ethnic type), *minqun* (ethnic cohort), *zhongren* (cohort), *buren* (tribal group) and zulei (national type). But the combination of *min* "people" and *zu* "group" as a stand-alone noun was something that came later. In 1903, the modern scholar Liang Qichao introduced the German political theorist and jurist J. K. Bluntschli's concept of nation to China. The term subsequently became a popular one in China, and its meaning was commonly mixed up with that of race and state, which was closely tied with the influence of western interpretations of nation (The Great China Encyclopedia, 1986).

Nowadays, most scholars agree that the Chinese term *minzu* should correspond with the term "nation" in English, and exhibit specialized modern political connotations that have only appeared in recent years.

8.2. What Does *Minzu* Mean in Modern Terms?

The term "nation" with modern political connotations was born in Europe, and in order to gain an understanding of this term, we need to start from the concept of "nation" in western countries.

Three major movements took place during the late medieval ages in Europe, which influenced its later development. These three movements were the Renaissance, the Reformation, and the Enlightenment. Originating in Italy, the Renaissance placed emphasis on human nature, utilizing the image of "man" to depict "God", as well as multiple artistic means to bring "man" to new heights. The Reformation, originating in Germany, helped people break loose of the various means of controls and emotional bondage of the Church. Originating among French philosophers, the Enlightenment propagated new ideas of democracy, freedom and equality, which all had modern political connotations, openly opposing the feudal monarchy and calling for a republican form of government. The three movements paved way for the emergence of republican government and capitalist production relations by providing necessary intellectual and public opinion preparation.

With the development of capitalism in some Western nations, the "lower class" and the "ruling class" wished to establish a new national system. In order to enable cash, raw material, labor power and products to flow freely according to the demands of the market, the newly emerged merchants wanted to escape from royal absolutism and the feudal government system that restricted their development, and, therefore, had a strong desire to overturn the aristocratic imperial regime. In order to establish a replacement of the royal absolutism and feudal government system, lower class intellectual leaders and thinkers of who rose out of the private industrial and commercial sectors proposed the idea of "nation". They promoted social movements using existing national boarders and common grounds in language and religion to encourage the masses to strive to build an independent "nation-state", which in other words, means to establishing a new political entity (state) representing the republican spirit, that would be made up of a "nation" segregated by geographic locations and demographics. This is the movement of "nationalism" that arose out of Western Europe in the early 18th century.[1]

8.3. What is Meant by "Nation" in Western Europe and What are its Components?

When thinkers and political leaders in Europe were ideating on the definition of "nation" and its geographic and demographic boundaries, they took many factors into consideration. Anthony Smith, a well-known British student of nationalism, has given a systematic account of it. He believed that there emerged a "civic model of the nation" during the development of Western Europe, which was made up of four components:

1. The concept of space or territory, which states that a "nation" must have clear geographic boundaries.
2. A nation is "a community of laws and of institutions with a single political will".
3. Completely equal "citizen rights" for all members of the community, which entitles the same citizenship rights into public affairs, legal rights, political rights and duties and social economic rights.

---

[1]The term nationalism was first used around 1789 in Europe by Augustin Barlow, a French clergyman exiled in England, to describe a social movement to overturn the aristocratic monarchy (see Yu Jianhua, 1999).

4. A common culture with respect to value systems, traditions and civil ideology.

The above mentioned four components form the standard Western model of "nation" (Anthony Smith, 1991).

8.4. The Goal of Establishing a "Nation": Building a Nation-State

Some European thinkers and their followers proposed the concept of "nation", and ideated on the geographic and demographic boundaries of the "nation", publicizing "national" consciousness to promote "nationalist" movements in the society. These actions had a sole purpose, which was to utilize the establishment of new political entities to escape from the long-standing institutions of traditional feudal government systems; break out of the old social system by building a new structure to empower the "nation-state" on the basis of newly formulated political principles and ideals.

The two authors provide a succinct summary of the ultimate political objectives of the nationalism movement. "Nationalism saw humanity naturally divided into nations which were, which had to be, the proper unit of political organization... nothing would go well with humanity unless each nation enjoyed an independent existence in its own state". "Nations are separate natural entities ordained by God, and the best political arrangement obtains when each nation forms a state on its own" (Elie Kedourie, 2002). "Nationalism primarily holds a political principle which insists the political and the national unit to be congruent... Nationalism is a theory of political legitimacy, which requires that ethnic boundaries should not cut across political limitations.[2]

"National" consciousness and nationalist movements first emerged in Western Europe, where the idea of "one nation, one state" was proposed. Nationalist movements utilized various social forces including young intellectuals influenced by the emerging bourgeois, the Enlightenment and traditional tribal leaders to build a series of "nation-states" composed of "nations" based on their own understandings and constructions of "nation" during the process of various political rivalries. At the time, there were various differences between diversified groups of people with respect to heritage, language/dialect, and historical origin within each "nation-state",

---

[2]The terms "nation" and "ethnic groups" are conflated by Gellner here (see Ernest Gellner, 2002).

but during the "nation building" process, all these differences disappeared and the groups started to accept the new concept of "one nation" and to establish a common understanding of this concept.

While pondering upon certain questions of how to establish the methods for ascertaining the boundaries of the "nations", how to understand the nature of differences between various groups that lie inside and outside of the national boundaries, and how to acknowledge the conflicts that arise between such boundaries and their historical backgrounds, ambiguities are more likely to occur. Why does a tribe or a region belong to one "nation" and not another? What was the most reasonable law-abiding way to establish the boundaries of a "nation"? There is no question that the new concept of "nation" that was eventually accepted by the majority of people and its implications must have some elements of "imagination" and "creation", similar to the "imagined communities" emerging from colonial rule as described by Anderson (Anderson Benedict, 1999).

8.5. "Nation-State" of Western Europe

The sovereign political unit set up in this historical period by the nationalist movements to overturn feudal monarchies was the norm of nation-state. As soon as it became a real political entity, the nation-state would rapidly solidify its political basis and legitimacy, gaining recognition as a sovereign unit by signing mutual agreements with other states under the new International Law. Political scientists generally see the signing of the Peace of Westphalia in 1864 as the birth of the nation-state.

After the success of the emerging nation-state political model in a few important Western European states, its impact on the manufacturing and commercial industries and on scientific and technological development was immediate, thus enabling these first states to adopt new political systems to rapidly gain strong comprehensive national strength and military strength, becoming dominant powers in Europe. These countries used their powers to bully other European nations, a classic example of France under the rule of Napoleon. Under these circumstances, although neighboring countries were lagging behind in terms of development of their capitalist factors of production, and limited influence of the Enlightenment movement on their elite and masses, they were forced to revolutionize their political systems in order to fight back against other Western European countries. Afterwards, with the expansion of economic power and its colonization of other regions, the imperial kingdoms, native states and tribes were also forced to adopt the same systems of the state.

8.6. The Second Model of "Nation": Forced Replication by Other Regions

The modern international order and political landscape led by the newly emerged nation-state having been set, attempts by other regions to rebuild their political entities have largely been attempts to replicate the Western European nation-state model by integrating various social groups into a modern "nation" within the existing territory of the sovereign, establishing a common political and cultural or historical identity among various groups, thereby soliciting identification and loyalty with this new "nation" from all members of the society. This practice was adopted by various countries in Eastern Europe after coming under attack by the Western European countries, newly created countries established by Caucasian European migrants such as the U.S.A., as well as newly established countries after the independence of the colonies, for e.g., India.

Smith argues that another "ethnic model of the nation" exists in the Asian and Eastern European regions. The characteristics of this model are: (1) identity based on origin and lineage is stronger than that is based on a territory. (2) Strong emotional and popular mobilization. (3) More emphasis on local cultural heritage such as the usage of language, value systems, customs and traditions than on rules and regulations (Anthony Smith, 1991).

This second model of "nation" is in fact the political reaction of Eastern European and Asian states, which are less developed in their capitalist production methods and political enlightenment, to those of developed and established Western European countries. In their interaction with newly established "nation-states" of the Western Europe, these states realized that this was an emerging and powerful model of state that they must follow. Under the influence of domestic thinkers and emerging political groups, Eastern European and some Asian countries started their own "nation-building" process. However, due to their lack of modern economic and intellectual foundations, their "nation" models are mere imitations of the political forms of Western Europe. On a timeline, the second model came later and was created in a passive way, as a recoil or response to the emergence of the first model.

8.7. "Nation-Building" of the Tsarist Russia

The Tsarist Empire was a grand one, with feudal traditions, imperial powers and aristocratic forces. If we pinpoint the start of this empire as 1613 with the establishment of the Romanov dynasty, then it had only some two hundred centuries of history. Over this history, this Empire expanded its territory significantly through invasions, and many regions of Russia were made up of different tribal groups, whose heads still held some power. These groups under the rule of Tsarist Russia are mostly tribes, and have not yet accepted the political ideology and structure of the modern "nation".

From the era of Peter the Great, Tsarist Russia actively copied from Western Europe, striving to respond to the latter's eastward expansion by turning its territory into a modern administrative system, and expediting its own modernization in order to get a piece of the pie in the world. Russia set up provinces in its territory, separating the population of each tribe into different administrative provinces and striving to weaken their independent political awareness so as to establish a "Russian nation", thus beginning the nation-building process. In other words, Russia was trying to turn a traditional feudal Empire into a Western European style nation-state, to turn traditional tribal regions into administrative provinces of the Empire to create a Russian nation.

Comparing the layout of administrative regions in Tsarist Russia and the Soviet Union in 1840 and 1900, we can see that in the territory presently occupied by Ukraine, there were nine administrative provinces during the Tsarist era, and there were five administrative provinces, where Belarus is situated today. The borders of these administrative provinces are not completely aligned, but we can still see the overall geographic region. There are, at present, 13 autonomous republics in the European part of Russia Federation, taking up around one-third of it. All these states were administrative provinces during the reign of Tsarist Russia, and there was no issue of them wanting ethnic region autonomy. The administrative region blueprint of that time indicates that Tsarist Russia at least tried to integrate those ethnic minority groups into the unified administrative system of Russia in order to influence the country into the nation-state concept, but this process was interrupted by the October Revolution.

8.8. Joseph Stalin Made the Soviet Union Into an "Ethnic Union"

Before the October Revolution, in order to overturn Tsarist rule, the Bolshevik Party adopted a key strategy for initiating revolution and seizing power. This was to entitle the various tribes under Tsarist rule as "nation" and encourage them to gain independence, thereby encouraging the Ukrainians, Georgians, and Kazakhs, with their differing cultures, languages and histories, to rebel. Suppressing these tribal rebellions would inevitably lead to a dispersion of military power and create a financial burden, thereby greatly increasing the chances of success for a worker's uprising. In order to encourage an uprising among the tribal groups, the Bolshevik Party declared all these groups to be "nations", which had natural rights to independence and sovereignty. The Russian working class would, it said, support them overturning the rule of Tsarist Russia to gain independence. The national theories of Vladimir Ilyich Lenin and Joseph Stalin, including the definition of "nation", "national equality", and "national self-determination" were all produced against this historical background.

After the official establishment of the Soviet Union, the process of "national identification" and the attendant institution building went forward under the leadership of Joseph Stalin. This was an approach of "politicizing" Tsarism's traditional tribal groups and turning them into modern nation. In 1922, the Union of Soviet Socialist Republics (USSR) was officially established. It was made up of 15 member republics including the Russian Federation, 20 autonomous republics, 8 autonomous regions, and 128 border area regions or states, all of which were termed nation. Federal system has been followed in some other states such as Western Germany, Sweden, and the U.S.A., but the division of territory in those countries was based on historical division of administrative regions, and the concept of "nation" was used neither for the division of territory nor for naming the regions. The only states that based the division and naming of their administrative regions on "nations" were the Soviet Union, China, Yugoslavia, and Czechoslovakia.

Recognizing those groups as "nations", and the groups having all established their own administrative units such as union republics and autonomous republics with rights to sovereignty and independence, the Soviet Union became a "multi-nation union" composed of many "nations" rather than a "nation-state". According to the Constitution of the USSR of 1923 and 1936, each "nation" had its own independent rights, and each union republic and autonomous republic had its own independent congress and constitution, as well as presidents and cabinet ministers. Therefore, the Soviet Union was a multi-tiered political system, the first tier being the Soviet Union, the second tier being various union republics, the third tier being autonomous republics, and the fourth layer being autonomous regions and border areas. The Soviet Union constitution clearly stipulated that the Union was a "consensual alliance of nations with equal rights" in which "each republic had the right to secede".

Under the new system of the Soviet Union, each group had accepted the theory and political implications of the modern "nation", and "national awareness" was growing steadily. At the same time, the Constitution of the Soviet Union provided the legal backing for these "nations" to secede from the Union and become independent. During the irresponsible reforms lead by Gorbachev, the original ideology ties, economic order, and political cohesion were all damaged, providing the opportunity for the "nations" that already established "union republics" to transform into independent "nation-states". Until this day, some established "autonomous republics" such as the Autonomous Republic of Chechnya of the Russian Federation and the South Ossetian Autonomous Republic of Georgia which are still fighting for their independence. We should carefully study and learn from the experiences of the Soviet Union with national theories and institutions.

The most pressing task of the current leaders of Russia is how to make a turnaround in "national theory" and initiate the "nation-building" process of the "Russian Confederation" from a new perspective.

8.9. "Nation-Building" in the Republic of China After the Late Qing Dynasty

When the Qing dynasty faced defeat in the face of European fleets and Western artillery, the dynasty was forced by the foreign powers to engage in "foreign (Western) affairs". Domestic students were sent for study overseas and Western ideas and publications were allowed to enter China. The Western concepts of "nationalism" and "nation" were also inevitably introduced to China during that time, influencing the academic community and masses of all ethnic groups in China.

Under the grim situation of national salvation, China's thinkers and elites naturally started to restructure their own state and nation using the Western "nation-state" model. Publications surrounding the topics of "the Chinese nation" and "state-nation" and several volumes of a *Chinese National History* published in the 1930s reflected the spread of the western "nation-state" ideology within the Chinese academic world, as well as the hopes of some individuals to strengthen the cohesion of the nation through the establishment of a *minzu shi* or "national history" (Wang Tongling, 1934). It was under such circumstances that the titles of "Chinese nation" and "Chinese" replaced the term "Qing Dynasty subjects". The Japanese would not use the term "Chinese" to describe Mongolians, Manchus, and Tibetans, purposefully limiting the area of "China" to the Han regions, and even proposed the concept of "mainland China" to lay down the seed for the disintegration of China. This is an important historical background that needs to be in the background of thoughts about China's "national issues".

The Republic of China was established after the 1911 Xinhai Revolution, and the idea of "Republic of five nations" was first promoted. In the first Chapter of *The Three Principles of the People*, Sun Yat-sen wrote "Zhongguo ren de minzuzhuyi shi guozuzhuyi" (China's nationalism is the state-nationalism). He also proposed in the *Interim Presidential Declaration*: "By joining Han, Manchu, Mongolia, Hui, and Tibet within in the same country, Han people, Manchus, Mongolians, Hui people and Tibetans are one people, this is what we call the unity of *minzu* or "nations" (Sun Yat-sen, 1981). He explicitly promoted using *Zhonghua minzu* or "the Chinese nations" as "national" units to build the "nation-state". Imperialist countries including England, Japan, and Russia who attempted to disintegrate China during the late Qin Dynasty and the Republic periods, all deliberately named the regions of Mongolia, Tibet, and Xingjiang as "nations" in an attempt to produce confusion and incite different regions to pursue "national self-determination" and "national independence". To refute this, Gu Jiegang, a renowned historian, penned an essay titled "The Chinese Nations Are One" in 1939 (Gu Jiegang, 1996).

8.10. Post 1949 "National Theory" and Nation-Building

During the formation of the Communist Party of China, China accepted the "nation" theory of the Soviet Party. In order to meet the needs of the revolution and the struggle to seize power, China at a certain point expressed support for the self-determination of Mongolia, Tibet, and Hui ethnic regions and elaborated a federal government system for China. After the victory of the anti-Japanese war, the CPC adjusted its national policy to promote "national region autonomy" and abandoned federalism. However, the core concepts of Joseph Stalin's "nation" theory and the national policies established by the Soviet Union were accepted and adopted by the new Chinese government during the 1950s.

After the establishment of the People's Republic of China is 1949, China replicated many successful experiences of the Soviet Union in many aspects including rural and urban ownership systems, government structures, higher education institutions, and military establishment, as well as in "national" theory and other relevant policies. Given the international environment of the day, New China could only "lean onto one side" and replicate the actions of the Soviet Union, which was a reasonable choice under the circumstances. Under the organization of the central government, China "identified" 56 "nationalities" during the 1950s. The meaning of *minzu* or "nation" could be interpreted into two ways — either as "the Chinese nation" or the unity of 56 "nationalities".

For citizens in pre-reform China, having few opportunities to appreciate the practical implications of being a "Chinese citizen" through international affairs, and being provided with many national policies and preferential guidelines, thereby lending practical significance to ethnic identity in a day-to-day life, the full meaning of the word "Chinese nation" in the practical sense was however, blurred. We have, in the past few decades, discussed the national theories of Karl Marx and Vladimir Ilyich Lenin, talking about the definition of Joseph Stalin's nation and Vladimir Ilyich Lenin's "right of national self-determination", these kinds of propaganda and education resulted in the citizens of the present day including the Han people thinking of "nations" in terms of the 56 ethnic groups instead of the "Chinese nation" that includes all Chinese people, as well as introducing the modern political view of *minzu* or "nation" to the scholars and masses of all *minzu* or "nations".

After the process of "national identification", the government established each citizen's "*minzu* makeup", delineating the boundaries between China's various *minzu*. By establishing "autonomous regions" for each *minzu*, the territorial awareness of each ethnic group was promoted, and various preferential policies such as family planning, extra credit for college entrance exam, bilingual education, and leadership positions in the autonomous regions also strengthened the "*minzu* awareness" among the people of each ethnic group. This was manifested by some in the following ways:

1. Failing to welcome members of other *minzu* into their "autonomous territory".
2. Protecting usage of native languages in schools, with special concern with members who cannot speak it.
3. Hoping to cultivate and develop "our national economy".
4. Reinforcing "national awareness" and cohesion by promoting religious, customary, and historical education.

In perfect conformity with Joseph Stalin's definition of *minzu* or "nation", they argue, if these were the four areas to be diluted, their *minzu* or "nation" would become weak or even perish.

The "national awareness" catalyzed in this way was most prevalent among ethnic minority scholars and political leaders educated in the government's "national theory"; average agricultural workers and herdsmen still held very simplistic loyalty to state and the government. Many ethnic minority students from rural and herding areas started with no idea of the modern political concept of "national consciousness". After taking systematic "national theories" and national policy courses, however, this consciousness gradually grew stronger. This caused the unified Chinese nation with its thousands of years of history to start losing cohesion.

Inheriting Joseph Stalin's "nation" theories and Soviet-style national systems and policies, China was unable to complete the process of building a "nation-state" in the early 20th century, but instead transitioned into a "multi-nation union" as that of the Soviet Union. This is the ideological and political foundation for the immergence of national related issues and national separationist trends in some areas of China.

8.11. The Crux of Current Ethnic Issues in China

Summarizing the points discussed above, the crux of current national issues in today's China is that after 1949, we followed Joseph Stalin's theory of "nation", national system and policies and conducted national identification in China, practically making China into a "multi-nation union". This structure led to "national" elites, who previously lacked any modern "national awareness," to accept this new notion and start to foment dreams of independence.

In nearly 60 years after the establishment of the country, China's ethnic relations have been relatively harmonious. This is related to China's basic national circumstances — a unified country with over 2000 years of history, China has extensive coexistence and integration among ethnic groups, Han ethnic group make up more than 90% of the entire population and holds significant advantages in economic and social development; the central government too offers support and preferential policies to ethnic minorities — and the results of the implementation of policies. In particular, "land reform" and "democratic reform" carried out in minority regions in the 1950s won gratitude for the Party and the government from a generation of minority groups. At that time, Han leaders who were sent to ethnic minority regions exhibited high political integrity, policy implementation standards and strong spirit of serving the people, building strong inter-ethnic ties. The influence of communist ideologies began to weaken with the Cultural Revolution of the 1980s and launch of the reforms. Both ethnic minority citizens and Han leaders were overtaken by a new generation, leading to changes in the tradition affective connections established back in the 1950s.

Theoretically speaking, if a group has been identified as a *minzu* or "nation" by its own government, foreign governments and the elites within the group, then, no matter if we follow the "national self-determinism" theory of Western capitalist countries or the Marxist principle of Vladimir Ilyich Lenin which says "unconditionally and firmly protect the self-determination right of each nation, which is the right of secession" (Vladimir Ilyich Lenin, 1958), the term "nation" will always invoke the desire to establish an independent nation-state through self-determination. After the launch of the opening up policy, Chinese study-abroad students and foreigners traveling or on exchange to China's West inevitably also became mediums for promoting nationalist ideas.

Within the 56 "nationalities" in China, some of those with smaller or more dispersed populations have never requested political independence, nor thought that such separationist movements would be feasible. But in the case of other larger, more concentrated "nationalities" who have histories of independent rule, their elite groups may initiate nationalist ideas and demands for independence under the guidance of "national theories" both domestic and foreign, not to mention encouragement from foreign anti-China forces. Strictly controlled and suppressed by the current government, these motions have been relatively covert. Among the union republics of the former Soviet Union after its disintegration, we can clearly see similar separationist trends. The real national separationist dangers that exist in China do not reside with the minority extremists who conduct terrorist attacks and create public unrest, but comes from the national awareness of ethnic minority leaders and scholars. In recent years, a few authoritative "national theory" scholars even proposed the idea of abandoning the "Chinese nation" — a trend that we should be vigilant about. The central government must carefully monitor proposals from these scholars such as further strengthening the national region autonomy system in China, and even setting up permanent national establishments for the national region autonomy institutions.

8.12. New Trends in China's Ethnic Relations

In recent years, in carrying out the "Western development" strategy, the central government and various coastal provinces invested huge amounts of funds into Western regions where ethnic minorities reside, and initiated many large projects to attract Han labor power from Eastern and Central to Western China. This has changed the economic and social structure of the Western regions, propelling communication between the Han ethnic group and ethnic minority groups in Western China into a new era, reaching unprecedented depth and breadth.

As in recent years, the work of various levels of government in conducting ethnic knowledge and ethnic policy education among the Han ethnic group has been extremely weak, therefore, the Han entrepreneurs, managers and construction workers lacked knowledge of the history, religion, and cultural customs of Western China ethnic minority groups, and some of these people held prejudices against local ethnic minority people due to their perceived lack of mandarin skills and cultural differences. We have seen in surveys conducted in cities (such as Lhasa), the income of migrated Han population was significantly higher than that of local ethnic minority populations. This kind of phenomenon will surely lead to the dissatisfaction from some ethnic minority members, and if we add on incitement and support from external hostile political and religious forces, issues of simple and normal cultural differences and benefit distribution would turn into ethnic unrest, and even promote the extremist actions of some extremist individuals. These extremist activities may appear in the forms of terrorist attacks or street riots, and as the target of these actions are specific "ethnic nations", it is easy to invoke distrust and put up emotional barriers between ethnic groups. This kind of ethnic emotion in the general public can easily be exploited by separationist extremists.

While events of 2008 — like the March 14th Lhasa incident and others in Tibet and Xingjiang — happened against a certain "ethnic" background, they were mostly public order cases and terrorist actions by individual extremists. However, discrimination targeted at Tibetans and Uighurs (such as cab drivers refusing to take passengers, hotels refusing to take guests and selective security checks at the airport that took place in large cities such as Beijing and predominantly Han regions reflected the prevalent Han chauvinism that is a cause for concern. This discriminatory attitude also hurt the feelings of many Tibetans and Uighurs who opposed violent actions such as the March 14th incident, and shocked more enlightened Han.

This exposed the consequences of the failure of post-Cultural Revolution governments to promote ethnic knowledge and policies as well as relevant education.

We feel that the efforts to educate the Han ethnic group on the "diversity and unity" nature of the Chinese nation and ethnic knowledge as well as the promotion of ethnic equality policies have been very weak. The history of China's ethnic minorities, cultural or religious heritages and China's ethnic policy in average elementary and secondary education in the Han regions have been weak or devoid of content, leading to pervasive ignorance of basic knowledge about minority groups among Han people and youth; Han consciously or unconsciously equate "Han" with "China". One-sidedly promotion of ideas about "Chinese" being "descendants of Huaxia", "offspring of Yanhuang" or "sons of the dragon" by certain government-affiliated cultural departments also adds to this slanted view. The worship of emperors was the product of the narrow-minded nationalist movement to "expel the Manchus" carried out by the late Qing Revolutionary Party (Sun Longji, 2004). Many minorities do not identify with Huangdi (Emperor) or the dragon totem; hence, these kinds of one-sided and narrow-minded promotions are detrimental to the cohesion of the Chinese nation, and are in need of attention and correction from the government.

8.13. Solution to the Root of Ethnic Issues in China

It is well known that some other countries in the world such as the U.S. and India, also have a variety of races and ethnic groups within their population, as well as different religions and language groups. However, the "nation-building" goal of these countries is to integrate all these groups into a common "nation", calling the different groups as "ethnic groups" and protecting and developing their cultural traits and customs under the banner of "multiculturalism". The common identity among all citizens is the "nation" and not "ethnic group", the national constitution and citizenship rights are emphasized, racial and ethnic differences are considered in cultural terms, and ethnic groups have no special political rights. This can be viewed as an approach to "culturizing" ethnic groups. Racial relations were once very tense in the U.S., however, when given positive reinforcement on racial equality and citizenship, racism and discrimination have gradually decreased. The ethnically African–American president Obama's landslide victory in the presidential elections was clear proof of this; his election slogan was to seek the interest of all American citizens, without any racial preferences. After the independence of India, Prime Minister Nehru's primary focus was placed on how to calm down the identity conflicts between ethnic groups due to differences in institution, language, religion and caste in an effort to establish the "Indian nation". This rationale of "culturizing" of racial and ethnic differences in order to downplay ethnic and political conflicts has had much success in the U.S. and India, leaves from whose books it would be well for China as a "multicultural" society to take.

In 2004, pursuing this line of thought, I proposed "culturizing" or "depoliticizing" China's ethnic divisions and ethnic identities, and suggested the preservation of the notion of the "Chinese nation" and restart the "nation-building" process for the "Chinese nation", building a "nation-state" for the entire Chinese population based on the core identity of "Chinese nation." In addition, the 56 "nationalities" should be renamed as "ethnic groups" (each ethnic group would be called so-and-so ethnicity) and gradually fading the national awareness of current ethnic groups. Only under such a conceptual framework can the "national awareness" of the Chinese nation be reinforced, and for the country to come together as the Chinese nation to face and take part in the fierce competition on the world stage. During this process, some groups who maintained the traditional mindset of "tribal nations" will transition into members of modern "citizens of the state", leaders and scholars of ethnic minority groups who have accepted the notion that their ethnic group is a nation will need a period of time in which to grasp and adjust to this new idea. This will be a lengthy process of historical development that will require more patience.

8.14. Rethinking *Minzu* Theories and Adjusting Ethnic Policies by "Liberating the Mind and Being Practical"

People have become familiar and accustomed to the national theories promoted after the establishment of China along with the various national systems and policies implemented; therefore, it would inevitably be difficult for people to accept any alternative suggestions. However, our times and societies are ever-changing; the Soviet Union established by Vladimir Ilyich Lenin and Joseph Stalin has disintegrated, obliging us to adhere to the scientific approach of liberating the mind and being practical in order to progress and keep up with the times. We should conduct research into social and economic changes in ethnic regions, conduct analysis into the transition of ethnic identity awareness of various ethnic groups, and also carry out theoretical discussions and policy comparisons between the ethnic relations of other countries in order to practically test and rethink the practical effect of national theories and practices since the establishment of our nation. During this discussion, everyone can express their different viewpoints without bringing politics into the picture. In this way, we will be able to reach a consensus in a robust scholarly discussion, and gradually adjust our related theories and ethnic policies according to the new rationale.

As for how to adjust the basic ethnic system and policies in China, and the order and speed of the adjustment, these are not the most pressing issues, and can be gradually resolved through research and experiment after a consensus has been reached. However, if we currently do not discuss thoroughly the core concept of "nation" in modern international politics and ideas of the state, with the development of inter-ethnic relations, intervention of external forces and the passing away of prominent figures well-versed in Republican era ethnic affairs, our ethnic relations will only become even more complex and exacerbated. Once ethnic separationist trends appear in China, all parties will become "losers"; as the case of the former Yugoslavia makes alarmingly clear. We must make it clear to everyone that the basic and long-tern interests of each ethnic group are completely in line with the overall interest of the entire Chinese nation. Only when we have clarified our basic *minzu* or "nation" theory can we start to rethink the new framework for China's "nation-building". The only future solution for China's ethnic issues is to gradually adjust the related systems and policies, and strive to make the 1.3 billion people identify with the "Chinese nation" as their core and most basic group identity.

In addition, the central government recently implemented a "national integration" class in elementary and secondary schools nationally, which is a necessary and timely measure. However, if these classes focus on Joseph Stalin's definition and theory of the "nation", their practical effect may turn out to be counterproductive. I would argue that the following principles must be followed in the curriculum of the "national integration" class: the first principle is to adhere to basic Marxist principles, which goes to the equality of all ethnic groups. The second principle relates to the coexistence structure of "diversity and unity", that the 56 "ethnic groups" have been unalienable components of the Chinese nation throughout history. The third principle relates to the Chinese nation being a "nation-state" unit in the current international political landscape, the differences between different ethnic groups mostly related to culture, lineage, and historical memories, and all ethnic groups should strive to strengthen the overall "national awareness" of the Chinese nation, as well as citizenship awareness. The fourth principle is that in the midst of the fierce competition during an era of globalization, the "unit" of international competition is the nation-state. The various ethnic groups in the Chinese nation thus have the same long-term and foundational interests, and all ethnic groups need to come together and collaborate in the effort to create a better future.

States and political forces that view China as a potential enemy or competitor will find various ways to play up China's domestic "national relations", and utilize the separationist activities of Tibet, Xingjiang, and Taipei as an attempt to slow down China's rise in the new century. When China becomes strong, these states and political forces will not hesitate to turn their backs on these separatist organizations, just as they have in the past. People and scholars of China's ethnic groups must be clearly aware of this fact.

References

Anderson, Benedict (1999). *Imagined Communities: Reflection on the Origin and Spread of Nationalism.* Taipei: Times publications.

Gellner, Ernest (2002). *Nation and Nationalism.* Beijing: Central Compilation & Tranlsation Press.

Gu, Jiegang (1996).*Collected Works*, pp. 773–785. Shijiazhuang: Hebei Education Press.

Kedourie, Elie (2002). *Nationalism.* Beijing: Central Compilation & Tranlsation Press.

Lenin, Vladimir Ilyich (1958). *On Issue of National Policy*, Vol. 20. Beijing: People's Publishing House.

Smith, Anthony D (1991). *National Identity.* London: Penguin Books.

Sun, Yat-sen (1981). *Collections Works*, Vol. 2, p. 2. Beijing: Zhonghua Book Company.

Sun, Longji (2004). *Meridian of Historians*, pp. 28–21. Guilin: Guangxi Normal University Press.

The Great China Encyclopedia (Nationality Volume) (1986). Beijing: Encyclopedia of China Publishing House, p. 302.

Wang, Tongling (1934). *Zhongguo minzu shi [Chinese National History].* Beijing: Cultural Society Press.

Yu, Jianhua (1999). *Nationalism: Intersection of Historical Heritage and Situation of the Time.* Shanghai: Xuelin Publications.

INDEX